MW01256178

Changeover

Changeover

A YOUNG RIVALRY AND
A NEW ERA OF MEN'S TENNIS

Giri Nathan

Gallery Books

New York   Amsterdam/Antwerp   London
Toronto   Sydney/Melbourne   New Delhi

G

Gallery Books
An Imprint of Simon & Schuster, LLC
1230 Avenue of the Americas
New York, NY 10020

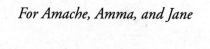

For Amache, Amma, and Jane

The trees are coming into leaf
Like something almost being said;
The recent buds relax and spread,
Their greenness is a kind of grief.

Is it that they are born again
And we grow old? No, they die too,
Their yearly trick of looking new
Is written down in rings of grain.

Yet still the unresting castles thresh
In fullgrown thickness every May.
Last year is dead, they seem to say,
Begin afresh, afresh, afresh.

—Philip Larkin, "The Trees"

CONTENTS

All quotes in *Changeover* appear as original, including those from our principal characters, who are non-native English speakers. I have not marked them with *sic,* as it would have roughly doubled the length of the book.

PROLOGUE

I had spent 10 hot, depleting days covering the 2022 U.S. Open, so I made a bad decision. Each morning I'd left my apartment in Brooklyn, taken the subway to Queens, and shuffled down the boardwalk to the Billie Jean King National Tennis Center. There I'd spent the next 12 hours hopping from court to court, occasionally ducking indoors to ask a player a question or refill my water bottle, absorbing as much of the tennis from as close a vantage point as I could. After the matches were over, I'd taken the subway home, stayed up until five a.m. tapping out a dispatch, and repeated the cycle. It sounds pathetic to be complaining about the weather when I was not the one swinging a racquet on court, but rather the one seated nearby scrawling in a notebook—and it is a bit pathetic—but by the second week I'd tired of navigating the sweaty throngs, of lurching awake from a sun-induced micro-nap in the stands. So on this particular evening of September 7, at roughly eight thirty p.m., with one men's quarterfinal still to come, I decided I'd watch from the comfort of my own sofa.

That was how I managed to miss out on the match between Carlos Alcaraz and Jannik Sinner, and with it, a chance to peer into an ecstatic future. There was Alcaraz, happy eyes sunk deep under a heavy brow, his body twitchy and muscled like a sprinter. There was Sinner, thin and laconic, pale as marble, flame-red curls trapped under a hat. I knew they were good but hadn't realized they could do *this*. I streamed the opening rallies on my phone, sitting on the 7 train, and knew in my gut I'd made a dire error. When I got home, I watched them fight until 2:50 a.m., still stabbing words of bafflement into my notebook as the match ended. Besides sleep, what could you do well, or do at all, for five hours and 15 minutes? How about the opposite of sleep: intermittent sprinting in every direction, batting a small projectile at 125 mph, tracking a projectile coming at you at 125 mph, making constant risk-reward calculations, clean emotional resets, energy and pain management decisions.

All this was done in solitude. When Alcaraz once looked in desperation to his coach, Juan Carlos Ferrero, after flubbing a pivotal point, he received a chilly half smile in return. He was then 19 years old and Sinner was 21. At ages when many people can't be trusted with basic self-preservation, these two produced tennis of the highest caliber, rallies so charismatic and coruscating that no other pair of players on tour could have replicated them. I saw Alcaraz leap midair to swat a shot behind-the-back, finding a solution where none existed. I saw Sinner strike the hardest backhands in the world, arrive within a single point of victory, and let his chance slip away. Alcaraz prevailed and went on to win the whole Open.

Reality got lazy with its metaphors: My pen ran out of ink. I'd gotten it only a month earlier. But it was forced to document every highlight, tactic, scoreline, atmospheric detail, and cathartic expletive for these five sets, and even then it caught only a fraction. The pen surrendered its innards and sputtered into retirement. I couldn't blame it. I was tempted to do the same—close my eyes, cross my arms like a mummy, and rest forever—after witnessing what Alcaraz and Sinner had accomplished in that same time span. I no longer feared the future, just my obsolescence in it. It was a smothering counterexample to anyone fussing about what tennis could even be after the old gods faded away. New gods take their place.

Trapped in the heat of that match, I saw only what Alcaraz and Sinner had in common, but in the following months I came to see just how vividly they diverged. The former ran hot and the latter lived in permafrost. One craved a crowd and the other sought privacy. With a racquet, Carlos chased sudden novelty, while Jannik aspired to calm regularity. Tennis was a passion for Carlos and a religion for Jannik, as the writer Owen Lewis put it to me. Like all the richest rivalries before them, each prodigy possessed some virtue absent in the other one; somehow each one appeared to be the antidote to the other's style of play. I detected more and more of these contrasts with every match and every passing season, as they chased not just historical records, but one another.

That 2022 U.S. Open quarterfinal was good enough to generate its own 45-minute highlight reel, which I watch from time to time. They should screen it in movie theaters. It was a vision from some sharp and fearsome new era that our eyes had not yet adjusted to. Now, at the start of 2025, I can see it more clearly. And I have written *Changeover* to document that new era in its earliest phase, as a primer for the tennis fans who either missed it firsthand or simply want to relive it someday. As my penance for missing that battle, the inception of a great rivalry, I am giving you this whole book. This time my pen won't run out.

CHAPTER 1

Empires

In the beginning, there was Roger Federer.

He was lean and composed, and seemed never to sweat. His feet moved over the court as do the feet of a water bug on the surface of a pond. His style was arty and aggressive. He always struck the ball a fraction of a second earlier than I expected. As a viewer, I was constantly taken aback by this, like a clap that landed just ahead of the beat, over and over. His opponents had no time to appreciate this quality, because the ball had already arrived at their feet. Many fans enjoyed seeing a hard game made to look so easy. But even Roger, at the outset of his career, was not yet so interested in toil. "Grit," as he'd later describe it, was something he had to learn. So he did. By his early twenties, the man from Switzerland was dominating the professional tour in a way few ever had. Ponytailed for a while, then with floppy locks tucked into a headband. Somewhat supercilious, keenly aware of his distance from the rest of the pack, Roger was aloft on his own cloud. He was the first one at the party.

Next to arrive was Rafael Nadal.

A strange chimera, who seemed ancient, yet terribly modern.

Feral, but also quite polite. Long hair, long shorts, no sleeves, big muscles. He applied spin to the ball with a fury not yet seen. His shots sailed high over the net and plunged back to earth with urgency. He was also curiously damp. On the island of Mallorca, the lefty Rafa was raised on clay, one of three main surfaces on which tennis is played, and he ruled it from the moment he set foot on tour. Tennis players are oddly fond of the term "fighting spirit," and Rafa was its living embodiment, a man who did not grasp surrender. Though he seemed impossibly full of life, he also grappled with injuries all over his body, causing many to question his longevity, which, in the end, would be no problem at all. He and Roger played indelible epics. Nadal unwound Federer's poise and forced the Swiss to evolve beyond his instinctive style. For a while it seemed it would be just these two, locked in permanent struggle, carving one another into genius as great rivals do.

Maybe it would have been so if not for Novak Djokovic.

To call him "limber" was too mild. He seemed to be composed of something other than flesh, some taffy-like substance that let him elongate and coil his body into confounding positions. He had short-cropped hair and close-set eyes that would widen as if in terror when he was about to return serve, which he did better than anyone ever had. His genius was less showy than the others, more attritional, but just as keen. And where the other two had grown up well-off in western Europe, he had emerged from Serbia during the Yugoslav Wars. His path to the high life of pro tennis had been more perilous. A wall he used to hit tennis balls against as a child had been struck by NATO bombs. He spoke of his family's experience with loan sharks. Early on, he would wilt in long or hot matches, which was funny in retrospect, because raw stamina became a defining trait. He liked to do silly impressions of his peers, eager to perturb the sport's sterile atmosphere. Sometimes he sparred with crowds. In time he relished his role as interloper. With his talent as crowbar, he pried his way into the Roger-Rafa duopoly. Where there had been one rivalry, now there were three, each of them distinct.

After him came—well, no one. For two decades, aside from the occasional guest stopping by for a cocktail and then getting shooed away, it would be just the three of them at the party, and a lot of people banging at the door.

The professional tennis tour runs all year long, across dozens of tournaments. The most important are the four majors. If you've heard of any, you've heard of these: the Australian Open, Roland-Garros (colloquially, the French Open), Wimbledon, and the U.S. Open. At the outset of each tournament, there are 128 players. Two weeks later, there is only one champion, who has won seven consecutive matches. A victory pays a few million dollars, assures a place in history, and improves or reaffirms a player's ranking. At any given time, a tennis player knows precisely where he ranks among his peers. He lives every day in a bare hierarchy that anyone can look up. Winning a match rewards a player with "ranking points." To get a sense of the relative importance of the tournaments, all you need to do is look at the points. A major is worth 2000 points. Beneath those are the Masters 1000 tournaments, which are unsurprisingly worth 1000 points. Beneath those, 500-level tournaments, then 250-level tournaments. You can imagine this as the pyramid that makes up the top professional division of men's tennis, also known as the ATP Tour. Beneath it are lower levels of competition—the Challenger Tour, Futures—that can be thought of as the minor leagues.

Perhaps I have given you an emotionally impoverished version of the story. No child drifts to sleep thinking of winning 2000 ranking points—they dream of winning a major. These four tournaments are the stuff of legacy, the currency in tedious debates about who is better than whom. For some fans, the simplest shorthand for a player's historic significance is the number of majors they won. There are many, many worthy feats in tennis outside of winning those tournaments, but in the popular imagination, and to hear many players tell it themselves, these four are untouchable. If given a chance, a player would trade any number of smaller trophies for just one of them. The exchange rate is infinite.

The tennis major is one of the hardest feats to pull off in contemporary sport. Winning seven best-of-five-set tennis matches is a profound physical and psychic ordeal, a truth that has only deepened as the sport's athletic demands have increased. To win those matches requires an alignment of circumstances: the tactical know-how to adapt to seven different opponents, the ability to recover from the wear-and-tear of each match, the mental acuity to play each point in isolation without getting overwhelmed by the enormity of the whole task. I have always thought about a major as a marathon run while engaged in hand-to-hand combat.

For roughly two decades, from 2004 to 2023, Federer, Nadal, and Djokovic won almost all the majors. As a result, they came to be known as a collective unit—the Big Three—like some cabal conspiring to hoard all the joy and prestige for themselves. It is not as though they were the only good tennis players born between the years 1981 and 1987. They had brilliant peers, players who would have won a major or two in other eras but had the blunt misfortune of being born at the same time as the three best ever to play. In any attempt to win a major, inevitably, a player would have to muscle their way past one member of the Big Three. Sometimes they'd beat one of them only to be evicted by another. Tomáš Berdych, the flinty, powerful Czech, once beat two of them in a row only to be eliminated by the third in the Wimbledon final. It was too much to ask of any one mortal.

Perhaps the most poignant way to understand the Big Three was to see the optimism steadily squeezed out of their contemporaries, as if by a juicer, a cup filled to the brim with hopes and dreams. You would hear the most extraordinary admissions of inadequacy. In pro sports, particularly individual sports, militant self-belief is a prerequisite for the job. And yet here these gifted competitors were, their confidence cracked, openly explaining to the press that their best efforts weren't remotely enough against these three adversaries. And that was only what they were willing to say in public. Who knows what macabre doubts went stalking through their heads as they took their post-match showers or car rides to the airport.

Broadly speaking, these valiant victims of the Big Three moved through recognizable phases of career grief. First in this sequence was Persistence; all it would take was some dedicated training, some tactical adjustments, perhaps a few more twists of good fortune, and an important match may well swing his way in the future. After said match definitively did not swing in his favor, nor the one after, nor the one after that, the player might admit to Cluelessness. At this phase, they would have no particular intuition about what they could have done to win, and would feel altogether lost on the court. There could be bright flashes of Anger or Despair en route, but in time, the player arrived at Resignation. Perhaps this was the reality of playing tennis in this era, as stark and immovable as the face of a cliff, and there was nothing else to be done. At the end of this path was Enlightenment, a lovely ego death. To play a game for a living, to travel the world, to be alive at all, was a privilege—what's that about a major?—no, he was content to sniff the freshly cut grass, kick the clay out of his shoes, and feel gratitude.

The players whose talent most closely approached the Big Three were the ones to most clearly see the chasm that still separated them. Often, these players would explain just how unpleasant their matches had been. Andy Roddick, a funny and frank American with one of history's great serves, who actually *did* win the U.S. Open in 2003, shortly before the Big Three shut the door behind them, battled with Federer too many times not to see the situation clearly. Once after a defeat in 2005: "I was bringing heat, too. I was going at him, trying different things. You just have to sit back and say 'too good' sometimes. Hope he gets bored or something. I don't know." Jo-Wilfried Tsonga, a barrel-chested Frenchman who looked a little like a young Muhammad Ali and had a pugilistic play style to match, was totally out of ideas in 2013, reflecting on two narrow five-set losses to Djokovic and Federer. "To be honest, I have no idea. You know, if you have some advice for me, I will take it because I don't know." That same year David Ferrer, a Spaniard blessed with uncommon foot speed and consistency, described the landscape dispassionately. "I am trying to do my best every match. But I know they are better than me. What can I do?" he wondered after being routed by Djokovic in an Australian Open semifinal. Five months later he would lose to Nadal in the Roland-Garros final. At season's end he was asked if he could envision himself winning a major the next year: "No, I don't think so." In a work culture defined by positive visualization exercises and constant gestures of self-motivation, this was hair-raising stuff. Years later, after Tsonga had retired, he was chatting with his countryman Gaël Monfils—also shut out by the Big Three, also immensely gifted—and the two discussed why they'd been unable to win a major. "I was not good enough," said Tsonga, and Monfils agreed.

But even if the Big Three's direct contemporaries suffered, surely there would be a path for the next generation of players. Time was on their side, theoretically. They were younger, and this was a game premised on agility and reflexes, qualities that do not age like wine. By mid-2017, Djokovic had joined Federer and Nadal as people in their thirties. That is the decade when a player slips out of his physical prime and reckons with the cumulative damage of a life on tour. And the trio seemed, for a brief moment, vulnerable. If you squinted, you could pinpoint 2016 as a year of hope. Two members of the cabal disappeared into injury exile. Federer had taken an awkward step while giving his kids a bath. He heard a click in his left knee and wound up requiring surgery on his meniscus. Nadal, nursing pain in his left wrist, missed big chunks of the season, even withdrawing midway through his favorite tournament, Roland-Garros. Not to accuse anyone in the locker room of celebrating a competitor's pain, but the youth saw an opening, a knife-width of light in the doorjamb.

Instead, Federer and Nadal returned the following season and split 2017's majors, two apiece, playing the most visionary tennis of their late careers. Federer had adopted a larger racquet, which souped up his sometimes vulnerable one-handed backhand. Nadal played a near-perfect clay season. The hair on their heads had thinned out, and their first step wasn't quite as explosive as it had been, but their self-knowledge was absolute, and they were still beating everyone on tour. It was a down year for Djokovic, who'd insisted on playing through an elbow injury that eventually required surgery. But he'd be back the next season, and as a unit, the Big Three were not budging. The story continued as it had.

The major tournament, historically a site of glimmery intrigue, became a fortnight of foregone conclusions. No matter how spirited some underdog looked at the start of a tournament, you knew, at the business end of the tournament, it would be one of three familiar faces holding the trophy. Time did not conspire in favor of youth, at least not quickly enough to rescue whole generations of players from doom. In tennis, the wealth is concentrated at the very top of the tour. And the Big Three were the first to play in an era when one could amass roughly the GDP of a small island nation, thanks to both prize money and endorsement deals. The nine-figure reward for dominating the modern game could then be applied to cutting-edge conditioning and medical care, prolonging careers beyond their assumed expiration dates. This was an emerging pattern across sports at the time—think of LeBron James or Tom Brady or Lionel Messi tearing it up well into their mid-thirties. Like them, the Big Three were scrupulous stewards of their own bodies. Federer's style of quick, punchy points was easier on the aging physique. Nadal carefully managed his complex suite of ailments, including a congenital foot problem he'd been working around since the start of his pro career. Djokovic was a seeker, living at the frontier of forward-thinking inquiry and batty pseudoscience, which would later manifest itself in knottier ways. But his emphasis on mobility was paying off, allowing him to continue his on-court contortionism well into his silver years, and his stamina was legend.

So this trio kept winning. And the career grief, like some inter-generational trauma, was inherited by the next batch of players, too. It was no longer just the members of the Big Three's direct age cohort, but then also the younger millennials, those born in the nineties, tasked with the same impossible labor. Among them was Grigor Dimitrov, the spry Bulgarian saddled with the nickname of "Baby Fed" due to strokes that resembled those of his frustrat-ingly overtalented colleague. There was Kei Nishikori, the fragile but deadly sharpshooter from Japan, and Milos Raonic, the ace machine from Canada. All of them managed moments of transcendence but never fulfilled the major dream. This generation followed the last into the juicer. And then yet *another* generation emerged. Surely, this would be the one to break the spell?

Reader, it would not. The same words of confusion and futility from 2004 were spoken by different men 15 years later: "His game style has something that it kind of makes the other half of your brain work more than it usually does," said Stefanos Tsitsipas, a dreamy, pseudo-philosophical Greek seen as potential heir to major titles, reflecting on a 2019 drubbing from Rafael Nadal. "I'm trying to understand, but I cannot find an explanation for that." That same year, another top prospect, Dominic Thiem of Austria, described "the unique and also brutal thing" in the structure of his job. He had just ended Djokovic's 26-match winning streak at the majors, only to run straight into another monster. "I beat yesterday one of the biggest legends of our game. Not even 24 hours later, I have to step on court against another amazing legend of our game, against the best clay-court player of all time."

As a writer, I began to feel a little stupid. There was a cycle. I was exhilarated by a young prospect, who was playing tennis that appeared fresh and audacious, and who seemed hardworking and shepherded by a smart coach, and I hoped to draw attention to their cause, only to know, in the innermost chamber of my tennis con-science, that they would be slain time and again by this geriatric elite. It was a narrative conundrum. Each time I could convince my-self to write the story, allowing myself to feel the frisson of novelty. But I knew that would fade. Each time I felt a little bit more like Charlie Brown approaching the football. At times, I could even be a bit ungrateful about these three great men, unfolding three of the most spectacular rivalries in the history of sport. But I wanted to see new players test them in new ways. Sometimes I just wanted to write about the new rather than the old.

We cannot advance another step without acknowledging those men who did manage to break down the door and enter the major title party. The Big Three were comprehensive, but not total. Chief among all other players was Andy Murray, the crotchety Scot who established a tier of his own. He made it to world No. 1, he beat all of them at the biggest events, and he clogged up the late stages of so many majors that the term was sometimes extended to "Big Four" to include him. He would end with three major titles. Then there was Federer's countryman Stan Wawrinka, a rumpled late bloomer who looked as if he'd rolled out of bed only to demonstrate some of the most hellacious groundstrokes anyone had ever seen. Though far less consistent than Murray, this occasional juggernaut won three majors also. Then there were four one-offs, all of whom managed to sneak in a U.S. Open title. First was Juan Martín del Potro, a soulful colossus with a forehand to pierce any defense. As a 20-year-old the Argentine had upset a swaggering Federer to win the 2009 U.S. Open, and seemed fated for many more such titles, only to be waylaid by injuries. There was Marin Čilić, a slightly hunched Croat with a mighty baseline game who peaked in a wild two-week run in 2014. There was the aforementioned Thiem, a hardworking bruiser who fashioned himself into the Big Three's most serious threat in the late 2010s. He won a 2020 tournament empty of fans due to the pandemic, and empty of Novak Djokovic, for reasons we will soon explore. And finally there was Daniil Medvedev, far too flavorful a character to relegate to an aside. We'll get to him later. But this is the end of our list of exceptions.

The era ended on a long fade, not a cut to black. In 2018, Federer won his record 20th and final major at the Australian Open, and in 2020, he was slowed down by another knee problem, this time for good. He played infrequently until the end of 2022, when he retired at an exhibition tournament, his hand clenching Nadal's, both blubbering. The two original rivals had become good friends. By then Nadal had already surpassed Federer's major record, setting a new standard at 22, his last coming at Roland-Garros in 2022, which he played on a left foot so quieted by pain-killing injections that he described it as "asleep." From there, his injuries, too, became unsustainable, and the prospect of retirement drew closer over the next two years, even though he played well in those rare windows of good health. Djokovic, the youngest member of the bunch, seemed as supple and motivated as ever. He had gained the upper hand in each of his rivalries against Federer and Nadal. He erased many of their other records, achieved new ones, and acted, even in the absence of his two counterparts, as a solitary "final boss" to test the mettle of all newcomers. They almost always failed that test. Djokovic kept stacking up major titles until he stood alone at 24.

If this last phase of the Big Three era was something of a predictable one-man act, it was also a fascinating full-spectrum character study of an eclectic figure. Djokovic could be intelligent and humane at one turn, cranky and dour the next. His thinking was sophisticated in some ways and regressive in others, a prominent example of what might be termed "jock epistemology," where elite athletes accumulate some useful beliefs for good reasons, some useful beliefs for bad reasons, and some bad beliefs for bad reasons. He could be quite generous to players at the outset of their careers. Sometimes he agitated as a labor organizer on behalf of lower-ranked players. He also professed his belief in telepathy and telekinesis. He once invited a man to explain to his sizable social media audience, on a live stream, that positive emotions could purify tainted water. He was skeptical of conventional medicine and did not want to vaccinate himself against the coronavirus, a conviction so firmly held that he skipped out on major tournaments that would have required him to cave. He attracted a new sort of fan in this era, people who fancied themselves to be raging against the establishment, who seemed always to locate him as the victim of a vast conspiracy, and expressed their love for him in paranoid style. (One prominent member of this fan base, whom Djokovic once shouted out by name, speculated that Nadal had colluded with Bill Gates and Joe Biden to prevent Djokovic from attending the 2022 U.S. Open.) He arrived in Australia for the 2022 Australian Open, under the impression that he had obtained a vaccine exemption, only to be detained and deported in a Kafkaesque legal saga that clearly wounded him. He won a lot of tennis matches in between all this. It was odd to see a man so frequently aggrieved even as he rose to the unquestioned status of Greatest of All Time, surpassing his two historic peers.

All the while, it had become more and more difficult to make sense of the future, which had been obscured by these three men for so many years. The tour had become littered with stunted, thwarted little careers, like a landscape of bonsai trees. When Djokovic stopped winning—assuming that happened before the heat death of the universe and the attendant end of organized tennis—would the major titles be distributed more erratically? Would the steady dictatorial rule of the Big Three be followed by a riotous free-for-all? Would fans, long invested in these three rich characters, lose touch with the pro tour? The only certain thing, it seemed to all of us, fans and journalists alike, was this: Whatever was coming next could not possibly look like what had just passed.

CHAPTER 2

Cabeza, Corazón y Cojones

At the 2020 U.S. Open, we caught our first glimpse of what we could only assume was the coming era of mortal tennis. Mortal tennis is flawed, raggedly human. Neither Federer nor Nadal entered the tournament, citing injury and the pandemic. And during the tournament, Djokovic was disqualified in odd circumstances. Late in the first set of his fourth-round match, he swatted a ball at the back of the court in frustration. Such tantrums were not uncommon on tour, and typically they would elicit only a warning from the umpire—except this particular ball had unintentionally struck the throat of a lineswoman, who fell to the ground in pain. His exit was a boon to other players in the draw. These included Dominic Thiem (who had beaten Djokovic in one major and taken him to the limit in another) and Alexander "Sascha" Zverev (who had not come close). As two of the brightest prospects among the twentysomethings, they met in the final.

Across five sets played in a pandemic-empty stadium, it appeared as though they'd heard the advice "act like you've been there before" and done the exact opposite. The match was occasionally high-level, but more often it was so technically sloppy and grotesquely nerve-ridden that I was compelled to queue up some Nadal-Djokovic highlights as a palate cleanser. Thiem won, and for all the match's shortcomings, plenty of fans were optimistic about a post–Big Three phase of the tour. In this hypothetical era ahead, there would be surprising champions instead of dominance and repetition, thrilling if temporary runs of form, a genuine fog of mystery at the start of majors about which man would be left standing at the end.

Then, circa 2021, a boy emerged, ready to reinstitute the hegemony.

To the tennis hardcores, those who scout the juniors, Futures, and Challenger tournaments in search of possible greatness, Carlos Alcaraz was no surprise. The Spaniard was like a meteor they had tracked for years, hurtling toward the pro tour, sure to make a destructive impact. If you hadn't paid attention all along, you might have been surprised to discover that the harbinger of tennis doom looked like such a cheerful adolescent doofus. But that was the feeling of early-career Carlos. So visibly happy to be there, so transparently living out a fantasy—a happiness that could infect any viewer, and a happiness that he channeled into his improvisational and blitzing style of tennis. Here were the pimples and bad buzz cut right out of puberty, and the racquet work right out of the Hall of Fame. He was as obvious a candidate for the word "prodigy" as I've seen in any area of human endeavor, sports or otherwise.

Early on I saw in Alcaraz a quality that Federer had once described to me, in a precious one-on-one conversation that lasted the length of a hallway, plus one right turn, plus the additional time it took to carefully step over a raised doorframe. He was urging young players to break free of their comfort zone at the back of the court and attack the net, where the ball could be struck out of the air. He wanted them to charge the net with the conviction that they could really win the point there. None of the would-be successors to the Big Three had met that standard. Alcaraz was not just willing to play at the net; he catapulted himself there as often as he could, even in situations where it was foolhardy to try. Yet he was so fast in his feet and so soft in his hands that he could pull it off. I had never seen such daring in a player so young.

That quality had been baked into Alcaraz's game since the start. Carlos—who prefers "Carlitos," or "Charlie," because, as he explained in 2020, "honestly, Carlos seems very serious to me and it seems that I have done something wrong"—was raised in a village called El Palmar outside the city of Murcia in southeast Spain. He first played at a club known as Tiro de Pichón, a reference to its century-old origins as a hunting society where rich men shot pigeons. There were in fact three generations of guys named Carlos Alcaraz who took up tennis at this club. Carlitos's grandfather helped build its courts and played recreationally. His father had bigger ambitions and competed domestically, but didn't have the funds to take his career past that point, and became a tennis coach. It was the third Carlos Alcaraz who actualized the father's dream. He received his first racquet at four and absorbed as much tennis as he could at the club his father administered. A visitor might arrive there, looking for Carlos Sr., and instead find tiny Carlos Jr. standing at the fence, coaching the elderly combatants on court, explaining their mistakes, telling them where to place their serves, as an Alcaraz family friend reminisced to the journalist Tumaini Carayol.

There are photos of Carlitos as a toothy squinting boy, holding a trophy. In most of them he is standing next to his first coach, Kiko Navarro. From the start, Carlos Sr. refused to mix the roles of father and coach, and for all his tennis fanaticism, he maintained a separation between church and state. Navarro, the boyhood coach, described his 10-year-old pupil as "a very innocent boy, without any bad intentions on or off the court, very happy." There was also a temper lurking. He broke racquets and was liable to storm off court in tears. He refused to lose at anything, be it tennis or board games. That trait, while unpleasant to deal with in the moment, is also necessary to become the top player in the world, Navarro observed a decade later, in a 2023 interview with France 24. And despite his issues with emotional regulation, the actual tennis technique came to him as if "innate."

From a young age, he was taught the trickier shots that require a subtle touch. There was the volley, struck in midair before the ball bounces, requiring a firm wrist and keen reflexes. There was the drop shot, a delicate bit of deceit that sends an opponent scrambling forward to retrieve a shallowly struck ball. Unlike other kids taught the same, Alcaraz immediately folded these shots into his repertoire for his competitive matches. When Navarro briefly considered switching young Alcaraz to a one-handed backhand, he was good at that, too. That remains an Alcaraz signature: a hunger to acquire new techniques, to arm himself with all the shots that can possibly be hit on a tennis court. And then also to invent some new ones, on the fly.

Becoming a top junior player requires both decent guidance and a good chunk of money. The Alcaraz family couldn't afford the frequent travel of a competitive junior career, so a local confectionery sponsored Alcaraz's early trips. (Yes, the tour's metaphorical kid in a candy store was funded by the literal candy store.) By the time he was 12, Alcaraz already had an agent, Albert Molina, who had to persuade his employer, the powerhouse agency IMG, that it was worth investing in such a young kid. He'd also had to persuade Carlos Sr., who felt it was a bit premature for his preteen son to have professional representation. But wherever he went, the tennis Carlitos played attracted an organic audience—a useful thing, for an agent—and Molina soon secured racquet and clothing sponsorships for his client. Molina remembered what it was like to watch a 15-year-old Carlitos play at the elementary level of pro tennis, a Futures tournament. "There were players of his age that only did two things, but they did them very well, really making the most of them," he said in a 2021 interview with the tour. "With him it was the opposite. He had such a variety that he would often get it wrong by not being organized, he would get mixed up. In one point he would approach the net, open up angles, play a slice, a lob . . ." Early Federer had been bedeviled by the same surfeit of options.

The most reliable indicator of elite talent: hitting milestones ahead of schedule. One rung above the Futures, and one rung below the ATP Tour you see on TV, is the Challenger tour. It is populated mostly by grown men, whose careers are not at a financial break-even point, fighting for the chance to enter the better-paid events on the main tour. Alcaraz won his first Challenger match at age 15, against a gangly ginger by the name of Jannik Sinner. Alcaraz fell to 0-3 in the third set, before reeling off six straight games. They wouldn't clash again for two years.

In 2020, at age 16, well past his usual bedtime, after three a.m. in Rio de Janeiro, Brazil, wearing a hot-pink polo shirt, Alcaraz won his first tour-level match. He had never before faced a player in the top 100. In a third-set tiebreak, he defeated fellow Spaniard, and world No. 41, Albert Ramos-Viñolas, who, it must be said, looked quite bummed to have lost to a child. He'd go on to lose to him three more times, though, so it was worth getting used to.

By that point, Alcaraz had fully professionalized his training. From his boyhood coach, he'd moved on to Juan Carlos Ferrero, a former world No. 1 who was running an academy in Villena, about an hour north of where the Alcaraz family lived. The young pupil briefly split his time between home and academy before moving in full-time. It's a quiet place in the mountains, where Carlitos could take his daily run on a dusty path accompanied by grazing chickens. A man of angular features and serious mien, Ferrero had won Roland-Garros in 2003. Because he was so thin and quick, an opponent once likened him to a certain insect. Ferrero wasn't necessarily thrilled, but the nickname stuck, and "El Mosquito" enjoyed a stint atop the tour in the early aughts, battled with the Big Three for a few years, and retired in 2012. Where some players struggle to locate meaning in life after retiring from the game that had defined it for them, Ferrero immediately transitioned into coaching, inheriting the academy that had been founded by his own coach, Antonio Cascales. It is very much a multigenerational concern; even the dog that lives there descends from Cascales's old dog.

Juan Carlos spent five years training players at the academy and not traveling on tour with any one player. That changed in 2017, when he decided to work with Sascha Zverev, who was then the sport's top young prospect, blessed with the big serve that his six-foot-six height would suggest, and the effortless lateral movement that it did not. They split after an eight-month collaboration. Ferrero later said that they had different views of how to conduct oneself off the court: diet, rest, comportment. Professionalism, in a word. He quickly received offers to coach other elite players. Instead, the following year, he chose to travel with the 15-year-old Alcaraz, ferrying him through the lower-level tournaments. The family could not afford Ferrero's usual rate, and while Alcaraz's agent sourced some funds from IMG to close the gap, it was still a big pay cut for Ferrero. That was one measure of his belief in his new pupil. He was making a long-term investment.

Alcaraz's tennis upbringing was thoroughly, even atypically, local. Yet, while he is a Spanish tennis player, raised by and surrounded by Spanish tennis players for much of his life, his game does not neatly fit the archetype of the Spanish tennis player. Such a player prefers clay, loads his groundstrokes with heavy topspin, and tracks down balls with raw foot speed. Brutally consistent, he relishes the physicality of this noncontact sport, the cardiovascular battles of long baseline rallies. The "dirtballer," as this type of player is sometimes called, a little derisively, might as well be a national tradition. There is an implicit ethos of steady attrition rather than abrupt gambits. David Ferrer epitomized the 21st-century dirtballer; Rafa Nadal took it to a physical and logical extreme that no one else could follow. Alcaraz presented a new paradigm once again. He shared many of those traits, but really his game was protean and unclassifiable. Ferrero's challenge, then, was to nourish this sui generis talent without feeding him irrelevant orthodoxy—to offer him a structure to climb onto without restricting what he might grow into.

Ferrero has vague memories of his first time watching Alcaraz play, when the boy was 12 or 13. He was told to look out for a kid who played a dynamic style, who liked hitting drop shots and charging toward the net. He was impressed by how quickly Carlitos accelerated the racquet on his forehand despite his tiny frame. And he also saw that Carlitos was quite emotional. In some ways the coach is the foil of his charge. Ferrero has described his own approach as "focused" and "restrictive" compared to Alcaraz's looser style. Ferrero prefers to anticipate problems and attack them ahead of time; Alcaraz likes to address them as they appear. Ferrero wondered whether his flighty student would ever learn to patiently build a point, shot by boring shot, without getting seduced by a shinier idea.

Mid-match coaching was not permitted on the tour until late 2022. Before that time, Ferrero—who believes coaching is more stressful than playing, because you cannot directly affect the outcome—suffered in the player's box in silence. But the rule change opened up a channel of incessant chatter and gesture between Alcaraz and Ferrero throughout their matches. It is a real-time collaboration that stands out in a sport of isolated problem-solving. It sometimes feels as though there is an umbilical cord connecting the two. It also sometimes feels like a liability.

Though I'd been quietly following Alcaraz's exploits since he won his first tour-level match in Rio in 2020, I was slow to acknowledge the scope of his talent. I'd been fooled so many times before, falling for the hype around so many false messiahs who wound up losing to the same three old men. Occasionally I would boot up some classic footage of the Big Three, like the 2009 Australian Open final, starring Federer and Nadal in their physical primes, as if consulting the fossil record. What remarkable beasts; this level of tennis had gone extinct. In 2021, I was enjoying the present state of mortal tennis, finding more than enough to chew on, but I was clear-headed enough to acknowledge that what I saw on court was not the same as what I saw in that 2009 footage. I figured *that* tennis would never come back again, and was simply grateful to have seen it. Until one Carlos Alcaraz caught fire.

As a witness to his 2021 season, I found it was impossible to resist the hype any longer. What a respectable pro might accomplish over the course of his career, Alcaraz compressed into the season he turned 18. That spring he broke into the top 100; in the summer he was racking up wins, seizing his first tour-level trophy, and still losing to the occasional journeyman; by fall he was regularly beating top-10 players. It was his five-set win over Stefanos Tsitsipas at the 2021 U.S. Open that flung him into mainstream consciousness. Tsitsipas, who looked as if he might be the superstar of the new guard, was the third seed in the tournament. But he was powerless against this noodle-built 18-year-old, and after losing, he announced in a press conference he'd "never seen someone hit the ball so hard." It was the first and last time that an Alcaraz win over Tsitsipas would be considered an upset. A few months later in Paris, Alcaraz stumbled into Sinner, their first-ever clash on the pro tour. Alcaraz won in two loud sets, and at match's end, Sinner leaned over to the victor, patted him on the shoulder, and said, "I hope we play some more." Alcaraz beamed back at him: "Yeah, yeah, yeah, for sure, for sure, me too."

During that 2021 season, Alcaraz ascended 99 spots in the rankings and ended the year at No. 32 in the world. It should not have been possible to further ratchet up the rate of improvement, but he did. He arrived in 2022 looking as if he'd been encased in 15 pounds of muscle, thanks to an intensive training block his trainer would later describe as the transformation from "boy to man." Soon Alcaraz entered the top 20, the youngest player to do so since 1993, surpassing even Nadal, the most recent standard for precocity. By the time he won the Miami Open, a 1000-level tournament, there was no denying his genius. Imagine any discernible tennis skill. It doesn't matter if you have the local jargon for it ("pace," "footwork") or just a general impression ("hits ball comically hard," "runs around well"). You could look at Alcaraz and see that skill perfected. A teenager might be a prodigy if he had just two of the following qualities: speed, pace, balance, improvisation, touch, consistency, anticipation. I didn't know what word to assign to a player who boasted all of them—except the serve, his one deficit—at a top-5 level. Every week of the 2022 season brought perplexing new developments, as the specimen mutated unpredictably in a hard-court petri dish. Is he now the fastest man in tennis? Suddenly he has the single best drop shot on tour? Now he can strike the ball between his legs while running backward—the "tweener"—to produce precision lobs? He was growing too much, too quickly, to track in real time.

Tennis is a terminally nostalgic sport, always trying to make sense of its future by using its past. Inevitably, Alcaraz began to earn comparisons to the Big Three: the touch of Federer, the physicality of Nadal, the pliability of Djokovic. I will confess that I myself harbored some blasphemous thoughts at this time. Could he be better than all of them? Certainly he was a more well-rounded player. But I prefer to try and see players on their own terms, to identify what is fresh about them, and there was something unmissably fresh about this one. Instead of visions of the legends, I had a much sillier image rattling around my head. Imagine the goalie on a foosball table, so explosive and responsive. Just that one little dude, gliding along a horizontal, ready to be spun at a furious pace with a light twist of a wrist. In his baseline exchanges Alcaraz stood on top of the line, never ceding more than an inch, waiting to meet the ball with lethal force, smooth in his movement but full of coiled rage. Then he reset instantly and did it again, melding caffeinated teen dynamism with a multi-major-winner's point construction. There was a fluid, unrelenting quality to his play that I did not usually ascribe to animate objects, or anything that needs time to recover from physical exertion.

Alcaraz then spent his spring turning 19 years old and closing the gap between "best prospect on tour" and "best player on tour." He won trophies in Miami, Barcelona, and Madrid in quick succession. His colleagues were increasingly willing to utter the obvious out loud. Sascha Zverev, after getting dissected 6-3, 6-1 in the

Madrid Open final, told Alcaraz in his runner-up speech that he was "the best player in the world, even though you're still five years old." Novak Djokovic said effectively the same thing. Stefanos Tsitsipas, four years older than Carlitos, and having lost to him two more times in 2022, wasn't shy about his feelings: "He inspires me a lot. I really want to be like him. I look up to him."

After Alcaraz won in Madrid, he went home to El Palmar and hoisted the trophy onto the balcony of his family apartment, to the roars of his neighbors. And then, having just rampaged through 16 wins in 17 matches, he sat out the following tournament in Rome, resting a sprained right ankle. It was strange. A teenager's rest week shouldn't have felt so consequential. It shouldn't have mattered remotely to players as accomplished as Djokovic and Nadal. But in this instance, it felt as though Alcaraz were granting his elders an opportunity. He had beaten both Djokovic and Nadal in Madrid—the first time any player had taken down both in the same clay tournament. Those matches were gristly three-setters with the greats in roughly B-minus form, which was typically good enough for them to dismiss most opponents. But Alcaraz was already challenging them as fiercely as they'd challenged one another. In the absence of the sudden superstar, Djokovic went on to claim the title in Rome.

Over the summer, Alcaraz's inexperience revealed itself in the best-of-five-set format of the majors. Rather than world-beating, he regressed to merely excellent. He lost in a quarterfinal at Roland-Garros. At Wimbledon, he lost in the fourth round to Sinner, evening their head-to-head record on the pro tour at 1-1. Alcaraz appeared to be charting a path that no contemporary could follow. But Sinner, two years his elder, seemed already like a potential rival, because he excelled in their specific matchup, even if he could not yet match Alcaraz's overall accomplishments. Later that summer, Sinner beat Alcaraz again, this time on clay courts in the final at the Croatia Open.

But as the U.S. Open rolled back around, it was the hour of Carlitos once again. Djokovic couldn't travel to the U.S. because of a federal policy that required noncitizens to be vaccinated against COVID-19. Nadal, who had suffered an abdominal tear earlier in the summer and played at the Open through visible pain, lost in the fourth round. Alcaraz became the favorite to win, but his path was laborious. In the fourth round, he played the veteran Marin Čilić, who had won the tournament eight years before, and dragged the wunderkind into a five-set slog that lasted three hours and 53 minutes. Alcaraz won to secure his place in the quarterfinal against Sinner—the futurist epic that I stupidly missed.

Alcaraz and Sinner were the No. 3 and No. 11 seeds, respectively. A fan coming to this match with fresh eyes would have seen that their gifts overlapped quite a bit. They had the finest groundstrokes of their age cohort, all precision and heavy spin, concussive power even when reaching for a faraway ball. But there were also some key differences. Alcaraz was superior in foot speed and vertical leap, and his shot selection skewed far spicier, thanks in part to his softer hands. Sinner had a longer wingspan, once-in-a-generation timing that produced outlandish power with minimal energy expenditure, and a sturdier backhand. They also shared one conspicuous flaw. The staple skill at the top of the men's tour is a consistent serve that earns low-effort points, because the returner struggles to put it back into play. For both players, the serve was a weakness that needed to be refined in the future; for the viewers, it was a boon to entertainment, because the points landed in neutral territory, where both players had to get creative to earn an advantage in the rally. Their lack was our gain.

To lay out every intricacy of the match would require its own book. Every surface of it was embedded with little experiments, regrets, and triumphs. Alcaraz toyed with an unconventional wide position on serve, which opened up an even more extreme angle for him; Sinner began slinging those returns down-the-line. One such return won Sinner the second set and left Alcaraz standing motionless. Sinner won every single point in the third-set tiebreak and led early in the fourth set. But he also blew a match point on his own serve late in that set, when Alcaraz began to play the high-pressure rallies with more clarity. Sinner led again early in the fifth set, only for Alcaraz to break back and high-five some courtside fans. He was developing a taste for crowd work; Sinner kept to himself. For both players there were discrete moments when victory seemed inevitable. But the win belonged solely to Alcaraz. The head-to-head had been leveled at 2-2.

After the match, Sinner remembered the crosscourt backhand he'd hit on match point, barely wide, thinking that if he'd kept it inside the court, he could have advanced to the semifinal instead of Alcaraz. But he said he had to "cancel" these ruminations so as not to get fixated on past mistakes. Though he'd lost, Sinner accomplished something more abstract with this match. He killed off any illusion that Alcaraz would rule the next era of tennis alone. Sinner had been just one ball away from beating Alcaraz in three straight matches on three different surfaces in 2022. In the early days, when sample size is small, rivalries are mutable, and the narratives shape-shift with every match. Or even with a single shot, missed by inches.

While Sinner was hung up on one particular shot he'd missed, Alcaraz was surely delighted by one particular shot he'd made, a highlight wild enough to turn tennis agnostics into converts. He was returning serve. Sinner's serve yanked him out to the left corner of the court. Alcaraz blocked the ball back and recovered to the middle. From there, he had to guess where Sinner was going to strike next, and he started moving toward the right corner. But he'd guessed wrong. Instead Sinner had put the ball clean down the center of the court, and Alcaraz was about to run *past* the ball. There was no solution for this puzzle. Except, of course, the absurdist solution: leaping straight into the air, wrapping the racquet behind his torso, and flicking the ball back over the net. This wasn't just a desperation behind-the-back shot that barely burbled over the net; it was an aggressive passing shot that genuinely threatened Sinner. Alcaraz won the point. His coach Ferrero shook his head and clapped, joining the rest of the crowd in a state of disbelief.

Many matches that stretch to five sets are hailed as classics, but closer inspection reveals their lulls and impurities. The thrilling fifth-set tiebreak gets enshrined in popular memory, and everyone politely forgets the third-set dud. This one, though, was euphoric from first ball to last. It was a match so good that fellow pro Coco Gauff tweeted that she had an early morning plane to catch, but refused to sleep and miss any of it. At the end it was a five-hour-and-15 minute odyssey. For the second match in a row, Alcaraz was on court past two a.m., playing for a thinned-out audience of diehards who were allowed to clamber down to the money seats, rewarded for their patience with a better view of tennis's future. Rueful on my sofa, I resolved never to miss another match between these two if I was within a 500-mile radius.

The American player Frances Tiafoe, who had entered the tournament unseeded but rocketed into the semifinals, awaited the winner of the Alcaraz-Sinner clash. He had joked earlier in the day that he wanted to see a marathon that would tire out the players, softening up whomever he'd end up playing. He got the marathon, but not a sufficiently soft Alcaraz. The Spaniard took him down in a Friday night showcase, not as incandescent as the Sinner match, but hitting similar highs. For Carlitos it was a third consecutive five-set match, this one lasting three hours, 50 minutes.

He had just one more task. In the final, he took on Casper Ruud. The 23-year-old Norwegian, who played a high-topspin style modeled on Rafael Nadal, was in his second major final of the year. Just like Alcaraz, he would reach the No. 1 ranking if he won the U.S. Open. He must have detected some fatigue in Alcaraz, because early in the match, Ruud was the decisive actor, cutting short lengthy crosscourt exchanges with his own bullets down-the-line. Carlitos had been avoiding his backhands, shifting his body perilously to the left to convert them into the forehands he preferred. So Ruud kept pushing him into that corner, deeper and deeper, daring Alcaraz to take bigger risks.

In a parallel universe, Ruud continued that path all the way to the trophy and the top ranking. But in our universe, Alcaraz was already solving the problems at hand. As he said later in press, he had grown "nervous" about Ruud's success from the back of the court, so he moved instead toward the strategy that had felt most natural since he was a small boy: Attack the net. At the crux of the match, late in the third set, he realized that Ruud's deep return position made him vulnerable to a serve-and-volley, so he surged forward again and again. (The ball would take longer to travel back from where Ruud was standing, affording Alcaraz extra time to run up and secure good position at the net to pluck the ball out of the air.) This was one of several good decisions that got him to a third-set tiebreak, where Ruud's consistency began to disintegrate. In the fourth set, without warning, Alcaraz began spewing aces on his serve, sparing his legs some hard work.

That's the thing about Alcaraz—there are so many possible versions of him that in best-of-five, an opponent will eventually have to beat several. It was baffling how many distinct parts of tennis he had mastered, how they cohered into this figure of ruin. My initial mistake was trying to fit him into my general schema for understanding tennis players: as human beings whose technical and physical specs grant some gifts and take others off the table. Big servers tend to be too ungainly to return nimbly. The lightest and fastest players often lack punch. The slow-surface specialists panic when the ball bounces faster. But none of these trade-offs seemed to apply to Carlitos. He could simply have it all ways. This was why he evoked a sense of impossibility more than any other player in recent memory, because he combined so many traits that don't belong together into a single psychedelic point. He shouldn't have been able to move his legs that fast while keeping his hands that quiet to sneak lobs an inch inside the baseline. He shouldn't have been able to contort his torso and racquet to scoop up a ball bouncing behind him, while in midair, having already sprinted past it. But he did all this and more.

At the end of the final, which he won in four sets, Alcaraz announced his mission statement. "I came here just to enjoy, you know? To smile on court, to enjoy playing tennis," he said. "I would say if I smile, if I have fun out there, I saw my best level, my best tennis." That broad, sharky smile was a dark omen for the rest of the tour. If he was enjoying himself, his tennis was probably unplayable. He had smiled right into the camera even after receiving an 18-shot battering from Ruud, lying flat on his stomach, taking in the show as if he were spectator and performer at once. In all, he gave the world 23 hours and 40 minutes of tennis to pore over in this fortnight. It was, at the time, the longest that any player had ever spent on court during any major. He would have cleaner major title runs, but this first one was all the more engaging for its stumbles. By winning it, he became the youngest man ever to reach world No. 1, at just 19 years, four months, and six days old.

We were meant to understand that this was a work in progress. Juan Carlos Ferrero said after the U.S. Open win that he thought Carlitos was only at "60 percent of his game." It was as though he'd announced plans to erect a skyscraper at the summit of a Himalayan peak. It was a slightly disturbing pronouncement, to be frank. But Ferrero, who spent the match looking like he'd explode from either paternal pride or digestive distress, depending on the scoreboard, had seen the long journey that culminated in that trophy. "When he arrived to academy when he was 15, he was like a spaghetti, very thin," Ferrero said. He himself had gutted through three five-set matches to make the U.S. Open final in 2003, only to lose. His player succeeded where he had failed. Alcaraz reciprocated the love: "Juan Carlos is my second father. He could train a lot of top players but he decides to be with me." This felt like humility wending into outright dishonesty. The coach was the lucky one to have been picked by this child. Even the sport of tennis was lucky he picked it, when his highlights left you wondering what he might've done as a striker or point guard or wide receiver. Having seen his lobs at a dead sprint, could you imagine his feel with a golf club—if he actually got to do his job standing still?

That title run left me with one indestructible memory. It was late in the first set of his semifinal against Tiafoe. The match already had the smell of war. Alcaraz was standing at the center of the net and Tiafoe tried to poke a ball past him down the right sideline. Alcaraz scampered back to collect it, then sprinted forward again to retrieve a drop volley fizzling into the left sideline, and then ran back the full diagonal of the court to rip a forehand passing shot against the momentum of his body. Imagine his side of the tennis court as a rectangle. Over the course of three shots he had inscribed a triangle—upper right corner, to upper left corner, to lower right corner. Two shots with soft touch, the last lashed with power. Alcaraz widened his eyes and raised his chin in defiance. The crowd raised every limb it had available. There were sounds unlike any I've heard in public. I know that my brain mashed every button on its control panel, that I stood up and clamped my hands against my skull and felt simultaneous urges to gasp, laugh, and cry, arriving at something like the average of the three. I even felt an esoteric urge to leave the stadium right then and there. But of course Alcaraz was then in the middle of this quest, the kind that screamed out to be witnessed.

And he went on to complete it. After his U.S. Open title, he tweeted a motto from his grandpa, words he'd eventually get tattooed on his body. Here it was expressed as emojis: a brain, a heart, two eggs. Or: *cabeza, corazón y cojones.*

CHAPTER 3

Boot and Rally

Eyes are so often deceiving in tennis. Sometimes it is better to trust the ears. The Italian talent scout Fabio Della Vida recalled standing at a tennis tournament, hearing a clamor behind him, and thinking there must be a construction site. He turned around, and it was just a twiggy boy, aged 13 or 14, hitting tennis balls with ludicrous power. The scout heard him before he ever saw him. That boy went on to startle opponents and fans on the pro tour. A frenzied mop of red hair, origins in mountain snow, a name like Sinner—how could I not be intrigued by this unlikely figure flying up the rankings in 2019?

In contrast to the Alcaraz clan, tennis had no sacred place in the Sinner family tree. It was just another game. Jannik Sinner was born to parents who worked as a chef and a waitress at a ski lodge in South Tyrol, which is Italy's northernmost province. South Tyrol borders Austria, and the majority of its residents speak German as a first language. It was a heavily contested territory throughout the twentieth century, and after decades of imperial ploys and separatist fervor, it settled in as an autonomous region of Italy in the 1970s. Sinner's hometown of Sexten rests in the Dolomite mountain range of the

Alps. Skiing was the default athletic pursuit there. "If you imagine coming from here, a tennis player, it's very, very strange," said Sinner during a brief visit home in the spring of 2024, when he returned as the No. 1 player in the world.

His journey to that peak was nonlinear; the racquet was not always a priority. He has described idyllic days as a kid who was good at many games: eating lunch at his grandparents' house, suiting up for ski training from two to four p.m., playing tennis just twice a week, overstaying his curfew to play soccer with friends.

Between the ages of seven and twelve, Sinner was one of the best junior skiers in Italy. He even abandoned tennis completely for a year, at age seven, to commit to the slopes, until he was coaxed back to the court by his father. In those days he idolized the brash style of the American skier Bode Miller, who either "won or crashed," in Sinner's words. Similarly, Sinner himself either wound up on the podium or didn't make it to the finish line. In time he saw how his slender build might put a cap on his potential. "So I was really good," Sinner recalled in 2024. "But then I had a couple of so-so seasons when I started competing against older athletes in slalom and giant slalom, and when downhill came into the picture, I weighed too little to compete."

As an adult, Sinner has been asked incessantly why he gave up skiing to commit to tennis, and he has fashioned a neat answer to be repeated ad nauseam: the margin of error. In a ski race, if you make one mistake, your race is over; in tennis you can make lots of mistakes and still win the match. Then there was also the question of physical danger: "When you go very fast and then you jump 20, 30 meters, you know, it's different. Then I had this fear. And then in my mind in tennis, it's nothing to be scared about, no?" Only at the late age of 13 did Sinner quit the mountains to throw himself into the blinkered, intense developmental pipeline necessary to become a professional tennis player. It is rare to find players on the tour who committed to the sport that deep into their childhood. But Sinner left an impression on everyone who saw him hit a tennis ball, including Riccardo Piatti, a don of Italian tennis who had coached a handful of elite players, including Djokovic for a short stint at the start of the latter's career. Piatti invited him to train full-time at his center on the Italian Riviera, on the opposite side of the country from Sinner's home. Like most people in South Tyrol, Sinner was a native German speaker. He would be sharpening up his rudimentary Italian to descend from the mountains and live by the sea, in Bordighera, his new home.

At the time, most players at the Piatti Tennis Center were older teenagers or adults. Sinner was their first-ever student who was too young to live on his own; his parents also couldn't leave their jobs in South Tyrol. So he lived for a time with one of his coaches, Luka Cvjetkovic. Sinner slid easily into the rhythms of the Cvjetkovic family, hanging out with his coach's two kids, vacuuming on weekends, taking the dog on hikes. Mostly, though, he worked. Cvjetkovic remembered Sinner as a child with an unusual capacity for work, and an unusual gift for simplifying that work. A technical detail that might take others six months to learn, he would handle in a week. Whenever he asked a question, it was aimed with purpose. He wanted to know the rationale behind every drill. This put some pressure on coaches; Jannik was not a pupil who could be pacified with generic drivel. "You need to be very careful what to say to him on the court. You need to be very secure! If you tell him something, don't tell something wrong or stupid," Cvjetkovic recalled. "He was the type of kid that if you ask him 100 questions, he will give you 100 precise answers." About food, about practice, about who he wanted to practice with, he was always lucid and direct. He was able to see distinctions that other kids couldn't, easily compartmentalizing the various parts of his training. He knew when to focus on technique, and then when to shut off that part of his brain that thought about technique, in order to practice match tactics.

After a six-hour day of tennis, conditioning, and recovery, he would come back to the Cvjetkovic family home and go to bed early. But not before continuing his monkish study of the pro game. There were rules. Never watch highlights, which pervert the reality of a tennis match, reducing it to its flashiest moments. Always watch at least one full set. And pick the syllabus carefully. Sinner watched only those "who have order, players with some sense," according to his coach, so he could understand how they approached different phases of the match and handled pivotal moments. Of the thousands of players Cvjetkovic has worked with, he told me he has never met another who sustained this kind of self-directed film study, sometimes for two or three hours a night.

Living and training at the Piatti Tennis Center meant that Sinner didn't have to just watch ATP players on TV; he could feel the forehands for himself. Pros often popped over to the Piatti Center in their sports cars for hitting sessions on hard courts that felt similar to those at the Australian Open. And Sinner took field trips to Monte-Carlo to train at a country club frequented by the pros. Even as a kid he was analytical rather than starstruck: "He was never the one who was using this [practice session] to be impressed. He was always the one who was doing this to understand where I need to be in three years, in four years, in five years," Cvjetkovic said. "He takes a lot from the practice. Because I know a lot of players doing practice like this, but they don't take too much from this except the Instagram photo." One day in 2016, Sinner trained for an hour with

Milos Raonic, then a top player on tour. When Raonic left, Sinner trained for two more hours with some Italians five years older than him, ranked in the 400s. Then those guys left and Sinner played for an hour and a half with the young son of his coach Piatti. "He played in one period, without stopping, from the No. 5 in the world to a 10-year-old, with completely the same attitude and focus and concentration," said Cvjetkovic.

Everyone noticed the same thing about Sinner's tennis then as they do now: the sound produced when he makes contact with the ball. I have listened to it up close. Depending on his effort level and the acoustics of the court, it has sounded to me like a firearm, a vehicle backfiring, or a hydraulic press. I can understand why that talent scout thought Sinner was a construction site. That such a lanky boy could produce such alarming noises is a testament to how power works in tennis. It is a question of technique, smoothly synchronizing every muscle in the body, from the foot to the torso to the forearm, to meet the ball with the dead center of the racquet, in its "sweet spot." To track a fast-approaching sphere, intuit its trajectory, and start a swing at just the right moment to strike it cleanly—this is known as timing. Sinner has perfect timing the way a singer might have perfect pitch. The impact of strings on ball is devastating and pure. Both his forehand and backhand are equally strong, leaving opponents no refuge. Working under Piatti, Sinner's innate gifts were refined until he became a ball-basher nonpareil.

For all his talent, Sinner wasn't a hyped junior player. That's because he was looking past the boys' tournaments, his eyes already fixed on the grown-up tour. "Playing juniors didn't interest me very much and I always wanted to make ATP points," he said in 2019, immediately after winning his first Challenger title in Bergamo, Italy, at age 17. That was just the fourth Challenger event he'd entered, and he hadn't won a single match in any of his previous tries. A few months later Sinner received a wild card to play the Italian Open, a 1000-level event, where he beat the American veteran Steve Johnson, then ranked No. 59 in the world. Five years later, on his podcast, Johnson happily described the misery of losing to a "super-skinny" 17-year-old. After the match he called his agent and said, "I just lost to this kid. This kid sucks. He's terrible." He threatened to quit tennis. The agent and a few coaches assured him that Sinner was for real, but Johnson wasn't having it: "You guys are so stupid, this guy's never going to make it anywhere, he's going to have one win and it's going to be me."

By the end of that year, Sinner had qualified, barely, for the Next Gen ATP Finals, an event that fishes around in the pool of promising under-21 players in hope of showcasing the next superstar. Sinner was the eighth and last player to earn a spot. He won the whole thing. By late 2019 he became the youngest player to enter the top 100 since Rafael Nadal did it in 2003. Sinner was 18 years and two months old; Alcaraz would go on to beat that record in 2021 by six weeks. But unlike Alcaraz, Sinner had not been steeped in tennis since childhood. He had gone full-time only five years earlier.

Sinner's early career trajectory was as steep as the mountains back home. He won lower-level ATP events with regularity. He developed a peculiar vegetable-themed fan base, inspired by one viral 2019 incident when he snacked on a carrot mid-match in Vienna. The Carota Boys, as the most devoted of this fan base came to be known, arrived at his matches around the world in full-body carrot costumes. By the end of 2020, Sinner was ranked in the top 40; by the end of 2021 he was in the top 10. And in 2022, he finally began to stagnate.

Early in that 2022 season, during the Australian Open, cameras on court captured proof of his fraying relationship with Piatti. "Stay fucking calmer," the otherwise tranquil Sinner snapped at his coach. After nearly seven years of collaboration, Sinner split with Piatti later that season. Reflecting on this moment three years later in an interview with *Corriere della Sera,* the coach said he'd been strict with Sinner but had no regrets. He felt it was inevitable that his star pupils would "one day tell me to go to hell." That was the job. Sinner later said of his decision, "I wanted to throw myself into the fire." He sought change, no matter the discomfort.

He hired a new pair of coaches. One was Darren Cahill, a veteran Australian coach known for his sunny bedside manner, who had already stewarded three players to major titles, and would offer Sinner big-picture psychological guidance. The more hands-on, technical coach was Simone Vagnozzi, an Italian in his late thirties whom Sinner had known since childhood. As a player, the five-foot-eight Vagnozzi had been undersized and underpowered, pushed to refine every facet of his technique to squeeze out every possible advantage. In the absence of power, he had to thoughtfully move the ball around the court, carve drop shots, and come to net. These happened to be the exact gaps in Sinner's game, which was defined by relentless, sometimes narrow-minded ball-striking from the baseline.

What Sinner needed was that elusive quality called "feel"—the ability to caress the ball rather than always pound it, to place it short rather than always deep, to volley it out of the air rather than always waiting for it to bounce. Alcaraz was an avatar of pure feel. Could something so instinctive be taught? Vagnozzi set out to cultivate it in his new pupil. At first, Sinner was overwhelmed by the flood of minute technical details Vagnozzi offered after each practice. But as with most things in his tennis life, he began to internalize these lessons quickly, and the evidence showed up in his matches: a short slice here, a sweeter volley there. Piatti had constructed the engine of Jannik's game, the baseline power. Vagnozzi now added an overlay of finesse and variety. And Cahill was there to keep Sinner feeling good in the punishing schedule of tour life. "Even if I don't smile a lot, but still, I have a lot of fun," Sinner attested. With this new team, he was looking to the future. In the summer of 2023, he debuted his own logo in the shape of a fox, a reference to a childhood nickname. It was the sort of move undertaken only by players who expect to make some outsize impact on the sport, and to monetize that impact.

And yet, as with skiing before, it seemed as though physical limitations were holding Sinner back, making the biggest titles look like remote possibilities. He still wilted when pushed to a fifth set. An easy draw at Wimbledon that summer helped him reach his first major semifinal; Alcaraz, still a step ahead, won the whole thing, notching his second major title. By September 2023, given the same set of facts, a tennis fan could tell two stories about the 22-year-old Jannik Sinner. The more pessimistic read: a solid top-10 player who thrived in the best-of-three format, had middling head-to-head records against elite peers and struggled with his stamina and late-game composure in best-of-five. A more optimistic read: the heaviest hitter on tour, a technical marvel who just needed to build up his body and serve, and then he'd seize multiple major titles.

There was no real consensus.

Sinner's signature red curls disappeared into a black trash bin one late October night in Beijing, as he vomited midway through his 2023 quarterfinal against Grigor Dimitrov. The player who emerged from the bin post-puke was an altogether changed beast. In the span of a few months, Sinner went from a talented second-stringer most notable for his ability to test Alcaraz to an undeniable prodigy in his own right. It later became a meme: When Sinner ducked into that trash bin, he was purging himself of the capacity to lose.

Sinner's 2023 season had been decent heading into Beijing: his first major semifinal, his first 1000-level title in Toronto after two runner-up finishes, and then a swing through American hard courts that was more grueling than gratifying. He lost in the fourth round of the U.S. Open on familiar terms: a draining five-set match against another top-10 player, Zverev, who beat him for the fourth consecutive time. After the Open, the tour goes to east Asia. Sinner had never even visited China, because its big tournaments had been halted during the pandemic. In the days before his first Beijing tournament, he was asked about his budding rivalry with Alcaraz. They'd split their two encounters that year, both big semifinals at the 1000-level, and the tally was three wins apiece. But responding to that question, Sinner was reluctant to discuss the topic, even deferential. "It's tough to talk about this rivalry because I feel he has won so many things," he said. "At the moment, he's still a better player, no? He has shown this. He was No. 1 in the world already a couple of times. I think at the moment the biggest rivalry is him and Novak." He said he would be happy to be a rival in the future, and felt he had the potential to do it, but insisted, with a smile, that he wasn't there yet.

For a 500-level event, the field in Beijing was treacherous, with talent lurking in every round. And even before the puke, there were other bodily woes for Sinner. He arrived in China already sick. He was hopeful he could recover for his first-round match against Dan Evans. During that match he fell hard, came up clutching his thigh, and requested a medical time-out. Evans, a prickly Brit with a slick game, was skeptical of the injury and antsy to keep playing. On tour there's a fair amount of gamesmanship when it comes to medical time-outs, which can be used dishonestly to break momentum or catch a breather. Evans expressed his displeasure by miming a limp and laughing darkly at the crowd. Sinner, who is sparse with emotion on court, replied only by beating him in three sets. The next match was the one against Dimitrov. Sinner was up 3-0 in the third set when nausea beat out dignity. The trash bin's large lid offered the barest shred of privacy from a rather aggressively positioned cameraman. Afterward Sinner said he "probably ate something wrong." He won in three sets, but it was a late finish and he looked in no state for his next test: Alcaraz, coming in hot off a U.S. Open semifinal, and having blitzed his two previous Beijing opponents in straight sets. Sinner's prospects were grim.

Sometimes it seems that the trick of playing Alcaraz is to strip him of opportunities to remember how original he is. Sinner, somehow recovered from his trials, managed to pin Alcaraz to the back of the court, as a butterfly to a corkboard. He used his power to deprive Alcaraz of his usual creative resources: wide angles, ample time on the ball, openings for a drop shot.

Even when forced into retreat, Alcaraz could still pull off defensive retrievals so ridiculous that each one landed like a punchline. The point had to be won several times over. Sinner stayed steady, however, and Alcaraz soon began to overcook his own shots in an attempt to outdo him. Sinner closed out the first set with a return winner, smearing the ball past an outstretched arm of Alcaraz, who'd skidded into a full split. From Sinner's player box came the sport's universal sign of coach elation: standing up with a taut, almost haunted gaze. This would really be a distressing expression, were it not accompanied by a celebratory raised fist. Here were two fists, belonging to two bearded Italians, Sinner's coach Vagnozzi and his fitness trainer Umberto Ferrara.

Sinner carried that same brilliance into the second set and met less resistance there. He won 7-6(4), 6-1, and of all his wins over Alcaraz, it was the most lopsided scoreline. For the first time in his career, he also led their rivalry, 4-3.

The relief was only temporary, since in the final Sinner would be playing Daniil Medvedev, who had won all six of their previous encounters. This was consistent with Sinner's struggles against top players at this juncture of his career: 1-4 against Zverev, 2-5 against Tsitsipas, and 0-3 against Djokovic. All week in Beijing, Medvedev had been in peak form: slapping flat and accurate shots, demonstrating a tremendous tolerance for cardiovascular suffering. For Sinner to finally win this matchup, he would have to maintain his power over a long period of time without losing his legs or focus. To exploit Medvedev's deeper court positioning, Sinner would have to use the tricks Vagnozzi had added to his game: following his serves to the net or sneaking up there mid-rally. Sinner did all that, played airtight tiebreaks, and won the title. Afterward he thanked Medvedev for letting him "win at least one match" and "making me a better player." The Sinner optimist's case had strengthened considerably. Still, it was just a 500-level tournament.

The following week in Shanghai, he lost early to the beefy and effusive American Ben Shelton in three sets. But Sinner then captured another 500-level title in Vienna, deposing Medvedev again in the final, clearly getting more comfortable in the matchup. At the season's last 1000-level event in Paris, he ended on a sour note. He won his first match, but it kept him up late. "I finished the match when it was almost three in the morning and didn't go to bed until a few hours later. I had less than 12 hours to rest and prepare for the next game," he wrote, about as close as he comes to outrage in a public statement, an ice cube releasing a single droplet.

After a match, players must cool down, often on a stationary bike, work with a physiotherapist to address their aches, shower up, field questions from the media, and get home. Finish a match late enough and the sun will be up when head hits pillow. Sometimes the tournament's scheduling gods try to accommodate this by pushing a player's next match as late as possible, but in this instance, there was no lenience. Sinner was slated for the next afternoon. Many players would grit through the situation, show up to the match, tolerate near-certain defeat, and collect a check. But a player at a certain level of financial security or self-possession might just blow off the tournament and quit town. That was the tack Sinner chose. He withdrew from Paris to prioritize his tournaments in the weeks ahead.

That might have been an auspicious choice, because the true Sinner magic came later that month, at the ATP Finals in Turin, where he didn't win the title but accomplished something psychologically bigger, a rite of passage for any ambitious player. The ATP Finals gather the top eight players in the world—the adult version of the under-21 Next Gen Finals that Sinner had won in 2019. It's played in a round-robin format, followed by a single-elimination bracket. It's difficult to pin down the precise reputation of the tournament. It's technically worth 1500 points, landing halfway between a 1000-level event and a major. The field is all killers, by definition. But it's also best-of-three sets, unlike the majors, and it happens at the tail end of the season. The event tests who has preserved themselves best for this sprint at the end of an ultramarathon.

Sinner came to Turin a sphere of heat and light, the home favorite, lustily cheered by Italian crowds. And the matchups continued to tilt his way. He took out the flagging Tsitsipas, who had won the title in the past. For the first time he beat Holger Rune, a Danish player born a week before Alcaraz, who fancied himself the third piece of their rivalry and had beaten Sinner in their two previous matches. On this day Rune looked like an afterthought.

Then came the gatekeeper. It was an axiom in men's tennis: If you do well enough in a meaningful tournament, there will come a time when you line up across the net from Novak Djokovic. He was the tournament's No. 1 seed, supreme after winning three of the season's four majors. It was a match of fine margins. Three sets, two tiebreaks. Djokovic had long reigned over the tiebreak format. He could enter a lockdown mode, lowering the risk of his own shots while still putting the opponent in unpleasant situations and still whittling away at their nerves. It almost always worked. But here Sinner triumphed, his first win over Djokovic in four tries, and the clearest indicator yet of his breakthrough. The thin, wilting kid had become a force.

Sinner's reward was yet another test against Medvedev, who likes fast courts like the ones in Turin. Medvedev delights in torturous backhand-to-backhand exchanges that have a faintly frog-boiled-alive aspect; opponents are doomed a half-dozen shots before they realize it. In the deciding set, Sinner accepted that challenge head-on. He was the frog unboiled. He never shied away from Medvedev's insidious two-hander, instead going straight at it with his heavier and angrier version, a frying pan meeting a sledgehammer. That second set from Sinner was as pure a sequence of backhands as you'll see this side of Djokovic. Speaking of that guy—he wasn't done. The unusual structure of this event meant that a player might have to defeat Djokovic *more than once* to win the overall title. And that was precisely how the bracket lined up for Sinner once he defeated Medvedev. Unable to produce two straight miracles and get canonized on home soil, Sinner lost to Djokovic in the title fight. But he would have an opportunity for revenge a week later.

The Davis Cup is a team-based national competition, which used to be more prestigious, drawing maximal effort from the game's best players. While it has dipped from that former prominence for reasons ranging from bureaucratic mismanagement to the increased rewards and demands of individual competition, its crowds are still loud with dueling patriotism. Serbia and Italy met in the semifinal, which was held in Málaga, Spain. Sinner had skipped the earliest stages of the event, but as Italy's best player, he parachuted into this late stage to take up the unenviable task of taming the GOAT. Djokovic, always keyed-up to play for his country's honor, hadn't lost a Davis Cup singles match in twelve years.

But Sinner had something most of Djokovic's prior foes lacked, which was fresh muscle memory of having beaten this man. Perhaps this was what the Italian drew on in the third set, when he faced three match points while serving at 4-5, 0-40. He stepped to the baseline, threw up a nervy ball toss, which sailed a little too far to his left, and let it fall to the court. The Davis Cup crowd, which runs much hotter than your usual one, possibly high off the fumes of nationalism, started howling and whistling. Then Sinner tossed the ball up again and hit it out. That made it second serve, down match point, against the most dangerous returner in the sport's history. Sinner put a safe ball right in the middle of the service box, then followed it with steady backhands until he saw a Djokovic slice float three feet long. A fist pump: one match point saved. Next: A first serve struck pure and wide, unreturnable for the man who returns everything. Still one more match point to go. On this one Sinner thumped his serve, crept forward to hit a forehand approach shot, and chose to test his fate at the net. His last shot hadn't been good enough. Djokovic had plenty of space to push the ball down the sideline, a shot he'd executed some hundred thousand times to perfection. Sinner started moving to cover that sideline—but for whatever reason, Djokovic instead sent his reply right into the middle of the court, and Sinner stopped his move midway, wiggled his body out of the ball's path, and knocked a volley into open space. Deuce—the fist pump now sterner, the lips pursed. Two big first serves, neither one returnable, and Sinner was free. Having leapt out of a seemingly fatal pit, he won 13 out of the next 16 points to win 6-2, 2-6, 7-5.

If that wasn't enough Djokovic for the year, or even a lifetime, Sinner came back for another helping. Later that same day at the Davis Cup they faced off in doubles, and Djokovic, never the most instinctive doubles player, looked frazzled. Sinner then basked in the improbable honor of defeating the game's greatest player twice in one day. Djokovic had suffered only three singles losses total since the beginning of Roland-Garros in May. It was now November. Two of those three losses were Sinner's doing. The only other was Alcaraz's. All told, Sinner had played Djokovic four times in 11 days and come up with three wins, a runner-up finish at the ATP Finals, and Italy's first Davis Cup trophy since 1976.

Far be it from me to discount a match win against Novak Djokovic; I've spent some portion of the book arguing that it is a big deal. But it must be acknowledged that the indoor hard-court season at the end of the calendar year is a sort of bizarro tennis season, an alternate plane of reality. Players arrive worn down and sometimes appear to be playing more out of financial obligation than competitive zeal, with the year's biggest prizes already in the rearview mirror. It's difficult to assess how success in these matches, played in controlled environments with predictable and quick bounces, translates to the rest of the tour schedule, played outside with fickle variables of weather, and on uneven and evolving surfaces like clay and grass. Sometimes there are fluky runs on indoor courts—late-season efflorescence that isn't followed up with proportionate success in the following season. Would Sinner be another indoor hero unable to deliver the same quality outdoors? The tour would have its answer in Australia.

Before that: some rest. In tennis, the more you win, the more you work. That unstoppable indoor season had put heavy mileage on those thin legs. And the tennis offseason is so short, players must approach even leisure time with intention. In late November, Sinner appeared at a Champions League soccer match, AC Milan hosting Dortmund. As he walked onto the pitch before play, waving to the crowd, his Davis Cup victory for Italy still top of mind, the fans welcomed him with what sounded like a war chant: *yah-neek, yah-neek, seen-air, seen-air.* By this point a bona fide national icon, Sinner then got to go home to the Alps and spend a bit of December in his happy place: on skis.

CHAPTER 4

Dancing in the Pressure Storm

The professional tennis calendar leaves no room for sloth. It is not an apt profession for anyone who prioritizes "a recharge" or "sleeping in your own bed for any longer than a few days at a time." Play deep into the calendar year, as Sinner and Alcaraz did in 2023, and you'll barely get a month off. And during that paltry offseason, the self-care will give way to sharpening up for the season to come.

The young stars spent a day in late December 2023 training together. Sinner paid a visit to Villena, Spain—incidentally, the site of their first-ever match, when Jannik was 17 and Carlos was 15—to hit at the Juan Carlos Ferrero Tennis Academy. Both players posted group pictures after the practice, the two of them flanked by their flotilla of coaches and trainers. Each player documented the moment in his own personal style. Sinner, a single pic, captioned only with "A good day of practice." Alcaraz, a full slideshow of images and earnest words: "Great morning and a great session! Warming up for 2024!" he wrote, which was more prescient than he could have realized.

For both of them, the season would start in Melbourne, site of the Australian Open. Roger Federer dubbed the Australian Open "the Happy Slam," because "people are happy to play again, happy to see each other." This is because it takes place in January, before the season has ravaged players' bodies and psyches, and after the off-season has temporarily renewed their optimism about career choice. Perhaps it's odd to place one of the four most important tournaments this early in the year, four months away from the next major, but it also gives the Open its singular mood. Everyone seems to arrive on equal footing. Nobody's bringing aches and pains, and nobody's bringing much match momentum. It often feels like a tournament of self-discovery, as if the players, briefly chipper and undamaged, are learning where they'll stand in the season to come.

As far as happiness is concerned, it also doesn't hurt that it takes place in a coastal city during the Australian summer, with logistics more manageable than in the urban sprawl of Paris, London, or New York. Players tend to fly down under just before New Year's to prepare for the task ahead. Before the majors, it's common practice to play a warm-up: smaller events, typically on a similar court surface and in similar weather conditions, which will help the players get into rhythm for the higher-stakes best-of-five matches to come. In 2024, Sinner and Alcaraz skipped the warm-up events in Australia and New Zealand, a move that many pundits questioned. Even Djokovic had played one, starting the season at the United Cup, winning two singles matches and losing one to a Alex de Minaur, a reedy Australian who managed not to lose a single point behind his first serve, despite playing such a gifted returner. It was a slightly out-of-character loss for Djokovic, but nothing that warranted genuine skepticism.

If there were any questions about the decision-making of Sinner or Alcaraz, they evaporated over the first week of the Australian

Open. Alcaraz, the No. 2 seed, won his first four matches mostly without incident. Sinner, the No. 4 seed, won his with conspicuous ease. He didn't lose a single set. He had lost only two games while serving. The man who was broken 11 times across five sets by Alcaraz back in their 2022 epic had become an elite server in roughly a year. And Sinner also had grown into a new grace, taking on the little rituals of superstar magnanimity, nodding and waving to the crowd, issuing the thumbs-up, all the details he might have eschewed in his more robotic past. Even a sly sense of humor was cracking open in public. "I made also a little bit of gym, even if you can't see it, I'm skinny, but it's okay," he said after his second-round win, holding up his pinky to model for his body type, then giggling and refusing to answer a follow-up about how much he weighed. "I'm happy with my physicality at the moment—of course you dream to have the *Baywatch* physicality," he said, buoyant in a way he hadn't been before. This was a man who had given stone-faced answers for years. He had seemed to resent the elision of his public and private worlds, brought on by his line of work. He liked to hit the ball and retreat back into ordinary life, despite his extraordinary talent. But was he suddenly having fun out there on court in Australia? It must have had something to do with the untouchably good tennis he'd been playing and the way he'd carried it into a major tournament, the site of so many past disappointments.

The real tests, though, were still to come: In the semifinals he would face Djokovic, who had set an ungodly standard at the Australian Open. He had lifted the trophy 10 times, and never lost after reaching the semifinal stage. Heading into the match against Sinner, he had won 33 matches in a row at the tournament, a streak that dated back to 2018. But in 2024 he had looked scrappy through the early rounds, dropping sets here and there. He lost one set to a promising but low-ranked 18-year-old Croat, Dino Prižmić, who looked fleet-ingly like a young Djokovic himself, before disappearing for the rest of the season. He lost one set in a testy second-round match against Alexei Popyrin, an Aussie enjoying a lift from the home crowd. Dur-ing the match Djokovic extended a personal invitation to one persis-tent heckler. "At one point I had enough, and I asked him whether he wants to come down and tell it to my face," he told reporters af-terward. "Unfortunately for him, he didn't have the courage to come down." He continued venting his frustrations in his fourth-round match against the Frenchman Adrian Mannarino, a tennis anomaly who has put up his best results in his late thirties, using unusually loose racquet strings and unusually short swings, and has attributed his success to not looking at his draw. He also attributed it to drink-ing tequila. By way of comparison, Djokovic, after toppling Nadal in a nearly six-hour Australian Open final a dozen years earlier, famously permitted himself just a single square of chocolate, letting it melt on his tongue. In 2024, Djokovic beat Mannarino so thoroughly that his behavior during the match made little sense. The crowd began to cheer the beleaguered underdog when he finally won his first game. When Djokovic complained to the umpire about a technicality with the clock, and the crowd then began to boo him—as they often do, even when it's a great player griping—he swayed his hands like a con-ductor of an orchestra. It was the sort of grandstanding that would feel appropriate if this had been a contentious match; Djokovic was up 6-0, 6-0, 1-1. While he closed out the third set, 6-3, for one of the most one-sided wins of his long career, the emotional tenor was not of a storied champion handling business with calm and grace, but of something cagey and defiant lashing out. Some of Djokovic's best tennis has always come from that place.

He carried that same disquiet into his semifinal appointment with

Sinner. When Djokovic is playing a best-of-five match, there's often a luxurious lack of urgency to the affair. So what if he starts flat-footed? He is inevitability personified. He knows, as he gradually gets the blood pumping and the synovial fluids flowing, that he has a dozen higher gears of tennis at his disposal, and he'll activate them as needed. He knows that his top gear can be matched by only a handful of people in the history of the sport. One of them was retired and probably eating fondue (Roger Federer), and another was busy rehabbing his hip (Rafael Nadal), and the youngest had just been upset the day before (Carlos Alcaraz).

Alcaraz had played a loose and distracted quarterfinal against Zverev, who remained a frustrating matchup for him. This match epitomized the Alcaraz puzzle. His losses can look worse than the losses of other top players. He can be capable of stupefying ingenuity while playing against the best opponents, even in the most tense moments of a match. He can also, in more pedestrian moments, play squirrelly and confused tennis. He might get fixated on ideas that amuse him but do not win him points; he might start peacocking prematurely. And his serve might go awry, as it did against Zverev in this quarterfinal, because that was a skill he still hadn't perfected, like Sinner had in recent months. Alcaraz flashed his iconic smile after he managed to break Zverev's serve for the first time in the match. Unfortunately for him, the scoreboard already read 1-6, 3-6, 3-5. He did go on to win an exuberant third-set tiebreak but went limp again in the fourth set, ending his run in Australia. The commentator David Law, summing up the match on the Tennis Podcast, deemed Alcaraz's performance in the first two-and-a-half sets "unprofessional." For his fans, these off days could be maddening. They had seen how sublime Carlitos was at his peak, and they couldn't believe just how far he could stray from the holiest version of himself. "It's a shame that I started the match like the way that I did, and ending the way that I did," he told reporters after. "But it's tennis."

Djokovic seemed to be joining Alcaraz in disarray. Sometimes it feels as though Djokovic donates his younger opponents a set or two just for sport. But even by his unhurried standards, his semifinal against Sinner began in a bizarre fashion. In short: He looked busted. This gifted contortionist, who eases in and out of full splits while running at a full sprint, was regularly losing his balance as he trotted along the baseline at low speeds. He was blooping mundane rally balls into the net. It was as if someone had designed a life-size marionette in the image of Novak Djokovic and was trying, rather skillfully but ultimately pointlessly, to pilot it through a world-class tennis match. It was about as badly as I'd ever seen him play, at a tournament he'd won 10 times. It took him 21 minutes to win his first game. He dropped the first two sets quickly. Sinner was doing good work, but it wasn't good enough to account for all this.

Finally, in set three, came the turn that tennis audiences have come to relish and/or dread, depending on their perspective on Djokovic. The champion eased his way back into the rallies and looked capable of turning the match around despite his two-set deficit. I was reminded again of how much the two players had in common. Djokovic's signature shot is the sliding backhand down-the-line. He sees a ball approaching the lower left corner of the court, sprints toward it, and then, while he is still two paces away, he plants his left foot, hard. He is done taking steps. They are too crude for the task at hand. Instead he allows both feet to *skid* on the court surface, ferrying him right into the ball's path, and with legs splayed wide, he punches the ball right up the sideline. Only a player as flexible and stable as Djokovic could have unlocked such a shot; Sinner is its true inheritor. Both are former skiers, and you can see it in their balance amid the chaos of a rally, their control over the edges of their feet, their soles seemingly more dexterous than a civilian's palms. Sinner sometimes even uses his racquet to propel himself when changing directions, planting it on the court as a skier uses a pole, and pushing off so forcefully that clay and grass get stuck in the top of the frame. (I once asked him if he intentionally borrowed that behavior from the slopes, which he found somewhat absurd; it was unconscious, of course.) Here, in Australia, both of them had begun to glide around as if the hard court were hard-packed snow.

At 5-5 in the third set, deuce, Djokovic serving, someone collapsed in the crowd. Play was paused for almost five minutes, escalating tension even more. When it resumed, Djokovic held serve, Sinner did the same, and they moved to the tiebreak. Sinner got a match point but wasted it. Djokovic won the set instead and lifted a fist. Sinner permitted himself what qualified, by his standards, as an extreme display of rage: gently knocking over one water bottle with another water bottle and tossing the first one to the ground.

A Djokovic momentum shift like this had destroyed many capable young players. Was Sinner about to become food like them, pushed around a plate for the next two sets, or could he banish the debilitating feelings of *what-if*? He'd beaten this guy recently but hadn't yet beaten him where it mattered most, at the majors, in the best-of-five format that Djokovic had mastered. The serve, the key to Djokovic's late empire, was fully operational now, carrying him through a match where his baseline game was fickle. Sinner's lead began to look perilous.

But instead of cracking, Sinner ran away with the fourth set. Down 1-4, Djokovic barked at the chair umpire, who in his view wasn't doing a thorough enough job quieting down the crowd: "You want a cup of tea? Relaxing up there?"

Sometimes a player will pick a fight with the umpire almost to jolt himself awake, hoping it will resuscitate their own tennis. It's a reliable technique for players with a certain cast of mind, and it had worked for Djokovic in the past. But Sinner rode it out. He won, smiled wide, and threw his hands up. He'd beaten better Djokovics before, but this time, he only needed to lock in and beat the facsimile in front of him. Standing on the court afterward, he said with a coy smile that he wouldn't be disclosing his tactics, because he hoped to play his elder again and again. He was that rare young player who genuinely craved more encounters with Novak Djokovic, like a sheep that had developed a taste for wolf.

The Djokovic postmortem was blunt. "Look, I was, in a way, shocked with my level—in a bad way," he said. "I guess this is one of the worst Grand Slam matches I've ever played, at least that I remember." It was also the first time in 15 years that he'd had to play a daytime match this deep into the tournament. He prefers when his matches are scheduled later, in the night session, when the air is cooler and the ball bounces slower, rather than under the burning Melbourne sun.

"I didn't feel really myself on the court during this tournament," he said. Feeling like himself at the Australian Open was a high standard. It had been 2,195 days since Djokovic lost a match in Melbourne. (He had, however, missed one tournament for vaccine- and detention-related reasons.) For all the numerologists out there, this is exactly the same number of days he stood unbeaten at Wimbledon before Carlos Alcaraz had managed to fell him there. The symmetry was mystical: two young rivals, taking out Djokovic at two different majors, breaking streaks of identical calendrical length.

Meanwhile, on the other side of the draw, Zverev had just beaten Alcaraz, holding on to his status as one of the few players with a winning record against the phenom, but he went on to lose to his own personal bugbear, Daniil Medvedev, in the semifinal. Zverev and Medvedev combine to produce some innovatively uncharismatic tennis. They look like two mantises entangled in a slow fight to the death, their rallies lengthy and tiring but devoid of pleasure. Whatever magic Alcaraz and Sinner make on court, consider these guys the spiritual opposite. But they played at least one point that stuck in the mind. Medvedev was two points from losing the match, and returning a serve, when he accidentally hit the ball with the frame of his racquet instead of the strings. This shanked ball behaved wickedly, dribbling over the net as a fluke drop shot that turned the course of the match. Medvedev prevailed in five sets instead.

The Australian Open final was familiar territory for Medvedev, who had appeared there twice before, losing to Djokovic and Nadal. It was new territory for Sinner, who had never before advanced to a major final and had barely met much adversity en route.

It was a match in two parts. In the first part Medvedev was unrecognizable. He came out playing ultra-aggressive tennis, striking his flat strokes with unusual venom and conviction, and Sinner struggled to find his usual baseline power when confronted with those low-skidding balls. A deep-positioned player often criticized for his reluctance to finish points in the front court, Medvedev crashed the net over and over, swooping in like a malevolent albatross to hit some of the best volleys I'd ever seen him attempt. Where was this coming from?

As Medvedev later confirmed, he played this aggressively because he had no other option. He didn't have enough gas in the tank to execute his preferred attritional style. He'd played three five-set matches before the final and decided that attacking Sinner early was his only way to win. And it was the right decision. It nearly pushed

Medvedev to victory over a much fresher opponent who'd spent six fewer hours on court heading into the final. (By the end of the tournament, Medvedev had accumulated 24 hours and 17 minutes on court, the most of any player at any tournament in modern history, breaking the record Alcaraz had set at the 2022 U.S. Open.)

Medvedev locked in a two-set lead. Early in the third, Sinner toweled off his sweat while announcing his own demise to his player's box: "Sono morto"—*I'm dead.* In fact, it was Medvedev who was about to succumb to the fatigue of his marathon matches. There was a subtle downshift in his endurance. Sinner leapt on this drop in quality from his opponent, breaking serve at identical junctures of the third and fourth sets, those tense 4-5 games when Medvedev had to hold his serve to stay alive in the set. Even deep into the fifth set, Medvedev was able to grind out defensive rallies for 20 shots, but he lacked the more explosive gear required to pummel the ground-strokes as hard as he had at the outset of the match. Sinner now had the legs to hang with him for a 39-shot rally and the higher-end power to deliver the coup de grace when necessary.

Despite having never been in a match with these stakes, and despite falling into a big deficit, Sinner endured, and nothing in his tennis faltered. He didn't deviate from his usual patterns, but kept at them until the points started going his way, mining belief from each incremental success, staring into his box with cold eyes. Ending points against a counterpuncher as sharp as Medvedev often requires changing the trajectory of a rally with a single decisive stroke. Sinner's down-the-line shots came in hotter and hotter as the match progressed, and he captured the championship, fittingly, with a volcanic running forehand ripped down the sideline. How would he celebrate? Many players lose their inhibitions to joy and hurl themselves forcefully at the ground. Upon completion of this childhood dream, Sinner responsibly and gently lowered himself onto his butt, using both hands for support, and then rolled back to assume the traditional starfish of relief. There were no tears as far as the camera could discern. As for the parallel drama in his player's box, his coaches, physiotherapist, trainer, and manager—who had been following the final point with queasy expressions—coalesced into a raucous embrace. This was their beginning.

"I like to dance in the pressure storm," Sinner said in his press conference. His gutsy tennis had reflected this philosophy. Instead of speaking about his life obliquely, as he often did, he delivered a poignant, specific message about his family. "I wish that everyone could have my parents, because they always let me choose whatever I wanted to, even when I was younger," Sinner said during his victor's speech. "I made also some other sports, and they never put pressure on myself. I wish this freedom is possible for as many young kids as possible." They're sweet, simple remarks in any normal context, but in the world of tennis, having normal parents is almost a flex. It's a sport notorious for intrusive dads (mostly) who have engineered their kids' lives for success since the racquet was first placed into tiny hands—a dark, teleological parenting style. It often takes years of effort for the grown-up players to extricate themselves from these relationships.

And yet here was Sinner, a sedate counterexample. A new, clearer picture of the Italian began to unfurl. Someone who came late to tennis, was never cornered into it, was at little risk of burnout compared to his peers, and instead maintained a gluttonous appetite for improvement. Even with the trophy sitting in front of his face, he was talking about next steps. "It's a great moment for me and my team," he said. "But in the other way, we also know that we have to improve if we want to have another chance to hold a big trophy again." Tennis was no longer the sport for gentlemen who liked a cigarette during changeovers; it belonged to single-minded ascetics.

Later, his coach Darren Cahill would say that he began to believe in a comeback because he could hear the difference in the sound of the ball coming off Sinner's racquet. As noted, his pure talent at ripping the tennis ball has always been apparent to those blessed with ears and some proximity to Sinner. But it wasn't until the 2024 Australian Open that he connected that central genius with the larger web of skills required for a major title run: consistent serving, energy conservation, recovery, tactical flexibility, endurance in both short bursts and long stretches. And also the irrational self-belief that kept him from preemptive surrender in the semifinal, when he played a champion who hadn't lost in that stadium in six years. Going into this Open, Sinner had an inglorious 4-12 record against top-20 players in major tournaments, but in this run, he beat all four such opponents.

When asked in a press conference if Alcaraz's conquest of two majors had motivated Sinner, coach Cahill was unambiguous: "Hell yeah." He expressed gratitude to Alcaraz for setting a course that they could follow. "We aspire to be as good as him and hopefully one day be better than him, but at the moment we're chasing Carlos, and we'll continue to do that," he said.

Even within the narrow category of prodigy, careers move at their own pace. Sinner had been moving steadily along when Alcaraz, two years his junior, arrived as a tour-warping force of nature and took dramatic pogo jumps from milestone to milestone. Sinner had kept up with Alcaraz in direct competition, but he lagged behind him in overall body of work. The chase intensified, however, once Sinner vomited into that bin in Beijing. Since then he'd booted and rallied to his first major title, solidifying the legend of Post-Puke Sinner.

Between the upchuck and this trophy, he had beaten all his most troublesome rivals, addressed the strongest critiques of his game, snagged a few smaller titles, brought national glory to Italy, and even begun to show early signs of a personality. He now joined Alcaraz on the highest plateau of the sport. This evolved Sinner was one of the tour's most balanced players, in every sense of that word: on both forehand and backhand, serve and return, defense and offense. And yet, according to a certain reductive but pervasive fan perspective, the scoreboard was clear: one major title versus two major titles. Get to work, kid.

Of course, nobody was more amenable to that imperative than Jannik himself.

CHAPTER 5

Smiling Through the Swarm

The slogan for Indian Wells is "tennis paradise." Some days I agree. The season's first 1000-level tournament takes place in mid-March in the desert landscape of Southern California's Coachella Valley. There is a high-contrast, hyperreal beauty to the tournament grounds. In good weather, you look up at cloudless blue skies filigreed with palm fronds. From the stands you can stare out at the San Jacinto mountain range, dark and crumbly, like piles of cocoa powder. It is honest dry heat by day, windbreaker weather at night. After sunset you can sometimes smell wildflowers on the breeze.

Fans see all the same players they'd see at a major, but in a more manageable, intimate setting. If they get sick of tennis, they can peel out to Joshua Tree National Park or stop by one of many date farms for a luscious milkshake in the local style. Players seem to like it here, too. They tend to have lots of obligations to their sponsors—photo shoots, parties—but there's also the proximity to Los Angeles, which widens the options for leisure. They can hang out there before the tournament, as Djokovic did in 2024, cheering on his fellow para- gon of Serbian sport, Nikola Jokić, and hugging him after his Nuggets beat the Lakers. Or, after an untimely loss, a player might drive coastward to spend away their woes.

But "paradise" is a little misleading. The elements are not always peaceful: a friend got caught in a sandstorm while driving, the windshield going blank and beige. The abundance of golf courses in such an arid place feels like an affront to the divine. In 2024 in particular, the desert took on a biblical aspect, as various plagues descended upon its tennis courts. It seemed like an apt setting for a man adrift to go soul-seeking.

Carlos Alcaraz arrived looking like one such man. After the Australian Open, he'd flown to South America to play some lower-level clay tournaments. He had fond feelings for the 250-level event in Buenos Aires, which his coach Ferrero had won in 2010, and which Alcaraz himself had won in 2023. But in 2024 he lost in the semifinals and sounded unusually dire afterward. "It's a difficult defeat, it hurt me a lot," he told the press. He worried about his own mind. "It's a shame to see that I haven't improved some things in my concentration since 2023." On the physical front he was suffering, too. The next week, playing in Rio de Janeiro, in just the second point of his first match, he badly rolled his left ankle. He was slow to rise. Slumping into his chair, he slung a towel over his face. The MRI ruled it a grade 2 ankle sprain. That was not enough to stop him from collecting a fat paycheck in Las Vegas, where he played an exhibition match against Nadal—two injured guys putting on just enough of a show.

At age 20, Alcaraz had already reached a point in his career when it was abnormal for him not to win titles; it called out for explanation. His wins were intoxicating, but his losses often looked intoxicated. Since his triumph at Wimbledon the previous season, he'd played 10 tournaments and won none. So despite coming to Indian Wells as the No. 2 seed and defending champion, Alcaraz was not looking like the favorite. The ankle injury lingered, preventing him from practicing at full intensity.

Jannik Sinner, by contrast, still bore his post-puke glow. The wider world had taken notice. Winning a major flings a player into popular consciousness. Even the pope gave Sinner a shoutout: "Today we have to congratulate the Italians because yesterday they won in Australia." Sinner had become the first Italian man to win a major in 48 years. Even after the victory, he seemed like the same old teenager who bought a machine to string his own racquets and save cash. "Before buying something I always look at the price, always. If I go to a restaurant and the pasta with meat sauce costs much more than the one with tomato sauce, I'll take the one with tomato sauce. Not because I'm stingy but because I respect money," he told *Vanity Fair Italia*. Nor had victory altered his tennis mindset. Immediately after winning his first major in Australia, he spent time on the plane wondering how he could have done better. Why had it taken him two whole sets to react to Medvedev's ultra-aggressive strategy? Sinner took two weeks off the tour, then went to the Netherlands to win a 500-level tournament in Rotterdam, which pushed him to a career-high ranking of No. 3 in the world.

He had won 32 of his last 34 matches. Sometimes it's easiest to understand a player's rise in the awe of their peers. No self-actualization goes unnoticed in the locker room, and praise for Sinner was widespread and unequivocal going into Indian Wells. Alcaraz called his rival "the best player in the world right now, without a doubt." Medvedev concurred, saying that Sinner was "the big one right now." Tommy Paul, a player from New Jersey with a fratty demeanor and fishing hobby, borrowed a fine expression from his

Argentinian fitness trainer for a player in unbelievable form. "He's absolutely playing naked right now," Paul decreed.

The draw at Indian Wells has 96 players; the top 32 get a bye in the first round. This bought Alcaraz some extra time to get his ankle right. His third-round match was against Felix Auger-Aliassime. Once upon a time, this sinewy, soft-spoken Canadian was hailed as the top player born in the 2000s. He went pro young, and at 14 years old became the youngest ever to win a match at the Challenger level. He soon found similar success on the main tour, rising as high as No. 6 in the world and making a major semifinal on the strength of his big serve and forehand. I felt somewhat sad as this man, who had at one time been considered the future of the sport, was devoured by the actual, undeniable future of the sport. Auger-Aliassime had the tools a scout might look for in a top player; he was up against someone who had tools nobody could have envisioned. Alcaraz won easily, and in his next round, too.

Sinner made quick work of his first two opponents as well. His fourth round against the American upstart Ben Shelton would be his first real test. Shelton was the only player not named Djokovic to have beaten Sinner in the past five months. He stands six foot five, topped by the broccoli-like coif favored by Zoomers the world over. A former childhood quarterback, Shelton is the answer to a funny old hypothetical: What if blue-chip American athletes trickled into tennis instead of the big team sports? He could've been throwing darts to receivers but instead found himself at the baseline, taking the first serve to bombastic extremes. Not that tennis was such an unexpected outcome for him. His father, Bryan, a former player who reached No. 55 in the world, coached Ben at the University of Florida before quitting that job to follow his large son around the world full-time. Only in his second pro season, the younger Shelton was already among the deadliest servers on tour. His service motion is a spectacle unto itself: the fluid range of motion in his shoulder, the sheer height of his racquet on impact. He doesn't wait for the tossed ball to meet his racquet; he rises up and hurls all of his 195 pounds into each delivery. Recently he'd begun to vary his pure power with change-ups of spin and placement, easing the wear on his body and making it harder for opponents to predict his next ball.

That did not mean he'd make much headway against Sinner, one of the best returners on tour, whose grand floppy wingspan and unshakable balance allow him to poke back into play huge serves that others would leave untouched. Shelton threw down 140-mph bombs that had the whole crowd squealing. Even the serves he missed felt like moments of emotional communion for thousands. Sinner's returns, however, were so strong that Shelton rarely escaped with a stress-free service hold. It was a close match until it wasn't. From 4-4 in the first tiebreak, Sinner strung together 14 of the next 17 points. Blind patriotism dies hard in American tennis audiences, particularly drunk ones, but the crowd support seemed evenly split between the two, a sign of Sinner's ascendence as a household name. As the evening chill set in, Shelton put on sleeves for the second set, and I expected him to fight. He relishes matches against top players, bringing some of the brashness and bluster of college tennis to the comparatively repressed professional tour. One memorable match against Djokovic from the 2023 U.S. Open got spicy enough that the champion impishly mimicked Shelton, who is 15 years his junior. (Shelton had been celebrating each win by hanging up an imaginary phone; Djokovic, who could actually recall life with corded phones, hung up one of his own after winning their duel.) But this match involved no such drama. Sinner broke down Shelton in set two, and the American shuffled off, just another casualty of the Italian's recent spree.

Speaking of Djokovic: The top seed had just spun out in the third round, losing to a different young Italian in a moody affair. Luca Nardi, a touted prospect with nice hands and feel, was not exactly some anonymous schmuck, but he was just 20 years old and ranked outside the top 100. Nardi was also what's called a "lucky loser"— a player who lost the matches that would have allowed him to qualify for the tournament, but managed to squeak in anyway because another player withdrew. Much of the stink of this match emanated from one specific incident in the second set. Djokovic hit a serve that bounced close to the line. Nardi initially stood there with arms slack, lead-footed, thinking that the serve would be called out—but it dipped in. Nardi lightly tapped the ball back into play, and Djokovic played a drop shot in response and then stood there, stunned into immobility, with his arms down and eyes on the umpire. Nardi ran up and nudged the ball past his frozen opponent. Djokovic felt wronged. He began to demand that the umpire do . . . what exactly? It wasn't clear. Possibly he wanted the umpire to call a hindrance on Nardi because he had paused in an odd manner while returning a serve. The umpire was not compelled by this line of reasoning: "Just because he stops doesn't mean the point stops." Nardi didn't point a finger, or call the ball out, or otherwise interrupt the course of play; he was just surprised, and it is not against the rules to be caught by surprise. Djokovic won the second set, so that point had no statistical bearing on the match, but it lodged itself in his mind.

Even when Djokovic isn't playing his best—in this match his groundstrokes lacked their usual depth and sting—it is never easy for an inexperienced player to beat him. Psychologically speaking, there are many ways an underdog can lose control of a match as he inches toward a possible upset of the old champion. He can tighten up, he can overhit, he can abandon the strategy that had taken him far. But Nardi stayed cool and won the third set, tossed his racquet, and rubbed his hands over his face. Later he'd admit that he'd had a Djokovic poster on his bedroom door since he was eight. Arriving at the net for a handshake, in the happiest moment of his career, perhaps the young Italian was expecting a golden phrase of wisdom from his idol. Instead, that idol, typically gracious in defeat, reprised his old gripe. Fluent in four languages and capable in many more, Djokovic killed the vibe in Nardi's native tongue. "It's not right, but bravo," he said repeatedly, motioning to the back of the court, where Nardi had taken his supposedly unsportsmanlike pause. Even the inveterate Djokovic apologists out there acknowledged that their man was being an ass for no reason, probably out of frustration with his own performance. "I was more surprised with my level. My level was really, really bad," came Djokovic's self-assessment after the match. "Every night I go to bed I see Novak," said Nardi, of the poster. "I think that I will keep it," he added.

Here was an anomalous moment in Djokovic's career: Deep into the third month of the season, he still hadn't picked up a title. But anyone whispering about decline still had to pinch themselves and remember that he'd won three majors and made the final of the other one in 2023. Whenever Djokovic loses early, the whole bracket blossoms with potential. Foregone conclusions fall away, and the tournament becomes a communiqué from tennis's future rather than its past. Carlitos, eager to rule that future and revive his slow season, cruised into the quarterfinals, where a tricky, familiar opponent awaited: Zverev, who led their head-to-head, 5-3.

This match would enter legend for reasons that had nothing to do with tennis. My colleague Patrick Redford first alerted me, pointing across the stadium at an apparition descending from the sky. Flitting in the sunlight, it looked like a cloud of gnats. But as it arrived at court level, and moved with sinister precision toward the players, the reality set in: bees. Alcaraz prepared to serve, then noticed them circling his head. He waved at them. The umpire announced the presence of the bees to the crowd. Soon poor Carlitos was getting stung, flailing his arms in self-defense, covering his face with his shirt, then grabbing a towel and skittering off to the locker room. Zverev had meanwhile flattened himself against the back wall of the court. Play was suspended. Concurrently, something strange was happening to the Spidercam, which slides along wires suspended above the stadium to capture overhead footage. It looked as if it were smoldering, casting off tails of black smoke. But those were more bees. They were swarming the camera in staggering volumes. The camera was retracted into a distant corner of the stadium. Fans fled that section, seen off by surly police and venue security. Bill Gates stayed put in his luxury box.

In time a bee expert emerged. His name was Lance Davis. He had wraparound sunglasses and a shoulder-length hairstyle best described as "glam rock." He drove up to the venue in a pickup truck painted with a huge advertisement for his business: "Killer Bee Live Removal." Alone, and devoid of any protective garments, he arrived in the evacuated section of the stadium. With the sun-drenched San Jacinto Mountains as our backdrop, I watched as this man, wearing only a long-sleeved T-shirt and jeans, serenely vacuumed the bees into a small cage. His work was meticulous and humane. He fiddled the vacuum hose into each crevice of the Spidercam, scouring it for every last bee. Some bees he even plucked up between forefinger and thumb and placed tenderly into the vacuum. He scooped up the queen bee as well. In the meantime, Alcaraz's agent had confirmed to reporters that his client had been stung on the forehead.

Later, Lance informed me that there were somewhere between 2,500 and 3,000 bees, and that this was a feral colony, loaded up with nectar and roaming the desert. It was a mix of African and European bees. I asked him about his game plan for approaching 2,500 to 3,000 bees. "Always keeping them alive and safe and saving anybody else around them. So they don't flash like steam and attack somebody, right?" He said he worked steadily, without overthinking anything, because that's when "something bad could happen." He'd been stung once on the cheek and a few times on the hand, but he didn't mind; he'd given up protective gear 10 years into this line of work. As for why they were so attracted to the camera? His guess was that this dark object, hanging in the sunlight, was hospitably warm to the bees on a chilly day. "They're cold-blooded insects. So you know, after about 57 degrees, they get really cold and lethargic, so they gotta cluster together and vibrate their wings. That's what makes friction to keep them warm."

After almost two hours of suspended play, Lance's work was done, and he jogged a victory lap of the stadium, shook hands with the two players, and got back into his pickup, where a cage full of bees now shuddered in the truck bed. Carlitos returned to court and promptly transformed the match into a whimsical circus act. Such was the splendor of his play—he had the crowd laughing throughout. At 5-2 in the first set, Zverev made him track down a ball on the opposite side of the court. Alcaraz started jogging, in no particular hurry, then hopped into a final step just a bit bolder and lungier than the previous ones and swatted a forehand down-the-line as lightly as you or I might swat a fly. This one clocked in at 100 mph. Alcaraz kept jogging off the court. In the stands, thousands of heads flew back, eyes were covered by hands, expressing not just awe but outright rejection of the reality before them. Zverev couldn't resist the charisma either, and applauded.

The drop shot, that Alcaraz specialty, had rarely looked more cruel. In many of their previous matches, Zverev had won the battle of groundstroke depth, pushing Alcaraz behind the baseline and preventing him from toying around with the court's north-south axis. Not this day. Drop shots dripped early and often from the Spaniard's racquet. Each one is a small joy. He rears back his racquet, pointing it straight up, as if preparing to strike the ball at full power. Then he begins to swing the racquet toward the ball—again, exactly as he would if he were about to hit the ball at full power. Only then does the deceit begin. Unbeknownst to his opponent, Carlitos has loosened his grip on the handle of his racquet and rotated it about 90 degrees clockwise in his palm. Now he has mischief on his mind. The racquet face has been "opened up," and he can treat the incoming projectile much more daintily. Instead of whipping the racquet up and through the ball, he is caressing down and under it. Instead of taking a purposeful step forward during the moment of contact, he takes an easy hop-skip, as if willing that gently scooped ball over the net, where it will land shallow in the court, demoralizing the player who has been fooled into thinking it would be struck hard and deep. All because of a little last-second swivel of the racquet in the palm.

Alcaraz pulled this off so often that by the home stretch of the match, Zverev sometimes saw the drop shot and bleated in misery, before setting off at a sprint, only to come up a step short. Other times he embraced futility and didn't even budge an inch. If Zverev cheated a few steps forward in anticipation of a drop shot, Carlitos would just punish him with power. It was Alcaraz's dynamic range, his command of both delicacy and brutality, that drove opponents into hopeless guessing games. In one rally, as Zverev struck three consecutive kill shots he expected to end the rally, and Alcaraz pulled off three increasingly preposterous retrievals, the kid started smiling. He was also smiling when, while preparing to serve at 4-1 in the third set, an observant cameraman zoomed in on a woman wearing a custom T-shirt. It was tiled with black-and-white glamour shots of Alcaraz from magazine covers and underwear shoots. She soon was cast on the stadium's big screen, mouthing, "I love you, Carlitos," forming a heart with her hands, and just about toppling over in delirium. Alcaraz, who'd been bouncing the ball to serve, looked up, grinned, and appeared to blush—a reminder that he was barely out of his teens. Maybe it made him feel good: He won eight of the following nine points to seize victory. (He signed the fan's shirt afterward.)

"I'm not gonna lie, I'm a little bit afraid of the bees," Alcaraz said immediately after the match. Later, speaking to press, he reiterated his fear. "I thought it was just a few of them, not too many, but I saw the sky and it was thousands and thousands, flying, stuck in my hair, going to me, it was crazy. One of them, it was hitting on me. I try to stay away from them, but it was impossible," he said.

I asked him about the range of emotions he provokes in the crowd and what effect that has on his play. "Screaming my name—then laughing—or they don't believe it, what's happening in the game—for me, it's great," he said. "My best level shows up when I'm smiling . . . sometimes I stay away from 100 percent focus on the match, probably watching some of the crowd, dancing or funny faces that help me to put a smile on my face, enjoying my time on the court. Having those different emotions from the crowd is really helpful for me."

Sinner, meanwhile, continued his study in minimalist emotion. In his own quarterfinal against Jiří Lehečka, a young Czech whose enormous legs are spiderwebbed with veins like an endurance cyclist's, Sinner struggled with his rhythm at times. Seated directly behind his team, I listened to his coaches offer exhortations in three languages. Tennis, which mixes and matches players and coaches from all over the world, has developed its own creole. "Allez" and "vamos" and "come on" belong to everyone in the sport. Jannik, being Italian, gets lots of "andiamo," which bursts from his trainer's lips so quickly it sounds like "jamo." Watching Darren Cahill, I could see how the coach must balance multitudes. While his legs stiffened in anxiety during points, Jannik couldn't see them below the half-wall of the stadium siding. All the player ever saw were tranquil facial expressions and hand gestures. When he hit a good enough shot the whole team all jerked up to their feet, as if by puppet strings.

After Sinner pulled off the win over Lehečka, I happened to stumble into his father. Though Jannik's family typically doesn't travel with him on tour, Hanspeter, a chef by profession, had spent the week cooking meals and watching television with his son. We shook hands. He told me it had been a rough day for his son, even though he'd won. I told him I was writing about Jannik; he informed me that Jannik was a nice man. I agreed heartily. As I asked increasingly logistical questions about setting up an interview, his English seemed to strategically degrade, until he was mostly just smiling, nodding, informing me good-naturedly, "I go home," and peeling off to rejoin the Sinner camp.

Not long after, Sinner arrived at his press conference. He was asked, given that he was on an impressive 19-match win streak, how much attention he had paid to Djokovic's win streak of 41 matches to open up the 2011 season. Sinner responded, with a laugh, that he had not paid much attention to that, because he was 10 years old then. He strenuously rejected a comparison to any feats of the Big

Three and said he started watching tennis more seriously only at age 16. (I've noticed that tennis greats aren't necessarily obsessed with the sport's history and trivia; with few exceptions, they don't have as encyclopedic a set of references as your average internet-savvy sports nerd.)

When asked about his potential clash with Alcaraz—that other quarterfinal had yet to finish—he cracked a smile, the first I'd seen from him all week. "We are good friends off the court. On the court, we just try to give 100 percent, no?" He said he'd struggled against Alcaraz in their 2023 match on this court, losing to him in straight sets.

The whole men's draw had been building up toward this clash: Sinner vs. Alcaraz, volume VIII. But the day itself had an ominous feel. There was so much cloud cover that the sun looked as though it had medical gauze stretched over it. The players rode together to the stadium in a golf cart, seated back-to-back, in matching blue-and-white Nike warm-up jackets. Despite having the next Federer-Nadal rivalry on their hands, the clothing sponsor hadn't yet figured out how to give these superstars distinct visual identities, the way they'd juxtaposed Rafa's capri shorts and muscle tees with Roger's off-white cardigan and gold trim in the late aughts. Alcaraz and Sinner looked pretty much the same.

By the time they arrived on court, there was no blue visible in the sky. During the first point, sparse pinpricks of rain fell, though the players themselves weren't fazed until the end of the second game. Sinner tentatively ran his sneaker along the baseline to test the traction there—the paint is the slipperiest part of a hard court. Just a few minutes later, play was paused. The combatants put their matching jackets back on and sat down in their chairs, shielded from the rain by ball kids holding umbrellas. In a gesture of chivalry caught on video, Sinner held the umbrella himself, while making small talk with the ball girl tasked with keeping him dry. The umpire formally suspended play. Carlitos was closer to the exit, but he stood on court, waiting for Jannik to catch up, and they smiled and gesticulated on their way into the tunnel, looking less like two rivals in a match worth $260,000 and more like two buddies en route to the bar after their hitting session was rained out.

The rain kept coming. There had been hard rain the night before, too. Was this the desert after all? Had we been deceived? We had been tested by insects and tempests; would we soon face frogs, hail, and the deaths of our firstborns? Unable to give up on the delectable prospect of Sincaraz, the fans stuck around, blowing their time and money however they saw fit, eating at the violently marked-up Nobu restaurant built into the stadium or flocking under a tent to dance to a DJ whose tunes had otherwise gone grimly unnoticed all week. After nearly three hours the players were back on court, in crisp air under clear skies, warming up their strokes again. Carlitos later said he and Jannik had spent some of their downtime chatting "about life."

Sinner came out with vigor while Alcaraz was sluggish, his serve a bit wonky. Sinner took the first set 6-1; he'd also won the last set they'd played, in Beijing, by the same lopsided score. Had he overtaken the entire tour, including his rival? This was not the contest anyone had been expecting. Early in set two, Alcaraz pushed yet another easy backhand long and roared "Venga," a bit of wrath from a player otherwise in steadfast pursuit of smiles. Minutes later he had figured out how to have fun again. The drop shot, a bellwether for his mood, was fully functional. He was starting to venture to net, breaking up the monotony of baseline rallies, resuming familiar hijinks. He moved his return position farther back and began to put more returns into play. Eventually he was rewarded with a break of serve early in the second set.

With Alcaraz up 3-1, he and Sinner revealed the main course to the drooling audience. It was the point of the year to date. Alcaraz served down the center; Sinner barely put a racquet on it. Alcaraz sped forward to volley the ball, leaving it short in the court; Sinner again barely put a racquet on it. Alcaraz, backpedaling slightly, pushed the ball back. This should have ended the point. The ball was too far away from Sinner. But he ate up all that distance with hunched, loping strides, looking like a highly task-oriented antelope, and he did not merely put a racquet on the ball but somehow punched a proper backhand down-the-line, abruptly taking control of the point. In reply Alcaraz got just as bold, volleying the ball at an angle so severe it basically moved horizontally across the court. Sinner was there again, scooping the ball back along the horizontal, his angle just as severe. Alcaraz, caught running the wrong way, corrected course, skidding into a last-ditch effort, but as Sinner jogged to retrieve that ball, I could already see his full-tooth grin, his pace slackening as he recognized it was sailing out. Alcaraz was smiling too, waving a sarcastic hand, as if to dismiss the miracles his rival had just performed. He still held on to the game, punctuating it with an unreturnable 131-mph serve and a yelp of "yeh!" As the tennis ascended into madness, the crowd responded with the same. Someone a few sections over from me offered the performers a real-time review: "Y'all are doing a great job." And they were.

Soon there were six points in a row that felt like a single hallucination, more vicious and vivid than the tennis we'd seen in the Big Three era. Alcaraz sprang a trap with a drop shot to lure Sinner in, hoping to hit a passing shot right by him, but Sinner, with his whole body still facing the back of the court, blocked a no-look volley into open space. I detected a new swagger in him—there he was, punishing another drop shot by slashing a slice hard crosscourt—as though Alcaraz were infecting him with his own way of life. Anyone who'd been watching tennis recently could tell they were doing something well beyond the usual patterns of the sport. They were inventing a new grammar all their own. Balls were struck hard at discombobulated elbow angles, immediate return winners were lashed off of big serves, sudden solutions were lobbed back at difficult questions. It was a matchup with no neutral shots, no peace talks. Attack or be attacked.

When Sinner found a break point at 3-5, Alcaraz, always emboldened by the dicey moments of a match, canceled it with a slap-happy backhand down-the-line. He then wrapped up the second set with a drop shot that left Sinner standing still as ice at the back of the court. In the third set they flew around as though gravity and air resistance were turned off in the stadium. They slipped around the rough hard court like air hockey pucks, occupying some frictionless and freer version of the world that we in the crowd could not access despite sitting just a few feet above them. But the show couldn't last forever. At 1-1 in the third, the match turned on a single misstep. Alcaraz got the better of a net exchange, and Sinner, tracking down the last ball, dove and fell hard. It was a stark reminder that this man was all thin limbs and knobby ends. Alcaraz had broken serve on the point, but he didn't celebrate. Instead he stood there with a raised hand of concern, as Sinner flexed his leg, pawed at his right elbow, but ultimately indicated that he was fine.

That did not seem to be so. Alcaraz took over the match, and in a late changeover, Sinner kept fiddling with his elbow as his camp looked on in distress. In the other player's box, Juan Carlos Ferrero was giving his charge a familiar "simmer down" gesture, a staple of his coaching language, a means of reining in the wildness of Alcaraz so that he might finish up the match in a more conservative fashion. Which he did in fact do. The last few games were more ceremonial than substantive, with Sinner still shaking out his right arm, and Alcaraz won 1-6, 6-3, 6-2. Despite the mild ending, that mind-altering second set had more than justified the hype. The two hugged it out at the net. Alcaraz engaged in the usual post-match rite, drawing with a marker on the lens of a TV camera. He produced a Cyclopean smiley face, one eye fusing into the grin—what a relief to learn that he was not a natural stylist in every medium. On court Alcaraz was asked about "how special a friend" Sinner is to him. "He means a lot to me," he responded. "I always say that first thing is you have to be a good person, and athlete comes after that. And I think Jannik is the same." The sun began to set over the mountains, in cotton-candy hues of pink and blue.

At the press conference following his first loss of 2024, Sinner looked more relaxed than he had all week, as if a great psychic burden had been dissolved. Talking to reporters, Sinner likes to lead off with a gentle objection to the very framing of the query—a "Look," or a nasally "No"—that makes the questioner feel a little silly for asking, before laying out his own view on the matter. He said that the late tumble he took hurt his elbow and made it difficult to serve, but that on the whole, he played too predictably. Reflecting on the state of the rivalry, he felt this match had been a "bigger test" of their relative merit—it had been five months since their last clash in Beijing, and they'd each had plenty of time to tinker in the interim. He saw some new things from Alcaraz. He was impressed by his heavy topspin, which works well on gritty hard courts that produce high bounces, like the ones at Indian Wells. "But this makes things really fun, no?" he said of the constant dance of adjustments and readjustments; to him this was the pleasure of their war. "Maybe there is one day where one of us wins three, four times in a row. Then the other one has to try to adjust a little bit, you know, trying completely new things, maybe goes completely wrong, that you lose 6-1, 6-1 or whatever. But I think that's good to see for me, trying to grow in the future." In loss he was more self-assured and meditative than he had been while carrying the weight of the win streak, and upon his exit, the tennis writer Gerry Marzorati turned to me and said, "That's one cool dude."

Alcaraz walked in soon after and joked about the various plagues visited upon him at the tournament. "Well, we were laughing about it with Jannik when it suspended, because I had bees, had the rain. Let's see what's gonna happen tomorrow. Maybe a random guy?" he said, the last bit slightly unintelligible, as even his rapidly improving English still retained some craggy charms. He said he felt nervous before the match against Sinner and that he always does, because beating him requires his maximal effort. But he was happy to end his rival's win streak, and he was aware that he'd leveled their head-to-head at four wins apiece. I had noticed that instead of exchanging rapid blows from the baseline, where Sinner is happiest, Alcaraz had been slow-rolling him with languid and loopy shots, almost testing the Italian's patience. It had turned the match in his favor, even before Sinner took his tumble. I asked him what felt different about this match compared to their previous encounters. Alcaraz said they did indeed play "more slowly" in this one, and then he stopped short, winkingly refusing to elaborate too much on his tactics in case they met again at the next tournament in Miami.

There was only one more obstacle to his title defense: the No. 4 seed, Medvedev. A self-proclaimed "hard-court specialist," Medvedev had surprisingly never before won the title at Indian Wells. It was a conspicuous exception, given how many other hard-court titles he'd collected. He had his own theories as to why—always, Daniil Medvedev has a theory. At the previous year's tournament, he'd mounted a days-long tantrum about the quality of the courts. He felt that the court was playing far too slow. The balls lost too much speed after making contact with its unusually rough surface, making it difficult for him to win points with his serve or hit winners. "I'm gonna pee as slow as this court is," he'd said to one umpire, threatening him with the prospect of an endless bathroom break. "So you can take 25 minutes. The court is slow, so I go slow." In another match he trudged toward the bathroom as if the court were mud as the umpire hollered at him to hurry up. But despite his flagrant distaste for the court, Medvedev was a gifted problem-solver. He had figured out a way to make it to the 2023 final, and he had done it again in 2024.

Despite a strong start, Medvedev was not up to the task of solving the hardest problem in tennis: a happy Carlitos playing in conditions that he loves. At 4-4 in the first set, he lofted a lovely lob over Alcaraz, who reared up to smash it overhead but mistimed his jump. Instead of aborting the mission, he turned around to chase down the ball. Who else was fast enough to jump up for a ball, whiff, land, and run back to retrieve it anyway? While scurrying back, he switched his grip as if to hit a forehand, which would have been impossible to do from that position—but he instead used the *wrong* face of his racquet and a nimble flick of the wrist to scoop the ball back into play. He went on to win the point. Having never seen anything like it, I later had to watch the clip several times at quarter-speed to grasp what he'd done. The point captured Alcaraz's blend of sloppiness and imagination. He gets himself into a bind, then works his way out of it, via some diabolical logic that no other player could follow.

After winning a competitive first set, Alcaraz began luring Medvedev into the front half of the court, where the latter had never felt
comfortable, and easily won the next set, securing his second consecutive Indian Wells title. In his press conference, Medvedev explained
what allowed Alcaraz to thrive in conditions where other players had
struggled. He said that when his previous opponents had hit hard—
Sebastian Korda and Tommy Paul had both served at him in the low
130s—he felt that their ball had slowed in the air so much that it
wasn't moving all that fast by the time it reached him. But Alcaraz
seemed to him immune to the basic problem of air resistance. He was
powerful enough to hit a ball that moved fast "from the beginning
to end"—fast when it left his racquet, and still fast when it arrived at
Medvedev's feet. "Mentally it's not easy to play against this. To be honest, in the second set, I felt a little bit out of solutions," he said.

When Alcaraz arrived in the same room minutes later, along
with the trophy, a huge hunk of rippling glass, he explained that the
tournament had renewed him. "Let's say the last two months it was
difficult for me to find myself," he said. "I was struggling to enjoy on
the court. My family, my team, people close to me was telling me,
what happened to me? That I was not smiling as much as I was doing
before." Through bees and desert downpours, Alcaraz had managed
to recover a crucial old feeling. He'd also found revenge. Since winning Wimbledon in 2023, he'd wandered for nine months without
winning a title. In that span he'd lost to all his chief rivals—Djokovic
(twice), Zverev (twice), Medvedev, Sinner—which invited specula-
tion about whether peers had found the holes in his miraculous play
style. His early success owed something to the element of surprise.
No teen had ever arrived on tour with such power and such sleight
of hand. But perhaps it's possible to sketch out a game plan for it the
third time around?

Not really, it turned out. Alcaraz beat Zverev, Sinner, and Medvedev in quick succession at Indian Wells, and he had relished the process. His return to joy had also been captured on tape. I saw cameras tailing him around the grounds, likely for a rumored docuseries. I can't recall if the cameras were there in the waning minutes of that final press conference, when an emergency alarm went off in the room, flashing a strobe light and sounding a siren so shrill that I could hardly think two thoughts in a row. But Carlitos sat there and offered generous, detailed answers to several questions, a smile in the flickering din.

CHAPTER 6

Triage Ward

Were Jannik Sinner and Carlos Alcaraz actually friends? It was a question I asked myself with some frequency in 2024. A lot of fans seemed to believe they were friends, or wanted to believe that they were; a lot of people involved in the Tennis Content Industrial Complex seemed committed to making it appear that they were. I was slightly embarrassed to discover that I wanted them to be friends, too, that I would burn precious questions at press conferences to hunt for a detail or two. It was a fun notion, that a friendship could coexist with a rivalry this fierce. It made tennis look good. How charming that its two prodigies could set aside the stakes of the job to enjoy a good goof or heart-to-heart. Over the season, countless clips of mundane Sincaraz interactions whirled around the internet. The fellas exchanging a banal handshake as they crossed paths on the practice courts; Carlos making a vaguely Italianate pinched hand gesture and Jannik duly mirroring it back at him; the two of them stiffly interviewing each other in the sort of icebreaker game that might be played at a corporate retreat; and in an extremely 2024 image, a hellish AI-generated video in which the two wore Christmas sweaters and embraced, with a light nuzzle.

Recall that, mere minutes after the Indian Wells win, the sweat still damp on Carlitos's brow, an interviewer stood on court and asked him about "how much Jannik means to you." The question wasn't completely unprompted—they had hung out during the rain delay that interrupted the match—but the almost romantic intensity of the phrasing made me laugh out loud in the moment. Imagine that you are friends with a colleague, but firmly in the water-cooler-buddy tier of acquaintance. A couple of inside jokes, some shared workplace gripes to fill any lulls in conversation. But then imagine that you are periodically interviewed, for the entertainment of hundreds of thousands of fans, about how much that colleague means to you. I mean, he's pretty nice, I guess? Alcaraz answered the question gamely, praising Sinner's character, but the moment revealed the ceaseless grind of the content mill, trying to extract A Poignant Moment from a rock.

That was not to diminish the pleasant working relationship that Sinner and Alcaraz did enjoy. Tennis rivalries have not always been compatible with basic civility, let alone light friendship. To take one especially noxious example: Pete Sampras and Andre Agassi. Apathetic toward one another in their playing days, they soured after the release of Agassi's candid memoir. A decade after their rivalry had subsided, when they were both retired and playing against each other in a doubles match for charity, their trash talk devolved into Andre pulling the pockets of his shorts inside out, dissing Pete for being a bad tipper. Roger Federer and Rafa Nadal, their doubles partners, had to fidget and wait out the enmity being aired in the middle of the stadium. Perhaps that was the precise moment when these two players resolved never to be like their elders. Their own rivalry was emotionally rich enough that Nadal, asked in 2017 what he admired most about Federer as a man, had to hose down the questioner by sighing deeply and saying, "I don't want to look like I'm gonna be his boyfriend." Their friendship had developed slowly, over the course of 40 bouts, until they wept hand-in-hand at Roger's retirement ceremony. But Sinner and Alcaraz seemed oddly congenial from the jump. Sinner sought out Alcaraz in the locker room after their first encounter on the Challenger tour; he said he was struck by Alcaraz's talent and precocity, already competing at that level as a 15-year-old.

There's a paradox in the friend-rival. On the one hand, it's hard to be close with someone with whom you are locked in zero-sum competition for all the prizes you most lust after in your career; on the other hand, there is no one else in the world who knows the pressures and predicaments at the top of the game, no one else who could relate as easily to the contours of your strange life. A coach might try to dispense wisdom from a past era, and some of the lessons might apply, but the scale of the prize money, the endorsement deals, the international fame, the nonstop performance of a personal brand, the online bands of trolls and devotees, was much bigger in 2024 than in, say 2003, when Juan Carlos Ferrero won his major. Being anointed the future of the ATP was something that only Jannik Sinner and Carlos Alcaraz could understand. That didn't mean they were sending each other memes every day.

So I was not surprised to hear Sinner deliver a sober assessment of their friendship early on in his devastating run at the Miami Open, the 1000-level event directly following Indian Wells. "We both try our best on the court, we have a lot of respect for each other. And yeah, that's it, no? Obviously off the court we don't speak that much. Because he has his own things and I have my things," he said in his judicious monotone. No matter how many people wanted it to be more, that was where the relationship stood, a week after their tough three-setter in the desert. Both Sinner and Alcaraz arrived in Miami in fine form. Alcaraz was ousted in the quarterfinal by Grigor Dimitrov, the veteran whose stylish and elastic game once seemed capable of winning majors. "He made me feel like I'm 13 years old," said a sheepish Alcaraz. Dimitrov, 12 years his elder, cracked up when the comment was relayed to him.

Sinner's semifinal opponent was Medvedev, whose career trajectory was growing more dire with every loss to his two outstanding junior colleagues. Sinner routed him in a startling 69 minutes. Later that day, Serena Williams, in her second year of enjoying tennis as a seated spectator rather than an on-court conqueror, came up to Sinner to congratulate him. Sinner wanted to peck cheek-to-cheek in the Italian style; Williams seemed to desire a standard American hug; their conflicting intentions almost resulted in a direct kiss on the lips. After the smooch was narrowly avoided, the 23-time major champion told Sinner she envied his racquet-head speed and power on his forehand, which put him in a bashful mood: "No, no, no, don't say that." Perhaps the small talk with legends would smooth itself out in time.

Dimitrov followed his Alcaraz upset with a win over Zverev. Heading into the final, he was feeling like a "rock star" thanks to the raucous crowd support he'd received all tournament long, playing some of his most aggressive and rapturous tennis in years—only to lose to Sinner straightforwardly. This was the story of the season. Players other than Alcaraz would unlock the optimal version of their tennis selves, would vibrate with confidence, and would then play Sinner, who met them with the sobriety of a librarian scanning a book, stamping a due date, and handing it back: 6-3, 6-1, see you next time.

After that loss in the Miami final, Dimitrov was asked to compare the feeling of playing Sinner with the feeling of playing the best players in history. Dimitrov stuck to the classics, citing prime Roger Federer at Wimbledon. "I wanted to dig a hole and disappear," he said of facing the Swiss. "I haven't had that feeling yet against anyone [else], so I'll leave it at that, I guess." A few weeks later Nadal was asked, "Do you think the level of tennis is getting higher and higher at a faster pace, with the rise of Sinner and Alcaraz?" A single skeptical Rafa eyebrow bounced up, as if it had been dropped from a great height. "No idea. Of course, they are amazing players, but at the same time, if we put in perspective that Novak Djokovic won three of four [majors in 2023] and played the final of another one . . . I mean, he's from my generation, so . . . that says that tennis has amazing new champions, but at the same time, things haven't changed that much." A polite but firm way of saying, let's give the kids their due, but don't get carried away with ahistorical praise—don't blaspheme the old gods.

Djokovic, the last remaining delegate of that pantheon, was having a gloomy year. After his upset at Indian Wells to the 19-year-old Luca Nardi, Djokovic jettisoned his coach of five years, Goran Ivanišević. This was not terribly surprising news. For the past few months the ambiance in his player's box could have been summarized as "awaiting firing squad." But it did signal the end of one of the great coaching relationships that tennis had ever seen. It had yielded 12 major titles and extended Djokovic's already excellent records to otherworldly marks. Ivanišević spoke freely and colorfully about that turbulent and demanding gig after the news broke, though at the end, he said, there was nothing all that dramatic to say. "We reached a certain level of saturation, as I like to say: 'material fatigue,' just as a car needs a regular service and tune-up, basically I became tired of him, he became tired of me," he told the journalist Saša Ozmo.

Amid this upheaval, Djokovic also withdrew from Miami, writing that "at this stage of my career, I'm balancing my private and professional schedule." He still had no titles in 2024 and hadn't started a season this poorly in over a decade. But on the strength of his 2023 season, he also still held the No. 1 ranking. And in April, a month shy of his 37th birthday, he became the oldest man ever to hold that slot, adding yet another line to his résumé. If the kids wanted to tear him out of the sport's hierarchy, there was still plenty of hard work to do.

After Miami, the tour moves to clay courts. If you're going to stare at a tennis court all day, make it a clay court. A hard court is a fixed surface accumulating nothing but sneaker scuffs; a clay court is made of ever-shifting sands. Its surface is overlaid with a fine powder of crushed red brick, which moves with every footstep and ball bounce. In this way the court takes a record of the tennis played on it. A divot over here where someone took a hard fall after a diving volley. A smear over there where a player slid to retrieve a drop shot. A small comma behind the baseline traced by the back foot while a player served. In the right light, the clay itself looks like soft velour and the footprints look like places it has been thumbed against the grain.

When the ball bounces hard on a clay court, it shoots up a plume of ocher. It also leaves a mark, which is helpful for getting line calls correct. The ball itself gathers up clay during a rally, and when it is struck hard enough, it abandons all the dust in an omnidirectional spray. Over the course of a day of play, sun and shadow can conjure new colors: the far corner of the court might look like a slice of smoked salmon, the afternoon silhouettes like dark chocolate. Or maybe I'm just prone to hunger after long days at tennis tournaments. Regardless, it's a visual feast.

Not every player has such a joyous review, because the experience of playing on clay is not to everyone's taste. Medvedev believed it was suitable only for animals, and one does indeed get dirty: shoe treads fill up, socks get stained, calves blush, shirts get spattered. Plenty of players are open about their disdain for the surface. But for others, clay-court tennis is the default and everything else is a deviation. Because even though rules and court dimensions remain the same, tennis does change when the surface changes. Relative to hard court, some game styles are punished and others rewarded. Temperature and humidity are important variables, but as a general rule, on clay the ball bounces higher and loses more speed after hitting the ground. The potency of the serve is thus neutralized. Rallies tend to get longer and gutsier. Footwork must be adapted. A hard court has the firmness of asphalt and a sandpapery grit, but clay courts, with their powdery consistency, demand that players get comfortable not just running but *sliding* across the surface. In the modern game, where alien athleticism has extracted every advantage, we see sliding on all court surfaces, but it is native to clay. A player takes his final step before arriving at the ball, glides right into its path, hits it, and comes to a stop, ready to recover to the middle.

Sinner and Alcaraz both spent a lot of their formative years on clay, and both have game styles well-suited to its specific demands. Neither needed to rely on his serve to win points, though the serve had made Sinner's life easier of late. They are both easy, aqueous movers, comfortable attacking from defensive positions. They both can hit the heavy topspin that is rewarded on clay with high, exasperating bounces. They are both adept at "point construction," the art of winning incremental advantage with a clairvoyant sequence of shots, each setting up the next—though Alcaraz could sometimes forget these fundamentals. They'd just split the two hard-court

1000-level titles in Indian Wells and Miami, and I expected to see them cresting on this surface, too.

But what might have been a window for twin excellence was instead an uncertain, banged-up, and bandaged time.

The first big clay tournament, and the most picturesque of the entire season, is the Monte-Carlo Masters. It is technically held in France, just outside the border of Monaco. Steep hills that once held olive trees were flattened into terraces to hold the clay courts of the Monte-Carlo Country Club, a sequence of words that might be sufficient to spark a socialist revolt. A seat in the stands offers a painterly tableau: the rich red of clay, the gemmed blue of the Mediterranean Sea, the chalky rock face and green of cypresses. Yachts float just offshore. A lot of top tennis players keep a permanent residence in Monte-Carlo, so it is also one of the most homey stops on tour. What rich person doesn't love a tax haven? And a ready supply of practice partners? Both of Djokovic's children were born there, and he trains regularly at the club. Sinner lives there too, and due to its close proximity to the Piatti Tennis Center, he has been familiar with this part of the world for half his life. Monte-Carlo is the one big tournament where Sinner can drive to work in his own car, from his own home—a luxury for people who spend the majority of the year in the transient churn of hotels and rentals.

Alcaraz arrived in Monte-Carlo eager to play on clay, but he had hurt his pronator teres muscle, on the inside of his right forearm. In an update to fans, he cited the muscle by name, though many players prefer to keep things vague, as if every anatomical detail offers exploitable intel to the opposition. That particular muscle, as the name would suggest, helps the arm pronate—imagine holding your arm palm up, and then turning it palm down—which is key to almost every stroke in tennis. He spent the days leading up to the tournament on the practice courts, with his right forearm mummified in tape, bunting his forehands gingerly, an adverb that typically would not come within a mile of the tennis of Carlos Alcaraz. His team chose not to push through the injury, and he withdrew right before the tournament began. After the bad ankle turn in Rio, here was another bodily woe to resolve.

Djokovic had won this tournament in 2013 and 2015 but, by his standards, had found little success since. He showed up and told reporters he had low expectations for himself and praised Sinner as the best player of the season. Djokovic went on a good run at Monte-Carlo but lost in the semifinal to Casper Ruud, the even-tempered clay specialist. Ruud hadn't managed to scrape even a set off Djokovic in their five prior meetings, but he won this one cleanly. He said he'd been emboldened by seeing Djokovic lose at Indian Wells. "He's human. Sometimes he doesn't seem like it, but he is like everyone else," he said. As he approached the end of the match, he remembered that vulnerability, and it amplified his self-belief. Djokovic's aura of invincibility, luminous for the last dozen years, had started to flicker in 2024.

Sinner's run in Monte-Carlo, meanwhile, got complicated in a quarterfinal against his young rival Holger Rune. The use of "rival" there is subject to dispute. Some people in tennis believed that Rune, Alcaraz, and Sinner would someday comprise a Big Three to replace the old one. At this point in time, that belief was mostly relegated to Holger Rune and perhaps his immediate family. But it wasn't all that outlandish. Rune, born a week before Alcaraz, had hit some intriguing benchmarks before his peers—beating Djokovic as a mere 19-year-old in the final of the Paris Masters, for example. His defining features are his backward hat, colossal thighs, clean groundstroke technique, and a resting facial expression that—through no fault of his own—makes it look like he's always complaining, locked in a permanent half scowl. Though he has, in fact, spent a big chunk of his matches complaining, bringing reality into alignment with perception, so perhaps it's not so unfair a fate. Rune's pungent personality has earned him a rep on the tour. The three-time major champ Stan Wawrinka once offered him a nugget of wisdom at the net after a tough match: "My advice to you is that you stop acting like a baby on the court, okay?"

That same pugnacious Rune reared his head in this match against Sinner. At a critical juncture, Rune made a mild gesture to a fan in the crowd—a chomping motion with his hand, as if dismissing an annoying chatterbox—and was dinged by the umpire for unsportsmanlike conduct. This had two consequences: first, an argument between Rune and the umpire, and second, a sudden upswell in Rune's tennis. He was sport-fighting with the umpire to get his blood pumping. Sinner, who seemed to operate with his heart beating at more of a smooth R & B tempo, frittered away a match point in the second set but fought through his resurgent opponent to win the third and earn a place in the semifinal.

It was in that match that his own physical woes began. He was facing Stefanos Tsitsipas, the spacey, leonine Greek. A few years ago, Tsitsipas appeared to be a top talent of this generation. Sensing this, I'd spent a week profiling him during his breakout season. I came to appreciate his world-class forehand, his fondness for fake-deep quotations, and his earnest travel vlogging on YouTube. On the strength of his intrepid all-court game, Tsitsipas got as high as No. 3 in the world. He'd beaten all of the Big Three and made two major finals. Through 2023 and 2024, however, he'd been thoroughly eclipsed by Alcaraz and then by Sinner, and he seemed to have spun into a zenned-out apathy, perhaps his way of coping with the new career obstacles. Sinner was about to bury him in the third set at Monte-Carlo. He had broken him once and would have done it a second time, had the umpire not botched a line call on a Tsitsipas second serve. But soon after the Italian fell apart. He even tanked a game, which I had never before seen from him. He called on a physiotherapist to treat his right leg. "I can feel something move," Sinner said, motioning to the leg, a suboptimal sentence to utter during a tennis match, but moments later he was smiling and praising the therapist's "magic hands."

Still, he never regained control of the match, or his body. As the match wound down he got treatment on the other leg, too, the physiotherapist pawing cream out of a tub and furiously massaging Sinner's hamstring, as if urging it back into service. It didn't work. Tsitsipas advanced, and won the final too, claiming his third Monte-Carlo title in four years. Collectively, Alcaraz, Sinner, and Djokovic had seized every title of note over the past two years, but here was one curious seaside perch that still belonged emphatically to the local resident Stefanos Tsitsipas.

Clay season is dense with 1000-level titles, three of them in quick succession. There are plenty of opportunities for a player to find his rhythm. Lose in Monte-Carlo and fly right out to Madrid, which is played in the Caja Májica—or magic box—tennis center, all high steel walls, austere modernism, and perpendicular angles. Madrid has its idiosyncrasies compared to other clay events. At over 2,000 feet above sea level, with lower air pressure, the ball moves through the air faster and leaps higher off the clay. These qualities seem to suit Alcaraz, whose many gifts include the ability to adapt quickly to conditions that might vex other players. He had won the Madrid title two years in a row. Nobody, not even clay king Nadal, had won it three times in a row. So Alcaraz arrived, a week out from his 21st birthday, hoping to make history in front of a smitten home crowd, who understood that he was the present and future of Spanish tennis. He'd just skipped the 500-level tournament in Barcelona due to his arm injury, so this was his 2024 debut on home soil.

Sinner, too, was making personal history in a more minor key: With Djokovic absent, he was playing his first-ever 1000-level event as the No. 1 seed. Over the past seven months he seemed to have immunized himself from early-round losses. At this point in the season, he'd played five tournaments: three trophies, two losses in semifinals. No lesser outcomes allowed. But his body began to falter in Madrid early in his third-round match. He won, and said afterward that his right hip had been nagging him, but he didn't think it was anything serious. After he won again, he changed his tune. He said doctors had warned him not to play on and worsen the injury. He withdrew before his quarterfinal. Even this was a fearsome index of where he was as a player: with a busted hip, he had beaten Karen Khachanov, the No. 17 player in the world.

Alcaraz, still nursing that arm injury, didn't advance any farther than Sinner. In the quarterfinal he lost to Andrey Rublev and his barrage of blind power. Bodily dysfunction was a theme of the tournament, because Rublev himself went on to win the title despite a handful of exotic ailments. He got his toe anesthetized. He said that heading into the final, he'd been ill for eight or nine days, unable to sleep or swallow food. After winning, he wrote a note on the camera lens that read "Samadhi now I'm free"—a reference to a rarefied state of consciousness sought by Hindu sages that is achieved, among other occasions, at their time of death. The next morning he checked into a hospital and stayed there two and a half days. "My throat was an ugly color, and the smell from my mouth, you cannot imagine how horrible it was," he later reflected. Sometimes from our sofas we forget what a punishing game this is.

From Madrid, the survivors flew off to play another 1000-level event at Rome. Except for our principals, because this was the physical nadir for both of them. Alcaraz had developed edema, or a buildup of fluid, in that same troublesome muscle in his right forearm. He was pulling out of Rome to recover. He'd later confess that he spent much of this clay season wondering whether he'd ever be able to hit his forehand properly again. Whenever a player has both an explosive style of play and a pattern of injuries, the pundit class is quick to draw a link, questioning the player's durability. Famously, this had been the line of critique on Nadal, and while he'd missed lots of tournaments here and there, the 22 majors over 17 years were sufficient to shut it up. Already in his short career, Alcaraz had dealt with multiple right arm injuries. Perhaps it was reasonable to wonder if his body would survive his own violent and beautiful playing style.

As for Sinner, this was meant to be his homecoming to Italy after claiming his first major title, the sort of achievement that can seduce even a soccer-crazed nation. In the past Sinner had endured some ribbing from the Italian press: He lived in Monaco rather than Italy, had skipped a few opportunities to represent his country in international competition, had mastered Italian late, and still chose the occasional clunky word in his unmelodic accent. But winning big has a way of erasing all prior concerns. Since he'd won his country the Davis Cup and won himself the Australian Open, Italy had been taking Sinner even more seriously. His freckled face was plastered over nearly every surface in public life: billboards, posters, screens. He peddled pasta, Parmesan cheese, sunscreen, Gucci bags.

Italy took him so seriously, in fact, that there was an official press conference to explain his absence from the Rome tournament. First to speak was the president of the Italian tennis federation, Angelo Binaghi. Glum, covered in gray stubble, in a dark suit and blue tie, he looked as if he were about to clumsily dodge responsibility for financial crimes. Sinner, sitting next to him in a green zip-up, his hair a frizzy pile, looked like his underdressed intern. Binaghi assured the assembled press that their star would come back stronger than ever, and then ended his remarks. With eleven microphones stacked in a jumble before him, Sinner fielded questions from despairing reporters, his words steady as ever. He wouldn't specify the exact nature of the injury, just that he'd gotten an MRI in Madrid and realized something was wrong, did more tests at home in Monte-Carlo and decided not to play through it. It was all standard-issue opacity except for one stray remark that caught the ear of concerned fans: "The situation is under control, I'll stop a little longer if I don't recover 100 percent. I don't want to throw away three years of my future career, I'm in no hurry." Three years? Was the injury that severe?

In the outlet *L'Ultimo Uomo,* the writer Emanuele Atturo wryly summed up the mood of his countrymen: "A strange phenomenon of collective psychosis has begun. A widespread feeling of anxiety, hypochondria, and medical alert on a national scale. His suffering has become ours, at least in the form of phantom pain, of constant thoughts about that hip. . . . All the orthopedists in Italy are gathered to have their say, draw on their knowledge, explain to us what Sinner has. All of Italy seems to have hip disease, a single hypochondriac body that searches on Google for information on the anatomy of the hip."

One indirect beneficiary of all this misfortune was Djokovic, who would enjoy a tidier path in Rome if neither of his young nuisances was in the draw. With the season he'd had to date, he was due for some rosier fortunes. Instead he took a large metal projectile straight to the noggin. After he won his second-round match in Rome, Djokovic had lingered on court to sign autographs for the fans who extended an arm—or a torso, or two-thirds of their body length—over the railings to get him to notice their hat or piece of paper. Djokovic was typically generous with his fans, but this time it hurt him. Video of the incident circulated online. A water bottle, apparently made of metal and about a foot long, had fallen from above and struck him on the top of the head. He'd crumpled onto his knees, hands clutching his skull, and was slow to stand, eventually helped off the court by tournament staff. A fan base that has historically had a somewhat gauzy relationship with reality initially treated the footage like the Zapruder film: Was this an ordered hit? Perhaps executed by the biased Western media? Or big pharma taking a shot at an oppressed truth-teller? In time another camera angle emerged, revealing an innocuous cause. A fan had leaned over the railing at such a steep angle that the bottle slipped out of a backpack sleeve and beelined to the dome. Painful result, but no ill intent. Djokovic arrived the next day for practice wearing a bike helmet, as a joke.

But he lost his following match to Alejandro Tabilo, a late-blooming Chilean who had never beaten a top-10 player. After praising his opponent, Djokovic spoke about the ramifications of the water bottle strike. "Today, under high stress, it was quite bad. Not in terms of pain, but just in terms of complete disbalance, no coordination, completely different player from what I was two nights ago," he said. "I have to do medical checkups and see what's going on." Instead of taking the following week to rest up for Roland-Garros, the crown jewel of the clay season, he entered a small tournament in Geneva. There he lost a woozy, seesawing third-round match. In the close-up shots, I could see a small indentation in Djokovic's thick hair, right around where the bottle had made impact. Playing Geneva at all was an unusual choice. In 17 of his previous 18 seasons, he had taken that week off to rest and train for the clay major. The man who had won almost everything in the sport several times over, and pared down his playing schedule to the most important tournaments, was now squeezing in a humble 250-level event to get some more reps in before the big one. All the favorites were ailing, and Roland-Garros looked like anyone's to win.

CHAPTER 7

Joy in Suffering

The crowd is the third participant in every tennis match. It can bend the outcome, like the sun or the wind. If players are shown love by the crowd, they can tap into new reservoirs of confidence. If they are shown scorn—and they happen to be named Novak Djokovic—they can also tap into new reservoirs of confidence. Sometimes there's hardly any crowd at all. The vast majority of professional tennis matches are played in remote outposts for sums that scarcely offset the costs of travel and lodging, with only a handful of ghosts populating the bleachers. But once you have made it to the highest levels of the game, fans start to travel and spend huge sums just to see you play. As an elite player, every day on tour is an opportunity to amuse, antagonize, or mystify those who have gathered to watch you work.

With Alcaraz, you get the sense that if there were no crowd, there would be no point to all this. His trade is tennis, but it is also spectacle. He never looks happier than when working a stadium into a froth of awe and glee. His tennis alone does most of the work for the fans, but he likes to embellish his genius with small gestures.

A finger pointed up to his ear, beckoning the crowd to roar, while the ball he's struck for a winner is still bouncing past his hapless opponent. A bright sharky smile, like a child who has committed a naughty deed but knows he can charm his way out of punishment. A silent raised fist. A cocksure nod. A single bellowed "vamos," his mouth open wide enough to eat the tennis ball. A nonverbal howl, the carotid artery pulsing like a garden hose on the side of his neck. Or his favorite: eyes narrowed and teeth fully bared—not a grin, more like a big cat reminding you of its fangs.

None of this seems affected. It is all expressive and improvised, just like his play. Sinner has said that he admires this aspect of his rival, his ability to enrapture the masses. As I've noted, the Italian's own forays into crowd work are humbler: a fist pump, a compact nod, an ashen gaze into the middle distance. After winning a 25-shot rally against Alcaraz at the 2023 Miami Open—possibly the best point of the decade, full of desperation and ingenuity—Sinner allowed himself a waggle of the fingers on one hand. I am not sure the pinky even moved. For him the goal seems never to leave a narrow band of calm, never to spike up or dip down out of the optimal emotional range for performance.

Alcaraz, who has admitted to moderate phone addiction, is aware that every iconic moment of his on-court life will be readily, almost instantaneously, available around the world. The highlight reel has become the fundamental unit of sports consumption and sports collective memory, and that has surely colored his approach to the game. He occasionally apologizes for his poor performances on the grounds that he didn't provide the people enough entertainment. He has confessed that he sometimes attempts his most audacious shots specifically to delight those who have assembled to watch him play. Judging by the love he gets from crowds on every continent, it's an arrangement that everyone finds acceptable. A few errors are worth an indelible memory.

By 2024 Alcaraz was already a crossover star, attracting actors and rappers and big names from soccer and basketball to his matches. Sinner, while of the same generation as Alcaraz—the first among pro athletes to be born in the age of smartphones—seems less adept, or interested, in performance as entertainment, celebrity guests as part of his show. And yet, I looked at my phone one summer day and saw him posing at his own Gucci-sponsored party with Salma Hayek and Ryan Gosling and thought, Okay, he's coming around to this lifestyle, too.

For a player eager to work the crowd, Roland-Garros, the clay-court major, is the ideal training ground. There, in Paris, the sport has preserved some of its rakish essence. It's the one place in the world where I have viewed best-of-five professional tennis through a fog of cigarette smoke. Tennis might be getting more international, but here the spirit remains resolutely French. Its crowds are well-schooled in the game, attuned to the merits and faults of its combatants. They are also unpredictable. To me the French crowd is like a baby: capable of baffling emotional 180s, oscillating from joy to hostility in a flash, for reasons mysterious to any third party. It communicates with a mix of whistles, howls, coos, grunts, claps, and shouted names. It is hyper-attuned to a moving ball, responding so minutely to the ebb and flow of these rallies that I sometimes wonder if I'm the one missing out on a subtlety. It will burst into solitary shouts of "ba-ba-ba-BA-ba-ba-BA-ba-ba-ba," in an approximation of an old bullfighting tune. It will cycle through seven rounds of the Wave, even though the umpire's stentorian s'il vous plaîts have been booming on the sound system, trying to restore dignity after the third one. And then the crowd will applaud itself to celebrate all the Waves it has just done.

Even though the venue of Roland-Garros, like all major tournament sites, has been somewhat bloated by the appetites of capital, the endless urge to house more and more paying ticket holders and lanyard-clad guests of corporate sponsors, it still maintains a certain purity. It still feels like a temple to clay-court tennis. And over the last two decades of the men's tournament, one player has been its chief deity. Rafael Nadal has a higher success rate winning matches at Roland-Garros than I do at tying my own shoes. Heading into the 2024 tournament, he had won 112 of his 115 matches there. It is not merely one of the great feats in tennis, but one of the most consistent performances in any competitive human endeavor. Being that good at something must make it difficult to stop, as Nadal's body now seemed to be urging him to do.

Nadal was so entangled with the tournament's history that in 2021 they'd erected a statue of him: 10 feet of gleaming, striated steel. His father, Sebastián, was seen admiring it in the days ahead of the 2024 tournament. If this was really Rafa's last appearance at Roland-Garros, then there were sure to be lots of people hungry to see the 14-time champion leave in style. His millions of fans would have liked to see him conquer a few foes on Court Philippe-Chatrier before saying goodbye. The tournament would have liked to sell out the stadium for a few more matches. The documentary team following Nadal to chronicle this last phase of his career would've liked some meatier material. There was a lot bound up in the notion of Nadal performing well here, of ending this long-running story on sufficiently beautiful terms.

Such an ending always seemed unlikely. Having previously said it would be his last season on tour, Nadal started 2024 surprisingly fresh, looking as brisk and lethal as he had in the preceding year and a half. But in just his third match of the season he pulled up limping with a hip injury. He sat out for three months and returned in time for the clay season, but even on his favorite surface he was unconvincing. In his last match before Roland-Garros, he was routed by the kindly and big-serving world No. 9 Hubert Hurkacz, 6-1, 6-3. He hadn't lost a match that badly on clay since 2003.

And yet Nadal has always played strange games with hope. By disposition, he isn't the type to close doors conclusively—he would not even commit to saying that this was his last appearance at Roland-Garros—and he likes to update his thinking based on his current sensations. He speaks a gnarled and intuitive English, a broken poetry full of rhetorical questions and bespoke idioms. His life has been dense and intense enough that he seems to have acquired wisdom at twice the normal rate. And while in the lead-up to the 2024 tournament he was honest about the ravages that tennis had inflicted on his body, he left open the possibility that he might restore his former glory.

His press conference before the tournament was a master class in his usual charms and optimism, and it left the faint but irrational impression that he could survive his first-round test. He riffed about the positive feelings he was having on court and the practice sets he'd been playing against other top players. He said Roland-Garros was magical for him and was asked if that magic made his body feel better. "No, unfortunately not," he laughed. "Is not that magic."

He would have required some dark and potent magic indeed to get past his first-round opponent. Because of his injuries over the last two years, Nadal's ranking had fallen to No. 275, which meant that he had to enter the tournament using a "protected" ranking, a tool intended to ease return to work for players recovering from injury or pregnancy. So for the first time in Nadal's career, he was playing the tournament unseeded. Every tournament has seeds for its highest-ranked players. The seeds are spaced out throughout the bracket, so as to eliminate the possibility of them meeting in the early rounds, ensuring richer matchups later in the tournament. In this way, a seed is a kind of armor. Gasps rang out at the draw ceremony where his first-round matchup was revealed: Sascha Zverev, the tournament's fourth seed, recent winner of the title in Rome, and a plausible winner of the whole tournament. Here was conclusive proof that these tournaments do not rig the draws to peddle tickets. Nadal would have no time to tune up his game against a middling opponent; Zverev was almost certain to end Nadal's career at Roland-Garros. What's more, Zverev made for an uneasy co-star in such a high-profile match. He was then in the middle of a trial in Berlin criminal court, appealing a penalty order for allegedly assaulting his former romantic partner.

On the day of the match, it was cold and rainy, so the retractable roof was expanded above the court. Nadal prefers open air, no clouds, and the hot sun baking the clay a little firmer so that the ball bounces faster and higher off the court, making his topspin all the deadlier. Even the weather was now conspiring against him. While this did seem likely to be his last match at Roland-Garros, he approached it like all the others, maintaining his famously eccentric, meticulous rituals. Right after the coin flip, most players simply walk to the back of the court, or jog if feeling frisky. But Nadal always opts for a zigzagging sprint—lunging left, then right, then left, then right, until he's back at the baseline. Throughout the match he keeps that baseline tidy, sweeping it with the bottom of his shoe, performing the roles of both player and custodian. Before every serve he adjusts his wedgie; during every changeover he arranges his water bottles along a diagonal. The old rites were all intact, even if the old tennis wasn't.

On this court Nadal used to rigorously delete his opponents. A No. 1–ranked tennis player historically wins about 55 percent of points in a season; that much of an edge equates to a dominant performance. In his prime, Nadal had on several occasions won nearly 70 percent of the points in his matches at Roland-Garros. In his prime, it sometimes appeared he was landing eight haymakers in a row on an insensate corpse. These performances weren't always beloved by the crowds—that kind of thing was hard to applaud. But such vigor from Rafa was now scarce, and thus precious. So precious that ordinary tennis fans like Novak Djokovic, Iga Świątek, and Carlos Alcaraz showed up in the stadium to watch the Zverev match in person and pay homage to the clay-court god. I have often felt that Nadal was the player I would design in a vacuum to succeed on clay. In his heyday, my imagination failed to conjure up any potential improvements. Watching him against Zverev, I could definitely imagine a handful.

There were heady moments in the second set when Nadal went up a break. That labile Paris crowd turned frantic and hopeful. Then, while serving for the set, Nadal fell into a 0-40 hole he could not crawl out of. Watching him hit his signature shots, I started to see a ghostly overlay of the 2013 Nadal projected over the present-day reality. The 2024 down-the-line forehand pass that bonked into the middle of the net post would have instead arced savagely outside Zverev's reach before dipping back into the corner of the court, following that infamous "banana" curve. It was possible to see the thrilling, crackling outlines of what Nadal once was, and occasionally the ghost and the present slid into serene alignment, before falling out of sync again. A slow and rickety recovery step, a belabored backhand falling a few feet before the service line, and the illusion dissipated.

Zverev won the match in straight sets. Nadal's lifetime record at Roland-Garros was now 112-4. At the end the crowd turned bleary and confused, as if unable to process the idea of a first-round exit from its forever champion. Immediately after the handshake, there was a stilted interview session on the court with both players, effectively drying out any wet eyes in the stadium. Anyone looking for an experience of deep feeling, or closure, was instead left with ambiguity. Some of that ambiguity was logistical: I remain puzzled by the insistence at tennis tournaments to use the question-and-answer format in moments of vivid life-altering emotion, when they could simply hand over the mic to the players and let them express themselves. Some of that ambiguity was in Nadal's own mind: He still would not rule out a future return and had nixed a more formal ceremony commemorating his career. He deserved to go out in a haze of fan delirium but got no such thing.

It was possible that Nadal had struck his last forehands on a court he had dominated as thoroughly as anyone had dominated any patch of earth. It was also possible that he would be back on the same grounds a few weeks later to compete in the Summer Olympics. After he'd recovered from the match and showered, he was asked in his press conference if he felt ready to play again in Paris. "I cannot tell you if I will be here or not be here in one month and a half," Nadal said. "Because my body has been a jungle for two years. And you don't know what to expect. I wake up one day and I found a snake biting me. Another day, a tiger. It have been a big fighting with all the things that I went through."

The second legend with his name in the 2024 Roland-Garros draw fell only a week later. Djokovic had just turned 37. No man younger than him owned a Roland-Garros title. Tennis used to be a young man's game until the Big Three colonized it. Despite coming into the tournament without much rhythm, he'd managed to win his first two rounds in straight sets. Nothing after that was straightforward. In the third round he had Lorenzo Musetti, the young Italian with a sweet, sinuous game. These two players had a curious history at this tournament. Three years before, Musetti had taken a two-sets-to-none lead, only for Djokovic to leave the court, change his clothes, and wrest back control of the match, with the crushing inevitability of a bear trap. Musetti retired from that match while getting blown out 4-0 in the fifth set. He said he wasn't actually injured but had simply realized "there was no chance that I could win a point." In the 2024 rematch, only a few details were changed: Musetti had a two-sets-to-one lead, but by the end, instead of packing his bags early, he stuck around and allowed himself to be wiped out 6-0 in the fifth set. It was yet another nightmare for a young player who thought he'd gotten the better of the legend in this format.

Djokovic had crushed dozens of dreams in the same fashion. He'd beaten Jannik Sinner from two sets down at Wimbledon two years earlier. And the year before that, he'd beaten Stefanos Tsitsipas in the Roland-Garros final from two sets down. "To be honest, I even liked the fact that I lost the first couple of sets," he said after beating Musetti back in 2021. "I like to play young guys in best-of-five, because I feel even if they are leading a set or two sets to love, as it was the case today, I still like my chances." It was almost as if he hunted them for sport, spotting them two sets to test his limits. The dicier the scoreboard, the more assured he was of his own eventual success.

Djokovic was apparently in the mood for five-setters, since he moved directly from Musetti to another one against Francisco Cerúndolo, an Argentinian slight in build but armed with one of the fastest forehands on tour. Early in their fourth-round match, Djokovic had asked officials to sweep the court more frequently, to ensure the clay was evenly coating the hard surface beneath and not exposing slick patches. Those concerns were legitimate, as he proceeded to fall down throughout the match, most severely in the second set, requiring lengthy medical treatment on his right knee. When he fell again early in the fifth set, he howled. Heading back to his chair to recover, he muttered, "It's not slippery at all, it's not dangerous at all." Still, despite all the falls, despite having finished his previous five-set match after three a.m., despite spending large stretches of this match unable to move laterally, Djokovic won in four hours and 39 minutes—another standard-issue miracle from him. The scope of that miracle only expanded the next day, when Djokovic announced that he was withdrawing from the tournament. It turned out that while winning he had torn the meniscus in his right knee.

Immediately upon hearing this, I looked again at the shot Djokovic had hit late in the fifth set the night before. Standing at the front of the court as a Cerúndolo shot threatened to fly past him, he took one long step toward the net and then with his next step descended into a full front split, as smoothly as a yogi, and scooped the ball up when it was hanging just inches over his right shoe. After winning the point with these elastic antics, he tipped onto his tummy and celebrated by spreading his legs wide and waggling them, like a child miming an airplane. (It was a gesture he'd invented the previous year after a similarly absurd side-split shot against Sinner.) He had done all that with a freshly torn meniscus? How was this man possible? Winning a seven-round major required an element beyond mere skill at hitting a tennis ball deep. It also took a survivalist's savvy, the capacity to win a four-hour odyssey, accept the physical damages, wake up, and prepare to do the same thing again the next day. Djokovic had honed that skill set more than any other player in history, marching through tears in his abdomen and hamstring until a sought-after title was in his hands. But this time, with the rip of cartilage, even he had met his limit.

Thus, Roland-Garros, which seemed wide-open at the outset, remained wide-open. Alcaraz and Sinner had arrived in Paris in low gear and with self-professed low expectations. Talking to the press right before the tournament, Sinner said that his hip was fine, but while recovering from the injury, he'd also fallen ill and lost his general conditioning. He'd started playing practice points only in the past three days. He reported all this in his typical matter-of-fact tone, but it was a startling update from the No. 2 seed. He'd be trying to get back in shape on a court surface known for demanding the most of its players cardiovascularly, and at a major, no less. The notion of getting into shape during a major is reserved only for the holy ones who can treat the opening rounds as a mere warm-up before the real work begins. The common joke was that Federer could use the early rounds of Wimbledon as a low-stress practice session to test out his whole repertoire of shots. Perhaps Sinner, at the age of 22, was verging on that greatness relative to the rest of the field. Probably not. Soon enough he would find out. He had said that clay courts asked more of him: more physicality and a more granular type of concentration from point to point, as it's harder to close out a rally with a decisive winner. His hip would be tested by all the sliding, too.

Alcaraz, meanwhile, was not his usual frisky self in his press appearance before the tournament. He often arrives at tournaments as if they're his own birthday party. Ahead of Roland-Garros, however, he was discreet, even a little guarded. He paid his dues to his idol Rafa, and then he was asked about his injury. If Sinner's report was clinical and plain, Alcaraz's was incomplete yet revealing in its own way. "Well, I think you're not going to believe me, but I don't know exactly what I have on the forearm. When I do the tests, when I'm talking with the doctors, my team, they 'splain me what I have on the forearm, but I listen to them, but I forget it, and I just focus to do the things that the doctors, my team, told me that I have to do. That's it," he said, smiling.

This enviable answer fit with the image he'd already built, that of a figure unburdened by the woes of the common man, frolicking about the world's tennis courts. But it was also consistent with the way that some players will intentionally outsource knowledge-keeping to their team. This happens with certain players' racquet setups. Even a weekend hobbyist knows his preferred strings and tensions and grips and lead-tape placements, and you'd think the best players in the world would want to know this stuff too, but some don't concern themselves with the details. The same can be true with health protocols. It isn't incuriosity, just a case of tacit bodily wisdom winning over explicit analytical fact. To tear around the court and hit balls at the speed Alcaraz does seems to require an uncluttered mind. Getting wrapped up in the minutiae of equipment or injury could only lead to overthinking, to the gestation of doubts. Alcaraz knew as much as he needed to know and would not be weighed down by a grain of superfluous information. In that, he was like so many other intuitive high performers: It was better to feel than to know.

At his pre-tournament practice sessions, however, the injury was preventing him from tapping into that usual unthinking flow. "I'm not feeling any pain in the practices when I step on the court. But I'm still thinking about it when I'm hitting forehands. Probably I'm gonna say I'm a little bit scared about hitting every forehand 100 percent," he said, noting he'd have to snap out of that mindset before his first match. I asked if he and Jannik commiserated about their injuries. He said he'd sent Sinner a text after hearing about his hip. It didn't sound all that deep.

And yet, no matter how hedged and cautious these two were before the tournament, once it actually started, they continued their characteristic dominance. Each of them lost only one set in their first five matches. Alcaraz faltered for a minute in his second-round match, but then he reminded himself that his job was to win, not just astonish. "The third set I needed to forget about putting on a show and put myself in the chance of putting myself in the rallies," he admitted afterward. Sinner, who spent his first match periodically clutching at his hip, looked more comfortable with every passing day. In the fourth round he had a tricky moment against the short, kooky Frenchman Corentin Moutet, known in equal measure for his experimental trick shots and deranged emotional outbursts. Sinner had never before played Moutet, who was liable to ambush opponents with an underarm serve or a drop shot at any time. The crowd in Paris lit up for their crazed countryman as he stole away the first set from Sinner, breaking serve three times. And then, as if humanely disposing of a mouse that had taken up residence in his pantry, Sinner dispatched him by winning the next three sets.

Sinner and Alcaraz were on track to meet in the semifinal. By this point in their careers it had become something of a joke among fans. Their last four meetings had been semifinals—when would these two ever get to meet in a proper final? By now, shouldn't they be the top two seeds, who get placed on opposite sides of the bracket, meeting only in a title fight? Not yet, said Djokovic, who often functioned as a wonderfully symbolic wedge. Because of his strong play in 2023, Djokovic was still the No. 1 seed in every tournament he entered, bumping Sinner and Alcaraz down to No. 2 and No. 3 respectively, which put them in the same half of the bracket. In this way the lingering presence of the past generation interfered with the ideal spectacle of the new generation.

However, by withdrawing early from Roland-Garros in 2024 with a meniscus tear, Djokovic lost a big chunk of his ranking points. This meant that Sinner had secured a place in history—a fact he learned in public, immediately after his quarterfinal win. "Jannik, I cannot leave you without telling you one thing," said the on-court interviewer, ex-player Fabrice Santoro. "Next Monday, at the age of 22 years old, you will become the first Italian ever to be No. 1 in the world." Sinner processed this—rapidly blinking, as if to shake some clay out of his eyes, then gave a long sigh, a smile. Typically he liked to glide right over his triumphs to stare down the next tasks on his agenda, but here for a moment, his stoicism cracked. He allowed himself the luxury of basking in this feat. The crowd hooted its approval, and he turned to wave back.

So the semifinal would be Sinner, at the apex of the tour, taking on his archrival, again. It wasn't the final, but it was still the first time they had met at this late stage in a major. They had never played a match with these stakes. Sinner had the better season heading in, 33-3 to Alcaraz's 24-4. If Sinner won their encounter, he would be favored in the final, too, and could level the major title count at two apiece. If Alcaraz advanced, he could go on to claim a major title on all three court surfaces of hard court, grass, and clay, becoming the youngest player ever to do so, validating all hype about him as an all-timer. His recovery was still ongoing. Alcaraz's coach Ferrero said ahead of the matchup that his charge's forehand was at "95 percent." That 5 percent deficit wouldn't be enough to curb the appetite of any fans. If the Indian Wells matchup was another piece of evidence for the file, by Roland-Garros, the case was clear: Sincaraz would be the best rivalry on the men's tour, the most telegenic and most portentous for the decade ahead. Every match they had ever played, dating back to their adorable Challenger circuit meeting in 2019, had been addictive, alien tennis. Were they even capable of playing a bad match against each other?

In Paris, for the first two and a half hours or so, they seemed intent on answering that question in the positive. Yes, we could bore you. This most alluring pairing had at last yielded an ugly baby. As they toiled and cramped up and fumed over errors, they offered a jarring visual reminder that they'd come into the tournament nursing injury, managing muted expectations. And while they'd both spent the last 10 days coolly chopping up the competition, they had each collided with the one opponent who could expose the limitations of their game. Tennis can be spectacular, but it can also devolve into the indelicate gnashing of one will against another, yielding few sparks. Sometimes a rival pushes a player to heretofore-unseen brilliance, feats they didn't know they were capable of. Sometimes they just make each other play like shit.

Nature was not helping matters, either. The tournament that had started out wet and cold was now dry and scorching. After the first set, attendants hosed down the court's arid clay. The players sat underneath umbrellas, catching their breath, towels draped around their necks like fat pythons. Tennis is the most towel-oriented sport, and it has devised a clever technique for its hottest conditions. Long towels are stuffed with ice packs, rolled up, and taped snug. An atypically pissy Alcaraz had been complaining to the umpire from the start of the match. Where were the ice towels? They should have been there! His tennis was just as tetchy. He spewed errors, losing the first four games of the match so badly that the crowd started roaring its support of him, as if he were some plucky underdog and not one of the great prodigies in the sport's history. Late in that first set Alcaraz absorbed a long monologue from Ferrero and snarled at himself in anger. If you held up a hand over your field of vision so that you could see only Alcaraz's side of the court, you'd have given him zero chance of beating the 2024 version of Sinner.

Fortunately for him, the dysfunction was mutual in the second set. Sinner lost all the depth on his shots. On the American broadcast, the word "diarrhea" was uttered, as if to apologize for the quality of the contest, in reference to the virus Sinner had before the tournament. In the third set, Sinner had a physiotherapist knead his right forearm and then his left hamstring. Alcaraz shook out his right hand, which had also locked up. A fan passed out in the stands and play was suspended. The unconscious spectator is a distressingly common feature of the live tennis experience under climate change—it makes you wonder how high-level tennis can be played in conditions oppressive enough to knock out stationary fans—but it felt especially apt on this day. Even the players' outfits were dire. Sinner and Alcaraz looked like they'd gotten dressed off the discount rack at a big-box store: solid-colored, utilitarian shirts and shorts in slate gray, banana yellow, persimmon orange.

Most puzzling of all was Alcaraz's tactical approach. I'd expected him to carry over his successful plan of attack from Indian Wells, where the grittier hard courts play a little bit like the clay they now stood on. Alcaraz had then hit slower and loopier shots that upset Sinner's rhythm and kept him from asserting himself. It was a patient and subtle plan. Instead, Alcaraz entered this semifinal in an itchy and willful mood, going for high-risk forehands from hopeless court positions, following every impulse. Most of the time, his ability to execute those shots justifies that audacity. He has earned the right to dream that boldly. But on those occasions where the balls consistently land five feet past the baseline or in the middle of the net, it's hard to accept such a grandiose vision. When Alcaraz plays badly, he can look uncentered and full of bad ideas. When Sinner plays badly, he looks like a machine just slightly miscalibrated, erring but with the right intent.

In the third set, Alcaraz continued to struggle but produced perhaps the single finest shot he'd ever hit against his rival. When he served at 3-3, 30-15 in the second set, Sinner's return of serve sent Alcaraz staggering. His next forehand broke the sideline and sent Alcaraz scuttling deep behind the baseline, into the lower left corner. Sinner paused, as if admiring his work, and then jogged forward in case there was a weak reply to clean up. He had played a perfect pair of shots. But it was possible to play Alcaraz perfectly and still lose. Because even on a bad forehand day, even when careening toward the walls at the perimeter of the court, Alcaraz could still fire off a passing shot that flitted right by an unprepared opponent, who had not realized that such a shot was on the menu of possibilities. And then Carlitos pointed at his ear.

Midway through the fourth set, with the match score two sets to one in Sinner's favor, Alcaraz began to hit more shots like that one. His execution rose to match his vision. He pulled off the screaming passing shots on the run, the cottony drop-shot-lob combos, the stinging wide serves, his racquet no longer a dull plank but a beam of joy. The crowd boomed. The tennis seemed to come out of nowhere. Writing about a match like this is attempting to impose a legible narrative on what is, effectively, two people trying to devise increasingly sophisticated ways of murdering one another for four hours. They were experiencing all kinds of small-scale spiritual and physical ups and downs, some of which would later make it into their comments after the match, and some of which will remain forever unknown, hard to articulate even for them, certainly in a second or third language. Often the real tennis match—its problem-solving, its private pains, its triage—resists after-the-fact comprehension. Deep in the fourth set it appeared Sinner had found the more reliable patterns of play and could win in a tiebreak; instead he threw in a few loose points and Alcaraz only amplified his own genius.

In the fifth set, at last, they both found beautiful tennis at the same time. Clay can have a gladiatorial quality, the combatants dirtying themselves in the toil, the long rallies leaving them too depleted to cheer. The traditionally silent Sinner began grunting, and once even reared back his racquet as if to smash it, which was a full-on evacuation of character. The unflappable had been flapped. By the end of the set, a big, serrated shadow had fallen over much of the court, blanketing the action in darkness. They had been playing for four hours. Alcaraz began to outclass Sinner at his own baseline game. On pivotal points, he kept sending his serve out wide, and Sinner never found a suitable reply. After winning the final point, Alcaraz closed his eyes, turned his face to the sky, threw up both hands, and grimaced, as though struck by a lightning bolt. Then he walked to his opponent and they embraced—a hug shorter and chillier than recent iterations. Tennis had gotten brawnier over the decades, but its competitors were still pressed into that display of genteel civility, just seconds after they'd spent four hours wired to kill.

"You have to find the joy in suffering," said Alcaraz as he was interviewed on court minutes later. It was a perfect and subconscious homage to Rafa Nadal, who over his career spoke volumes about the masochism of tennis, his worldview still evidently looming over his tournament. Alcaraz reiterated, "That's the key, even more so on clay, long rallies, long matches, five sets. I told my team many times, 'You have to enjoy suffering.'" He went on to say that the toughest matches he'd played in his career had been against Sinner. Though it was Sinner crowned No. 1, compiling one of the best seasons in recent memory, Alcaraz had still won both their meetings thus far in 2024. He was advancing to his first-ever Roland-Garros final.

Given that he had conquered his true rival and biggest obstacle, I expected a buoyant and purposeful Carlitos in the championship match. Instead he arrived to face Zverev, the man who had ousted Nadal, in a salty mood again. While squandering a big lead in the third set, he told the umpire that the courts weren't being maintained well, that the wind had exposed patches, just as Djokovic had complained about. "Do you think it's normal? We are playing a final of a Grand Slam on clay court, but it seems like it's hard court," Alcaraz declared. "It's unbelievable. It's unbelievable. Unbelievable."

Only a few days earlier, Zverev's assault case had reached a settlement, and the charges against him were dropped. "I never ever want to hear another question about the subject again," he'd told reporters. Zverev had an enormous serve stapled to a consistent baseline game. It was a player archetype that did not really exist in the sport's history but had lately come to occupy a slot high on its food chain: "big-serving counterpunchers," as the tennis writer Matthew Willis put it. Throwing down serves in the 130s and backing it up from the baseline was a style that seemed to work against Alcaraz. With

Zverev leading the championship match two sets to one, it was clear that winning would ask more of Alcaraz than he had shown thus far. Possibly more than he had shown through the whole season up to that point. He had no more margin for error, no more sets to burn.

Pressure can be immobilizing even for the elite on tour. Look no further than Zverev himself for the perfect illustration. Playing in his first major final, the pandemic 2020 U.S. Open, in an eerie stadium devoid of fans, Zverev, then just 23 years old, saw his tennis fall apart. The serve he could strike harder than 130 mph started rolling in the 80s, 70s, even high 60s. Serving for the championship at 5-3 in the fifth, he made four unforced errors and went on to lose the match to Dominic Thiem, despite having led by two sets to love and a break in the third. This was human. To wilt under pressure, for the body to compromise technique once the mind comprehended the gravity of the moment, was understandable. It happened to nearly every player at some point.

Harder to understand is how Alcaraz responds to pressure. For him, pressure seems clarifying. It forces him to stop temporizing. He stops surveying his various options on court and commits to the lucid, slashing style that made his name. It's as if pressure snaps a lens into focus, revealing his own identity. Often he'll look to his box for some insight, something to settle his young mind, but in the end, at Roland-Garros in 2024, it fell to him to stay loose and play free and push this match to a fifth set, which he did.

That deciding set left us with one cinematic image. Zverev, down 2-4, pounded a backhand approach shot and ran up to the net. Alcaraz fired a forehand right at him, testing his foe's shaky net skills, but Zverev snapped off a nice volley that sent the Spaniard sprinting in the other direction. Skating across the clay, Alcaraz didn't even have time to put both hands on his backhand. Instead, with his back facing his opponent, arching his head over his shoulder, he flicked it back with one hand. It was a shot of pure Alcarazian feel, nonchalant but crisp. The ball struck the top of the net. And then, like a stone skipping off a pond, it kept hissing right past Zverev, who glared back in frustration, wanting the Spaniard to acknowledge his stupidly good fortune. Alcaraz threw up the standard hand of apology, the usual etiquette when a player wins a point after his ball strikes the net cord—and then, when Zverev looked away, he cunningly curled his apology hand into a fist pump. No time for guilt. Some luck, sure, but also a glorious jolt of improvisation, the type of shot that explained why I'd overheard some French fans describe him as "pétillant"—sparkling, fizzy, like wine.

Not long after, Alcaraz collapsed on the clay in triumph. A Roland-Garros champion for the first time, he hauled himself up, paid respects to Zverev, and bunny-hopped over to his player's box, shouting "Vamos" again and again as he went. Upon arriving among his platoon of Spanish men—brother, agent, physio, coach, coach's coach—they each embraced him, ruffled his hair, and hollered into his ear, the court's red clay still coating his back like dried blood.

An old video circulated after his win. A 12-year-old Carlitos, sitting on a bench in a polo shirt with the Spanish flag, was asked about his life dreams. "Ganar Roland-Garros y Wimbledon," he said, his trilled *r*'s like the revving of a tiny engine. Not even a decade later, he'd accomplished the task he set out for himself. At 21 Alcaraz was the youngest man ever to hold a major title on every surface. Even more staggering was how he'd won this particular title: coming fresh off injury and without summoning his peak tennis for longer than a few minutes in a row. He concentrated his brilliance into a few critical doses and timed their delivery perfectly. That was enough. Carlos Alcaraz was capable of transcendence, but he was now also capable of winning a major title while far from transcendent, defeating many of his best contemporaries along the way. He won choppily, even unhappily at times. The happiness came a few days later, at a nightclub on the island of Ibiza, where Alcaraz stood surrounded by friends: "Weeeeee are the chambyons," he howled tunelessly into the mic, into his future.

CHAPTER 8

Meddy in the Middle

There is an image of Daniil Medvedev that I return to like a sacrament. It's a screenshot of a slow-motion replay from the 2021 Australian Open semifinal. The camera is positioned along the baseline. Daniil is running toward us, having just struck a miraculous backhand winner. He looks not so much triumphant as crumpled. Bent over, back rounded into a turtle shell. Legs buckling, knees nearly knocking together. Feet pigeon-toed and pointed at angles that elicit a sympathetic wince. Thin arms drawn forward like long beans. It looks like what you'd get if you'd asked a child to draw a tennis player from memory—in the dark. It is not an image that inspires great confidence. That's why I love it. No layman would ever conclude that it depicted one of the most hand-foot-eye-coordinated people on the planet.

Look at a similarly timed freeze-frame of Rafael Nadal and you see a form that might have been sculpted in antiquity. Look at the one of Medvedev and you see a software engineer encouraged by his wife to pick up a hobby. Whereas Nadal's rigorous and explosive style can be intuited from his build, Medvedev's uncanny and innovative style must be seen to be understood. And even then, it rewards watching and rewatching, where it reveals new wrinkles and anomalies. I have always been drawn to athletes who defy visual bias. Who cares whether their body types match the textbook illustration? What matters, in this arena, is what you can do to a tennis ball. Watching Medvedev marooned 10 feet behind the baseline, maneuvering his jangly limbs all over the court, swatting his flat, skidding shots, over and over, it is hard to grasp how these parts sum up to a world-class tennis player. Medvedev himself is as bamboozled as we are, saying, "When I see myself in videos, I'm like, 'What am I doing?'"

It's not just his tennis that resists easy comprehension. His personality, too, has left casual fans convinced that he is some enemy of the game. Perhaps they are reading too much into the expansive plain of his forehead, those cunning beady eyes, the physiognomy of a supervillain plotting to take down the power grid.

What could have left those fans with this unsavory impression? What evidence could they find for it? Perhaps they'd caught the match from his 2019 U.S. Open run, when he'd subtly flipped the bird to the crowd, as though he were scratching the side of his head but happened to use only one finger. Or the end of that match, when he provoked that same crowd with the best on-court sermon in recent history: "If you were not here, guys, I would probably lose the match because I was so tired. . . . I want all of you to know when you sleep tonight I won today because of you," he said, to a cacophony of boos. "The energy you've given me right now, guys, I think it will be enough for my five next matches. The more you do this, the more I will win for you guys. Thank you." He spread his arms wide and waggled his fingers, as if he were a plant photosynthesizing their hatred.

Or perhaps those fans saw the match in Miami where he skirmished with Stefanos Tsitsipas in an iconic English-as-second-language scuffle, which saw Daniil coin such phrases as "He's a small kid who doesn't know how to fight" and "Man, you better shut your fuck up, okay?"

Or perhaps it was one of the many, many times he screamed at an umpire? Like the time at Wimbledon he pulled out his wallet and threw coins at the umpire chair to imply that the official had taken a bribe. Or the time in Australia when he slurred an umpire on his way off the court, infuriated that his opponent hadn't been penalized for illegal coaching, by saying: "Next time it should be a code violation. . . . If you don't, you are a—how can I call it?—small cat."

Or perhaps it was his years-long campaign against clay courts, against the very material they were made of. In Madrid, after Medvedev banged his racquet against the clay, an umpire chastised him for damaging the court. "It's bad surface. Me, I cannot do damage against bad surface. Bad surface is bad surface." Here he is making a metaphysical point about clay—can you really break a pile of already broken brick?—in the middle of an unabashed hissy fit. But in spite of his personal distaste for the clay, he tried to keep an open mind: "But if you like to be in the dirt like a dog, I don't judge," he said in Rome.

Surely some of his outbursts were a crude form of moral protest. Like the time he objected to intolerably hot court conditions at the Tokyo Olympics: "I'm fine. I can finish the match but I can die. If I die will the ITF take responsibility?" Medvedev asked, holding one of the sport's governing bodies accountable for his imminent demise.

Alas, the evidence is overwhelming. I concede that he has given the world legitimate grounds for thinking that he is an ass. But I'd like to at least amend that statement: He is an ass with lethal comic timing. And those who have witnessed his toddler-style loss of control but haven't had the chance to speak with him mere minutes after those tantrums are missing something important: He transforms into a warm, attentive, and disarmingly funny interlocutor. Regardless of whether he has won or lost, he walks into the press conference with an open smile, floppy body language, and ready apologies for whatever scandal he might have just enacted on the court. As soon as he enters that room, everyone perks up, because he is the rare player who treats it as a space for real-time reflection rather than a contractual obligation, who doesn't seem to resent the process of answering those questions.

Nicknamed "the octopus" for his tentacular body type and play style, he also holds conversations the way I imagine such an inquisitive animal might. Lob a question at Medvedev and he will ensnare it with one tentacle and turn it around like a bauble—answering it in keen detail, or negating its premise, or asking an even more interesting question and answering that instead, always amusing himself and the asker. He does all this in three languages: English, French, and Russian, often in quick succession. His off-the-cuff remarks reflect a penetrating tennis mind, a talent for jarring metaphor, and bitterly blackened humor. His insights into other players offer a more transparent view into their minds and their tennis than those players do themselves. I have often wished he could hold press conferences on behalf of everyone else on tour. A psychoanalyst and performance coach who consulted with Medvedev when he was 20 years old recalled leaving the meeting struck by his "monstrous mental potential, that is to say, a rare ability to explore his thoughts."

At the outset of the 2024 season, Medvedev publicly declared his intention to become a more civilized and less rageful colleague. Nine months later—after he'd perpetrated too many absurd antics to fit within these dashes—I planted my tongue firmly in cheek and asked him how his New Year's resolution was going. He was a little bashful about falling short but promised to keep trying. He also explained what it's like inside that big head of his. "When I'm on court, my mind is boiling, constantly boiling. Sometimes it's frustration. Sometimes with good emotions. It's like tea. It just comes out, comes out even if I don't want it. It just boils."

The man with a mind full of tea has had plenty of reasons to boil over the years. He was a nonconformist trying to find his way in a very conservative game. Not everyone has believed in him or the way he went about things. As a junior player in Russia, his potential was not fully understood. Most elite athletes leave traditional schooling at 12, but his mother wanted to keep him studying, so he graduated early from a specialized math and science high school, then enrolled in an economics program in college before dropping out to commit to tennis. He left Russia to train in France. He has said that he was terribly conditioned as a younger player, cramping early in matches, staying up late, addicted to his PlayStation. In his first few years as a pro he was unremarkable. It was in 2019 that he emerged, suddenly, as one of the best players alive, at age 23, on the strength of his irreplicable play style.

Nobody could have taught him this style; it had to be discovered. Nobody would have taken a six-foot-six guy and stationed him a kilometer behind the baseline to play in this weird, patient, siege-like fashion. Someone that big would have been pressed into a high-powered, bang-bang approach to the game. That guidance would have grossly misunderstood the athlete at hand. Medvedev's specific brand of athleticism can't be divined from a superficial once-over of his frame. He has an ultramarathoner's endurance and tolerance for discomfort. His peculiar combination of foot speed and pterodactyl wingspan allows him to cover large swaths of the court as a defender. His fate was not to become a quick-point power player but rather an oversized counterpuncher, scheming his way through interminable rallies.

In a world of topspin, Medvedev is a subversive. Topspin is produced by brushing the tennis ball upward so that it spins forward. It is the foundation of the modern game. It allows players to hit the ball even harder while still ensuring it will dip back down inside the court. It allows them to hit the ball a comfortable margin over the net. It also enables them to hit shots with even more severe angles. No high-level tennis player could go without it. But Medvedev often uses the minimum viable amount of topspin, instead hitting some of the flattest shots on tour, as measured by the ball's revolutions per minute. The ball coming off his racquet behaves unlike the ball coming off anyone else's. It flirts close to the net, skids off the court, and stays low after bouncing. While nearly everyone else on tour is hitting balls that trace large curvaceous arcs, Medvedev lands perfectly weighted linear bunts on a desired quarter inch of space. Without the benefit of topspin to bring his shots down into the court, he simply stands farther behind the baseline to give them more distance to travel. He has figured out the interlocking tactical choices to make his style work.

Perfecting that game was a slow process of refinement, but its skeleton was always there. "It's how I've been playing since I was 10, 12," he told me back in 2019, when he was on the cusp of the top 10. "I don't know why did I start playing like this. Because usually you come to a coach when you are six, and he tells you, you have to come under the ball," he said, evoking the swing that produces topspin. "So I have no idea how I start playing like this." It was good that he did. As he pointed out, he can hit it flat, but still quite powerfully, and it's difficult to attack his low-bouncing balls. The squiggly strokes themselves seemed to reflect Dadaist influence. When he follows through on his forehand, his arm rises up and encircles his neck, like a spaghetti noodle encircling the tine of a fork. This technique is not going to send casual observers into rhapsody—good luck working that into a slo-mo luxury watch ad—but wonkish fans could enjoy its delicious idiosyncrasy. So too could his frustrated opponents. "He has a very weird game. It's very sloppy, but a good sloppy," said his rival Stefanos Tsitsipas. "He has this completely different way of playing, flat and low, without giving you much angle to work with. It can be very disturbing to play against him. He can make you miss without understanding why you missed." As the octopus, he traps his opponents in long, sticky rallies, steadily strangling their will.

Medvedev's other innovations involve court positioning. When he was first breaking out on tour, he liked to experiment with his serve position, scooting from the hashmark at the center of the court all the way out to the doubles alley, which allowed him to find unusual angles. Most memorable, though, is where he chooses to stand when returning serves. He positions himself so far behind the baseline that, on certain camera angles, his body disappears entirely from view, and the ball pings back as if off some unseen force field. The ingenious thing about standing this far back is that by the time the ball reaches him, it has slowed down considerably, allowing him to strike it more like a normal groundstroke and less like the hasty abbreviated swings that most returners must use when standing in a traditional position. Hilariously, he has said that he can't even train this tactic when practicing on normal-sized tennis courts; it can be employed only on the stadium courts at the biggest tournaments, and even then, he sometimes worries about bumping into a cameraman or ball boy. These are not ordinary mid-match concerns.

A player like this requires a coach who can accommodate his

peculiar vision and temperament. Medvedev found his in Gilles Cervara, a Frenchman who joined his team in 2017 and has since navigated the peaks and troughs of the Meddy experience with admirable cool. In a sport trending toward massive entourages, full of auxiliary therapists and trainers, Cervara is often the solitary figure seated in Medvedev's player box, his beard and sunglasses poking out from beneath a low-slung cap. He placidly oversees the tirades and meltdowns. Player and coach seem to enjoy an intimate bond. Which is not to say it is always a happy relationship; Medvedev has banished his coach from the court at tense moments. "It's like to coach a genius," Cervara said in 2019. "Sometimes a genius, you don't understand them." He knew that Medvedev wouldn't respond to a dogmatic approach, with blank appeals to authority. Cervara had to listen to Medvedev and understand how his mind worked. In the course of summer 2019, the two realized their potential. Medvedev made six straight finals, in one of the great hard-court summers in history, announcing himself as an unorthodox assassin on the tour's most common surface. Cervara went on to win the tour's coach of the year award for this metamorphosis.

"They ask me 200 times but my answer will always be the same, I don't have an idol, just want to be myself," Medvedev said in 2020. Reverence does not come naturally to him. But it's hard to be an iconoclast in a sport that is so square and so fetishistic about its own past. In particular, it's tricky to be an iconoclast in an era defined by the three most worshipped icons ever. They set a decorous tone for the whole sport. Once, when asked about his prickly rivalry with Tsitsipas, Medvedev suggested that his predecessors had dampened self-expression. "Especially because of the Big Three, tennis is considered as a super, super conservative sport, super intelligent. So we as young guys, we need to follow this because otherwise we get destroyed by media, by people." And it wasn't just that he didn't want to follow them as a template for behavior; he actually had to figure out how to beat them on the tennis court, too, using his home-brewed style. In 2019, when Djokovic and Nadal were closer to their primes, Medvedev began to regularly confront them. And unlike so many from his generation, he fought quite well.

In that 2019 U.S. Open run, the one that began his supervillain arc, Medvedev arrived in the final against Nadal, lost the first two sets, and rooted around for solutions until he resorted to serve-and-volley tactics, the polar opposite of his preferred style. But it worked. His performance was so bold that he almost won the match and wound up wooing the same New York crowd that had despised him throughout the tournament. He addressed them in a classic runner-up speech. Asked how he nearly pulled off the comeback, he said, "To be honest, in my mind, I was already okay, what do I say in the [runner-up] speech, it's going to be soon, in 20 minutes." He then called back to his crowd taunt from the previous week and flipped it into sincere appreciation. "I know earlier in the tournament I said something kind of in a bad way, now I'm saying in a good way: It's because of your energy, guys, I was here in the final," he said. "In the third set where, as I say, I was already thinking which speech should I give, you guys were pushing me to prolong this match, because you want to see more tennis. And because of you guys, I was fighting like hell." The stadium pealed, this time in approval. He acknowledged that he was human, that he'd made mistakes and said he was sorry.

From that point forward, Medvedev stayed at the front of his age cohort. He was the tip of the spear poking through the Big Three barricade. His attainment of a major title seemed inevitable. And two years after the Nadal loss, he completed the work he'd left unfinished in New York. In the 2021 U.S. Open final, he faced Djokovic, who was looking to collect all four major titles in the same calendar year, a feat that hadn't been accomplished in the previous 52 years. Djokovic had won 27 of the 28 matches required to pull off this formidable feat; all that remained was Medvedev, whom he'd beaten easily in the Australian Open final at the outset of the season.

Instead, in New York, Medvedev was the one to accomplish a different Herculean labor: A person born in the 1990s had finally beaten Novak Djokovic in a major final. He was the one youngster sent into that dark wilderness who emerged alive. And after beating the elder Djokovic—who had sobbed into his towel during a changeover late in the match, moved by the underdog support he'd received from the crowd—Medvedev celebrated the win in a style befitting the youth movement. He collapsed on the court, but not the usual, happy way. He flopped like a dead fish. A sudden, sideways collapse onto his hip that looked a little painful, his tongue lolled out and his eyes glazed over. Why behave this way at the peak of his professional career? It was, naturally, a celebration used in the FIFA soccer video game. "Only legends will understand what I did after the match is L2 plus left," he explained, the first major champion to cite a controller button combination in his victory speech. Gamers had found representation among tennis's elite. Medvedev loved gaming so much, in fact, that the studio behind the first-person shooter *Rainbow Six* later brought him on as a product tester and promotional partner. The studio also revealed that he was in the top 3 percent of players worldwide. Somehow he found the hours to do that while also being the No. 3 tennis player in the world at the time. Some people are good at all the games.

Having already surpassed his own contemporaries, and having conquered Djokovic on hard court, both players' favorite surface, it seemed as though Medvedev was due an enjoyable reign at the top.

Time to savor the fruits of the toil. But for a number of reasons, matters were instead about to get a lot more difficult. At the next major tournament, the 2022 Australian Open, he again made it to the final. This time his opponent was Nadal. Medvedev led by two sets to none and had three break points early in the third set. Yet, in one of the most dramatic comebacks of the 21st century, Nadal still won the match in five wrenching sets, with the crowd spurring him on. Afterward Medvedev led his press conference with a monologue both cryptic and poignant. He said he was going to tell the story of a "young kid who dreamed about big things in tennis." He wove in specific memories of his junior days on tour—moments of happiness, moments when he was puzzled not to find a warmer reception from media or fans, moments of doubt when he wondered whether to continue dreaming. Then, abruptly, he declared that this very day the kid's dream had died. "From now on I'm playing for myself, for my family, to provide my family, for people that trust in me, of course for all the Russians because I feel a lot of support there," he said. "I'm going to say it like this. If there is a tournament on hard courts in Moscow, before Roland-Garros or Wimbledon, I'm going to go there even if I miss the Wimbledon or Roland-Garros or whatever. The kid stopped dreaming. The kid is going to play for himself. That's it. That's my story. Thanks for listening, guys."

He'd left his fable deliberately vague, but it was possible to reconstruct the authorial intent. For all his bile and sarcasm, Daniil Medvedev still had a basic human desire to connect. And he had rarely been met with affection from crowds. In the final, the crowd had vigorously backed Nadal, while also vigorously abusing Medvedev between points, hissing between his serves. "Go back to Russia," screamed one heckler. (At that time, Russian troops had amassed on the Ukrainian border, just a few weeks out from eventual war.)

Later in his press conference he threw in an addendum. "I remember there were a lot of talks . . . people saying we really want young generation to go for it, to be better, to be stronger," he said. "I was like pumped up. Yeah, let's try to give them hard time and everything. Well, I guess these people were lying because every time I stepped on the court in these big matches, I really didn't see much people who wanted me to win." For all the enthusiasm about young talent who could challenge the Big Three, the people sitting in the stadiums didn't actually want their gods killed. That monologue, then, was a confession from Medvedev. The tangible xenophobia and disinterest from crowds had killed off whatever was left of his childhood idealism. Tennis was now just a mercenary pursuit. Clock in, clock out.

Time might have healed the traumas of that match; time should have eventually bent the Nadal and Djokovic matchups in his favor. For a moment, that appeared to be the case. At just 26, Medvedev was in his physical prime, and those men, already in their mid-thirties, were drifting further from theirs. Just three weeks after the Australian Open loss, Medvedev became the No. 1 player in the world. For the past 18 years, that slot had been held exclusively by men named Roger Federer, Rafael Nadal, Novak Djokovic, and Andy Murray. Of all the men to break their hegemony—an era of sportsmanship, clean technique, and outward politesse—how glorious that it was *this* man, with the hysterics, the unseemly technique, and acid disposition. That wasn't to last long, though. Medvedev held on to that spot for only three weeks before Djokovic snatched it back. It was one of the three shortest-ever stints at No. 1.

Later that year, Medvedev regained the top rank for another 13 weeks. And in the middle of this fretful moment—scrapping with the greats, wondering if he would ever be loved, announcing his disillusionment—he was dealt another devastating fate. Enter the biggest prodigy in decades, seven years Medvedev's junior, permanently a-grin, and instantly beloved. Why him? Why now? Medvedev had spent the first half of his career fighting off the Big Three and could have reasonably assumed that he'd never have to deal with anyone that talented ever again. And yet here was Carlos Alcaraz, his raw skill and career trajectory arguably surpassing theirs in some respects. He would only get better.

Medvedev could not catch a break. He first encountered Alcaraz at Wimbledon in 2021, before the Spaniard had truly ascended, when he was still an 18-year-old unfamiliar with grass courts. Speaking to the press afterward, Medvedev spent more words explaining his own mid-match misbehavior than describing his young opponent. They did not meet the following year, which was Alcaraz's breakout season, but starting in 2023, the junior began to dominate the elder in every encounter. Not only was Alcaraz winning, Medvedev couldn't figure out how to win a set, getting swept at Indian Wells, Wimbledon, and the ATP Finals—three different court conditions, with the same grim result.

One exception to this new rule was the 2023 U.S. Open semifinal, perhaps the single most ferocious of Medvedev's career. It required him to summon an aggression he had rarely tried before and has barely tried since. The greatest players, like Alcaraz, have this effect. Opponents know their ordinary game plan is hopeless against such a player, so they must adapt or perish. Medvedev, typically the patient counterpuncher, chose instead to proactively attack the little offensive dynamo. He struck his forehand harder than usual, took his returns sharply crosscourt to punish Alcaraz's forays to the net. After Medvedev won, Alcaraz was in awe. "He's amazing. And when I do serve and volley, he always finds the passing shot, from his house," he laughed, referring to Medvedev's bizarrely deep return position near the back wall of the court.

By the middle of 2024, though, Medvedev had absorbed several more losses to Alcaraz and decided that he was "the toughest opponent I have ever faced"—high praise from a guy who had taken lashings from the greatest players ever. Had it only been Alcaraz in his way, it would have been a manageable state of affairs for Medvedev. He was still superior to the rest of the tour, and when needed, perhaps he could call on the extreme tactics that helped him defeat the genius child in New York. There would be plenty of titles to scoop up in those inevitable weeks when the volatile Alcaraz had spun out in an early round. It was only in late 2023 that Medvedev's situation deteriorated completely. That was when Jannik Sinner joined Alcaraz on the plateau of anointed ones.

There was a long period when Medvedev seemed to regard Sinner as a talented peer but basically a terrestrial talent, no real trouble. The Russian beat the Italian in their first six matches. Sinner was a strong baseliner, but knowable, fallible. He didn't present the novel, complex problems that Alcaraz did. While Sinner always possessed more power than Medvedev, he would break down earlier in their rallies, never piercing that defense of crazed scrambles and flat strokes. Finally, in their 2023 Beijing final, Sinner broke the streak and thanked Medvedev for "making me a better player." Medvedev probably regrets making Jannik Sinner a better player. Just three months later, the two met in the Australian Open final. On paper this should have been a relief. At last, an opportunity to play a major final against an opponent not named Djokovic (four times) or Nadal (two times). And Medvedev took a two-set lead, only for Sinner to rage back and beat him. Perhaps some scar tissue was forming. It was

Medvedev's second time losing that particular final in Australia after having a two-sets-to-none lead.

Six months later, at Wimbledon, Medvedev was discussing Alcaraz and Sinner in the same breath. They were the successors; they had leapfrogged him in the queue. He noted that Sinner used to just be powerful but lately had forgotten how to miss. He said that to beat him, you had to be willing to step up and hit winners yourself, a tack that had worked in Australia until Medvedev's embattled legs, carrying a full 24 hours of on-court mileage from the tournament, gave up. When asked which of the two kids he feared most, Medvedev seemed to find the question sort of insipid—"Every time I go, no fear"—though he did dish on the state of the rivalry. "It's not even talent, 'talent' is not the right word, but I would say, quality of the shots, I would say Carlos. I never saw something like this. I would say bit more up and down than Jannik," he said. He still wasn't giving up. "I will try to put trouble to them." He suggested that he had his own prediction of who would win the most majors but didn't want to say it aloud, despite the prodding of several journalists in the room, who offered to keep his secrets.

As Sinner and Alcaraz rose, Medvedev faced some structural challenges, too. For a while, his big serve was the only discernible six-foot-six aspect of his game. He used to hit one serve right after the other, hardly pausing between points, as if exasperated by the notion of an opponent catching his breath. It worked for him, and having such an effective serve saved him some energy that could be expended instead on the long, brutal rallies he liked to engage in as a returner. But after a 2022 procedure to repair a sports hernia, that serve lost some of its sting. An injury can have a short impact on the body but a long impact on technique, he explained to the press at Roland-Garros in 2024. Without a serve he could weaponize for quick points, he was having to toil on both serve and return, which, even for a player as fit as him, was not a tenable model for dominating the tour. It was too much to ask of the human body.

Medvedev began to speculate that the tennis ball itself had changed, in a way that further imperiled his style of play. He noticed that during the pandemic, it had become harder to get the ball to move quickly through the air. He believed that the quality of manufacturing had declined. So he changed to softer strings on his racquet in 2023, which upped his power and helped compensate for what he had lost. This fix satisfied him for a while, but in 2024, once again, Medvedev decided he'd lost his competitive advantage. With the ball moving sluggishly, and players getting to those balls more easily, his defense was not so special anymore. "Literally everyone can stay in the rally with me right now," he said. "Tactics matter less." He even theorized that the ball in 2024 favored players such as Alcaraz and Sinner, who had enough power to attack even a "dead ball" and get it moving at an unreturnable speed.

"Every practice is a struggle. Every match is a struggle. I was holding [serve] for a long time. Now I feel zero pleasure of being on the court," went his lament. I investigated his notion that the ball had gotten worse and found that several other players agreed with him. One company that manufactures balls for the tour even conceded that they'd had supply chain issues but assured me they'd been fixed. Perhaps there was some truth to the theory. Perhaps, also, it is easier to stomach a professional decline by building a theory that the game had changed structurally to favor some other set of players. Was it really about the ball, or was he really just coming to terms with living the rest of his career in a permanent underclass, well below the Teutonic ginger destroyer and the ebullient happy artiste? My fascination with Medvedev only grew. As sad as I was for his plight, I was also enjoying his point of view. Tennis's funniest and most perceptive observer happened to be stationed right in between two great generations. He would explain to us anything we ever wanted to know.

It is odd to feel pity toward an intelligent, wealthy, charismatic, athletic, and famous person. But I did. In what should have been his prime years, Medvedev was receding from relevance, his trophy count stagnating, his press conferences thinning out despite his lovely personality. It was sad to see a player I regarded as a one-of-one, avant-garde talent get pinned gruesomely between the Big Three and the Next Two, with barely a season in between to get his bearings.

One boy wonder was a healthy challenge; two of them muddled the future. Long ago, Medvedev had declared that his dreams were dead. Now he observed that tennis no longer held any joy. What was this melancholic Russian novel of a career? He had timed his birth poorly. He should have planned that out better. That would have been the Medvedev joke.

CHAPTER 9

Tossing Out the Syllabus

"Hey, Carlos, nice to see you," began the journalist's question, innocuously enough. "Can you tell us—did you go to any nightclubs in your holiday?" The kids might call such an inquisitor a "narc." Alcaraz, sitting at a press conference for his first tournament since his Roland-Garros victory in June, swept his fingers through his new haircut and snickered. "I did." He said he spent three days partying in Ibiza with his brothers and friends, that it was important for him to separate his tennis from his personal life, to put down the racquet and reset his mind. Jannik Sinner, by way of comparison, has said that he doesn't go out at all: "I've never been to a disco, I don't like going to sleep late. I prefer playing cards with a friend." The homebody Sinner was in a relationship with the top-20 player Anna Kalinskaya—though it might have been an on-and-off affair, according to the fans who studiously tracked how often they followed and unfollowed each other on Instagram. (Sinner seemed so resistant to apps that I wondered if he'd tasked his social media manager with such details.) Alcaraz hadn't publicly acknowledged any romantic partner since becoming a star, but Rafa Nadal did once tease him for his tendency to "like" women's photos online, and on an Australian talk show, Alcaraz bashfully confessed that he used tongue on the first kiss. It's unclear how much money Sinner would need to be paid to even utter a sentence about a hypothetical kiss in which he was involved.

At this stage of their careers, Alcaraz was more prone to burning out psychologically, and Sinner physically. A few days on a party island is about as much of a release as a tennis player can manage during a busy summer. Even there, they must be on reasonably good behavior, as far as diet and recovery are concerned. Carlitos often wears shirts featuring Michael Jordan, either his photo or his silhouette, but there's no way he could follow the Bulls legend's protocol—smoking cigars and eating entire pizzas during the course of the NBA Finals. If Carlitos was lighting up Havanas in the backyard of his rented house in southwest London, he would not survive until the second week of Wimbledon.

The life of a professional tennis player in 2024 was quite monastic, as far as pro athletes are concerned. A lot of time is spent in transit, surrounded by a support team, and no matter how much you like them, it can be stifling. Part of the team's job is to do the stifling, too. Alcaraz's agent, Albert Molina, a bald man with a vigilant and hawkish expression, said in an interview with Spanish TV that his player's outings made him a bit nervous. Not because of the behavior of Carlitos himself, or that of his friends, but because of the outside world. "When so much of your life is exposed to the outside world, there are always people with a phone that can record something that might be taken out of context, or it may not be reality." Yet, at the same time, there was no sense in instilling paranoia. "What I also can't transmit to Carlos is that life is fearful, and everything is rubbish, and that people are going to take advantage of him. Because in the end, a noble boy, a boy as nice as he is at 21 years old, you start to put fears in your head and you start saying 'watch out for this, watch out for that'—well, you can hurt him in the end."

Thus far Alcaraz seemed to have struck a balance of trusting extroversion and insulation from the world's worst. When he arrived at the grass season, he seemed content and rested. If clay is an evolving surface, changing with every step and slide, then grass upped the ante once again: It is literally a living surface. A layer of gravel is topped with a layer of soil, which is packed firm, seeded with carefully selected strains of grass, and grown to an exacting standard. At Wimbledon, it is perennial ryegrass, chosen for its durability, and shorn to exactly eight millimeters. White lines of titanium dioxide are rolled onto the grass to transform it into a tennis court. Tennis originated on 19th-century lawns, but by 2024 grass had been relegated to a tiny stretch of the professional calendar. Most players had limited exposure to it in their developmental years. It was more of a quirky detour than a foundation of the game, which was a tragedy for the old-school purists and for the players with the particular skill set to thrive on it.

Grass-court tennis is not for everyone. Some players, even elite ones like Casper Ruud or Iga Świątek, seem to have decided that it's not worth the bother to deform their clay-optimized game styles just to master those arcane lawns for a few weeks a year. They treat the grass season, short as it is—one or two tournaments—as a brief and exotic jaunt. Among the eccentricities of the grass court is the muted bounce of the ball, which you can intuit, in a crude way, by throwing a tennis ball at a driveway and then at an adjacent patch of lawn. Blades of grass flatten on impact, so that the ball slides along their slick surfaces, rather than kicking up like it does when it meets the grit of a clay court.

Players must tune their eyes to the altered bounces and speeds when moving on to a new surface. They also have to tread more carefully on grass, more of a pitter-patter. If you wish to see a pre-ternaturally coordinated person faceplant—cruel of you, but I don't judge—watch them play tennis on a dewy court early on in the grass season. These paragons of movement turn temporarily doe-like, their legs flying out from underneath them, which can be perilous for hips and knees. Medvedev, true to form, is forthcoming about such matters: "Usually the first tournament I play on grass, I cannot hit a forehand. [The ball] is so fast. It's sliding through the court. Where on clay, it's bouncing high. It's completely different." Because rapid change of direction on grass can be so treacherous, defensive strategies are also less viable. Instead: bold shots, net attacks, and quick hands. The muted bounces reward good slices, which almost seem to cling to the turf. Big servers thrive on grass, too, as the ball doesn't lose much on impact, staying fast, low, and irretrievable.

Neither Alcaraz nor Sinner arrived on the pro tour with a big serve. This was a charming aspect of their rivalry in its earliest phase. It made for longer, somewhat psychotropic rallies. But they were too ambitious for that phase to last forever. The serve is a shot that many players tune steadily over the course of a career. It is a shot struck in isolation, without any opponent input—you toss the ball up yourself, you go up and hit it—and thus it is amenable to offseason tweaks. Back at the time of their seminal 2022 U.S. Open clash, I suspected Sinner would be quicker to improve his serve, because he's taller and had a smoother motion.

Their initial lack of serving prowess would, theoretically, make it a bit harder to navigate Wimbledon. So did their inexperience on the surface. Grass courts are rare in Spain, and Carlitos barely played on them as a junior. In 2021, ahead of his first grass season as a pro,

Sinner estimated that he had played just 15 days on the surface in his life. That year both of them entered the main draw at Wimbledon for the first time; neither one made it out of the first round. The next year, they met in the fourth round, and Sinner, less hyped at the time, prevailed in four sets. I felt as though I were watching only lightly sedated versions of Nadal and Djokovic; I knew they were each capable of winning this title someday. But I also knew they would have to better attune their games to the surface.

Midway through 2023, Sinner had his serving breakthrough. He switched from a "platform" stance, where the ball is struck with the feet roughly shoulder width apart, to a "pinpoint" stance, where the ball is struck after the back foot has dragged forward to meet the front foot. As a younger player he had experimented with both, but the pinpoint had now stuck. On YouTube, a cottage industry of coaches began to forensically analyze the other changes he'd made. He tossed the ball lower; his legs exploded off the ground a tick earlier than most players', before his racquet had even come up to rest briefly behind his head. A serve is a bespoke piece of choreography, and players seek out the rhythm that works for them; some never quite find it. Sinner had. With this stronger delivery, and a fairly soft draw, he got to the semifinals of Wimbledon in 2023, where he lost to Djokovic. Then, in 2024, I heard a consistent compliment among his slain peers: He used to serve pretty well, but now it was "big big big," to use Medvedev's term of art. It was sure to win Sinner some easier points.

All the while, Alcaraz was already solving the grass, finding ways to thrive on the surface even though his own serve wasn't developing as naturally as Sinner's. In 2023, he approached the grass season with new intent, and for the first time, he entered a warm-up tournament ahead of Wimbledon. It was the 500-level event at

Queen's Club, also in London. Before the tournament he said he'd been studying the footwork of grass-court greats, looking up videos of Roger Federer and Andy Murray. (Less of Novak Djokovic, who preferred to slide on grass, a technique Alcaraz had yet to embrace.) "I have to be really focused on every move, every shot, so for me, it's more tiring when you're moving on grass, I have to do a specific work to move on grass," he said. After winning his first round at Queen's Club, he said, "Honestly, my expectations in this tournament are not too high." Halfway through that week, he wrote on social media that he was "learning and having fun on this surface!" followed by emojis of a face in mustached disguise and a face with a party hat. By the weekend he was holding aloft a massive silver urn, big enough to bathe a newborn, the champion's trophy. At that point he had spent only a cumulative 25 hours and 54 minutes playing grass-court matches as a professional, and he had already won one of its biggest titles. Alcaraz is an alarmingly efficient mechanism for turning matches into useful muscle memory and actionable wisdom, I thought at the time.

Seven matches later, he had won Wimbledon, too. It had taken him five absorbing sets to dispatch Djokovic in the final. But even then, as Alcaraz lifted the golden cup, he was just 46 hours and 15 minutes into his grass-court career. He was flying on sheer feel and animal instincts. True prodigy gets to skip the trial-and-error phase.

Most impressively, Alcaraz had completed a perfect grass-court season without the benefit of a consistently big serve. As traditional wisdom had it, grass courts were the happiest time of year for the slow-moving, big-serving players often derided as "servebots." Picture tall, unwieldy fellows trading aces for hours. It doesn't make for the most compelling television. Often, these bots managed to infiltrate the second week of Wimbledon. Back in 2018, two of them went ace-for-ace in a match that lasted six hours and 35 minutes. Eight years before that, one of the participants, John Isner, had played a match that lasted 11 hours, five minutes, which the tournament had memorialized with a solemn plaque. They even changed the rules for the fifth-set tiebreak so that such a thing would never occur again.

Carlitos is the furthest thing from a servebot. He is just six feet flat with a somewhat gawky motion. As of 2023, he could serve well on certain days—particularly his kick serve, loaded with topspin. But in general, it was one feature of his tennis that didn't seem to have sprung into the world fully formed. (Once, the two rivals were asked to interview each other on camera. Sinner had to pick which of his rival's shots he would *not* borrow; he picked the serve without hesitation.) That's also what made Alcaraz's success on grass courts so pleasurable. He had no steady stream of aces. No cheap points, all pure sorcery. In fact, aside from his serve, Alcaraz had, encoded in his tennis DNA, all the other stuff of a grass-court champion: sensitive hands, improvisational instincts, and unflagging aggression. Evidently those things could compensate for what his serve lacked.

My first thought, every time I see the grass of Wimbledon, is that I want to touch it. I don't want to eat it, the way that Djokovic did after each title—plucking a few blades off the lawn and chewing them in celebration—but I am open to being convinced. Mowed both directions into alternating bands of mint and emerald, with white lines rolled on, they are beautiful to look at even without beautiful tennis happening on them. And when there is tennis, one hears only quiet where there should be sound. Muffled by the vegetation, there are no sneaker squeaks or thuds of the ball hitting the court,

just the clean blast of the ball hitting strings, a serene simplicity to
the audio. Absent are the garish sponsor logos that mar the sidelines
of every other tournament; Wimbledon is snooty about advertising,
keeps it to a minimum. The players, clad in mandatory all-white,
further reduce the sensory input. The crowds in southwest London
generally have a diminished, chastened presence, sticking to polite
applause until a couple rounds of Pimm's Cups have upped the collective blood-alcohol content and reminded them of their capability
to yell in public.

When I arrive in 2024, I know that these courts are as pristine
as they'll ever be, until next year, at least. Under the care of the All
England Lawn Tennis and Croquet Club, they have taken on an
uncanny evenness I can only associate, in a backward way, with ar-
tificial turf. Not even the vainest McMansion dweller could achieve
the purity of these lawns. Yet match by match, they will be chewed
away by the hard work of so many monochrome sneakers. Unlike
hard court, which sits inert, or clay, which is groomed and restored
between matches, the grass cannot be reset. Wimbledon is a story of
degradation. Before advances in racquet and string tech, back when
serve-and-volley was the principal game plan here, you could see
a funnel of brown starting at the baseline and opening out to the
net, tracing the path of the players. Now all the damage is wrought
behind the baseline, where the bulk of contemporary tennis goes
down. The blades of grass are first trampled to a dull brown, before
drying out to a nearly ash-white, before abandoning the premises
altogether, leaving just dirt. The destruction of the grass reveals, in
aggregate, the tendencies of the players who toil on it for glory—big
data in little blades.

Thus far in the grass-court season, Sinner's souped-up serve
seemed to have closed the gap between him and Alcaraz. Both of

them played a warm-up event, and the Italian looked far better in his. Alcaraz had crashed out of Queen's, losing in the second round to the big-serving British lefty Jack Draper and snapping his 13-match win streak on the surface. The day had not been happy: Alcaraz felt he was being rushed by an umpire starting the serve clock too early. "For the players it's something bad," he explained after the match. "I finish the point at the net, and I have no time to ask for the balls . . . something is crazy." His team worried that his brief Ibiza getaway had taken him too far afield of a disciplined tennis mindset.

Sinner, that same week, won a 500-level title in Halle, Germany, fighting through a tough slate of opponents. In two different matches, he'd won points by completing a full-on barrel roll in the grass. Tennis players dive only occasionally, but it's a much less painful proposition on a lawn versus a hard court. The first time, Sinner lunged forward, hit a winner mid-stride, rolled right back onto his feet, and stood there, chuckling. Two days later, he dove again, sprang up to his feet, and just kept playing out the point, sprinting back to the opposite corner to rip a backhand winner. This time he threw up a hand to titillate the crowd, and they happily obliged. By winning that Halle title, Sinner entered Wimbledon with a win rate above 90 percent for the year to date, a mark that had been achieved only in the best seasons in tour history. The Big Three each had one such season. The year before, Alcaraz had a 90 percent win rate at the end of Wimbledon but squandered it in the last stretch of the season. Thus far, Sinner's 2024 tournaments had ended in only three outcomes: win the title (four times), get injured (two times), or lose to Carlos Alcaraz (two times).

Despite his new habit of kvetching about work conditions, Alcaraz did not lack confidence, either. He was coming to Wimbledon as defending champ. I remembered he had studied the footwork of Federer and Murray last grass season, so I asked him if he'd been studying anyone else this year to pick up a new micro-skill. Wearing a baggy white tee that would've worked in a mid-aughts Houston rap video, Alcaraz first said that he hadn't been looking at anyone else for inspiration. Then he clarified that he had seen some videos of the Big Three and Murray, but he wasn't trying to pick up anything in particular. And then he came clean: "And I put in videos of myself last year. I'm not gonna lie," he laughed. "To see what I did, and how I did it." From him, it wasn't arrogant, just sensible. Tennis's most brilliant pupil had decided he didn't need a syllabus anymore; he had become his own assigned reading.

To the surprise of many of his peers, 2023's runner-up was also alive and well. Djokovic had already been seen training on the grounds of Wimbledon with a gray compression sleeve on the knee he'd torn at Roland-Garros. Three days before the tournament, he practiced with Sinner on Centre Court, site of his seven Wimbledon titles and celebratory grass bites. During the practice he got ornery a few times, but it was generally productive, and he flashed journalists a thumbs-up on his way out when asked if he would be ready for the tournament.

In a press conference later, Djokovic appeared fresh-faced in a mustard polo shirt. The moderator began by asking how he was doing, and Djokovic deadpanned, "Fine, and you?" before answering the question that everyone chuckling at his joke had been poised to ask. How did he get himself ready to play Wimbledon just three weeks after knee surgery? He said he spent those weeks in rigorous rehab. He'd talked to other athletes who'd undergone similar surgeries, colleagues like Stan Wawrinka and Taylor Fritz,

and also the skier Lindsey Vonn. And he'd determined that a return was feasible, if not the medical ideal—which was more like six
weeks, compared to his riskier three. Asked why he was returning so
quickly, given that he'd played dozens of majors before and would
likely play many more, he wasn't sure. "It's a very fair question," he
said, smiling slightly, "that I don't know the answer to, and that I
do know the answer to." He was peering into his own inky depths,
assessing what he saw moving in the murk. "I wouldn't call it a fear
of missing out. I would just say it's this incredible desire to play,"
he said, emphasizing that Wimbledon was his specific childhood
dream. He also said that because this injury was a new one in his
career, he was curious to see just how fast he could recover. He saw a
chance to test his body's limits in a new way and could not resist. It
takes an eccentric cast of mind to keep going at work this grueling
when there's so little left to prove.

Over those three weeks he had escalated the intensity of his
training, with no setbacks, until he felt good enough to deliver a
firm verdict: "I don't see myself holding back, being calculating or
a bit cautious in the movement. I go all in. That's the way I've been
playing my whole career." Djokovic was aiming to tie Roger Federer's
record eight Wimbledon titles. This year he had an easy draw, which
would allow him to play his way into shape during the tournament,
the way Sinner had managed to do at Roland-Garros. And his presence here, once again, shunted the two rivals into the same half of
the draw, as the No. 1 and No. 3 seeds, ensuring that they could
meet only in the semifinal. Novak Djokovic, always the wedge.

Playing his first-ever major as the top seed, Jannik Sinner had a vicious draw ahead of him, with menace lurking as early as the second
round. When I arrived at that match, the press box was densely,

vibrantly Italian. That was only right. Before us on the turf were Sinner and Matteo Berrettini, an all-Italian contest so alluring I wished it were taking place deeper in the tournament. For several years, Berrettini was at the vanguard of a strong Italian cohort. Six-foot-five with a parsnip-like physique, broad chest tapering down to slim calves, he played heavyweight tennis, reliant on a hammer forehand and serve, which had taken him as high as No. 6 in the world in 2022. He was especially keen on grass and reached the Wimbledon final in 2021, which is to say, he was yet another youth mowed down by Djokovic in an only briefly interesting major final. Berrettini had taken one set before the laws of nature ran their course. That was three years ago, and injuries had since scuttled his rise. His latest six-month injury layoff meant that he was out of office while his friend Jannik abruptly became the best player in the world. "At the end of last year I was injured and I wasn't on tour to see him live with my eyes. And then I had the chance to go to the Davis Cup and it was unbelievable," he'd said earlier that week. "We [the Italian team] were looking at each other saying, 'Is this guy real?' Because he wasn't missing. Hitting every ball full power." It had gotten realer with every passing month. Sinner carried Italy to Davis Cup victory and had scarcely lost since. Now it was Berrettini, five years the elder, saying that he'd drawn inspiration from Sinner.

Despite having fallen out of the top 50, Berrettini exhumed his old self for four clamorous, lovely sets. Berrettini's opponents gravitated toward a common game plan: attack his stiff two-handed backhand, the weakest part of his game. Sinner had clearly set out to do just that. But on grass, Berrettini could protect that weakness with a strength: his backhand slice. A well-struck slice is one of the most hypnotic sights in tennis. The racquet slashes under the ball, causing it to spin backward in the air. A ball with backspin creates a pocket of low air pressure above it and a pocket of high air pressure below it, giving the ball gentle upward lift. A sliced ball might fly off Berrettini's racquet and travel through the air slowly, as if passing through gelatin, slowly enough to buy Berrettini time to recover in these brutal rallies against the quicker Sinner. And once that ball landed, that same backspin ensured that it would take only the tiniest bounce off the grass, staying frustratingly low for the opponent. Berrettini had one of the finest slices on tour, and Sinner tested it over and over with his own topspin backhand, a match-long cross-examination that barely elicited a flinch. In the rally of the match, Berrettini even curled a slice *around* the net post, rather than over the net, one of the holy grails of shot-making in tennis.

Sinner won his three sets in tiebreaks. The tail end of each set ratcheted up to brilliance. The Italian journalists were chirping, pontificating, passing a pair of brass binoculars from hand to hand—and lightly admonishing one another not to openly cheer for Berrettini. This struck me as odd. Setting aside the fact that journalists were not supposed to cheer in the neutral space of the press box—a rule mostly just enforced with dirty looks—I'd expected more of an even split among the Italian corps. Why did they all seem to be rallying behind Berrettini? One possibility did occur to me. The dark-eyed Berrettini is a level of handsome where he probably would have made his way onto billboards and commercials even if he had no talent for striking tennis balls. "My grandma, of course, she spoils me. She still thinks that I'm the most handsome guy on the planet," he said in 2022, and perhaps these journalists simply agreed with his nonna's assessment. I then had a slightly more sophisticated thought. Was it possible that he inflamed their patriotic passions more than the No. 1 seed did? Berrettini was a grandma's boy born and raised in Rome; Sinner was a German-speaking skier who had descended from an autonomous border region in the Alps, long contested by Austria. It was the center versus the periphery.

I bounced this theory off the journalist Claudia Fusani, who writes on both tennis and politics, and she dismissed it, explaining that their sympathies had more to do with Berrettini's underdog status and his recent injuries. No one here was so parochial. The parochial viewpoint had already been expressed—and, for these journalists, would remain—elsewhere. In September 2023, *La Gazzetta dello Sport*, a leading daily paper in Italy that focused on soccer, veered into tennis to launch an invective. On the cover of that issue was a picture of Sinner with the breathless headline "Caso Nazionale"—which could be read as "issue with the national team," or "issue with nationality," depending on your point of view.

Inside was a strange piece by the septuagenarian writer Giancarlo Dotto, which began by criticizing Sinner's absence from some round of international competition on behalf of Italy. It then called into question Sinner's essential Italianness. Dotto portrayed him as an opportunist playing on Italian hearts and declared an absence of "the romantic feeling" evoked by Lorenzo Musetti or other Italian tennis players. Elsewhere in the paper, other athletes were quoted about how happy they were to represent Italy—only they hadn't been told about the context in which their quotes would appear. As a piece of journalism, it was savaged by other corners of the Italian press. Reached by *MOW* magazine for a follow-up interview about his piece, Dotto insisted that he was not making a moral judgment. He used to be obsessed with Sinner, found his fame fascinating, and felt he had to point out that Italy had embraced him because of his "diversity."

"I am talking about the beautiful story of a boy so different from us and from the typical Italian who becomes the idol of a nation," Dotto said. "He who was born into a family where our language is not spoken, when he started to become important at a certain point said, with a beautiful slip of the tongue, 'I am very happy because this thing makes Italians happy,' rather than 'I am very happy to play in front of Italians.' So, he himself pointed out this difference." Supposedly, in this psychoanalysis, Sinner still conceived of himself as separate from the Italian people, rather than one of them. Time passed; *La Gazzetta* never acknowledged any misstep and smoothly transitioned to covering Sinner's accomplishments; the article became a punchline for many Italian tennis fans. In any case, Sinner soon appeared in the later stages of that very tournament where his absence had struck Dotto as such a national disgrace. He beat Djokovic and won the Davis Cup.

It's not that Italians don't acknowledge his distinct regional flavor at all, though. Some in Italian tennis see Sinner's origins as a clear advantage. Diego Nargiso, a former player and current commentator, told me that Sinner's territorial origins might have shaped his disposition. "He's learned that in their lives there, if it doesn't snow, they probably won't work," he said of the seasonal ski-adjacent work that Sinner's family did. "Things cannot go always the right way, but you have to still be living. The resilience is something that can come from up there, you know—it's cold as hell." This idea of geographical character-building was echoed by Francesca Schiavone, the ex-player who had won Roland-Garros in 2010, in a documentary on Sinner produced by the Australian Open. "In the north in Italy, in general, are more attention to the details, and that's a good power to be a champion," she said. Before Sinner, the province of South Tyrol had produced Andreas Seppi, the embodiment of unglamorous consistency, which paid off in a fruitful two-decade career, three titles, one upset of Federer, and a peak ranking of world No. 18. Sinner had a similar work ethic, plus an overlay of freakish talent.

Sinner, perhaps blessed with a Südtiroler's consistency and attention to detail, perhaps just good at tennis, won the Wimbledon match against Berrettini. It was a delight to see him bob and weave around the huge service bombs, a test of his talent as a returner. One minute he was hurling his gangly frame out of the path of a body serve, the next minute he was smothering a second serve with gorgeous timing. I asked him afterward how he approached a server as good as his friend Matteo. He said that the way the ball slips off the grass made it hard to get too experimental with positioning, but he tried to mix it up on second serves. "It's also a little bit a gut feeling, no? Which can help you, and you just have to go for it." Alcaraz was famous for playing on instinct, and Sinner was learning to do the same. In a match against a server like Berrettini, you might just have to have the correct gut feeling five or six times to turn the whole contest in your favor.

When I asked Berrettini what had changed most in Sinner since they had last played, since his vault to the top of the tour, he pointed to his softer touch with the racquet and his ability to "read the moments" in the match and detect when to deviate from the script. "I think he missed three balls in the whole match," he said. "It didn't give me that oxygen that sometimes you need." Often Djokovic's game was described with similarly stark images of oxygen deprivation. They both could suffocate an opponent by hitting ball after ball deep in the court. As Berrettini left the press conference, he was treated to full-on applause by the Italian journalists in the room. I couldn't help but remember the words of a journalist who at the outset of the tournament told me quite colorfully that despite knowing Sinner well since his junior days, he would rather sleep than watch his matches. Maybe some tennis fans, Italian or otherwise, wanted to see oxygen breathed into a match, instead.

. . .

Alcaraz was in peril early on in the 2024 tournament. By round three he found himself locked in another battle with his pal Frances Tiafoe. The gregarious American was the player Alcaraz named as the funniest on tour and the one he would pick as his "wingman" on a night out. It came as a surprise to Tiafoe that he was so competitive in this match, because he'd been in a nasty funk for months. He'd spent 2023 sharpening his focus and rising into the top 10 for the first time; he spent most of 2024 losing touch with that, and his ranking had plunged. By the time he arrived at Wimbledon, he had lost to 11 players ranked outside the top 50. Perhaps these were the opponents referenced in the lament Tiafoe let loose after his first-round Wimbledon win: "Literally this week last year I was 10 in the world and now I'm barely seeded here. Losing to clowns. I hate to say it, but I'm just gonna be honest." That's about as spicy as peer review gets on the tour.

He who calls his fellows a clown must immediately declown himself. If Tiafoe really was better than those guys, then he could demonstrate that by winning matches; otherwise he was just another variety of clown, the self-deluded kind. Tennis is unambiguous that way. No loss can be blamed on a teammate or coach or external force. You are only as good as your wins. As Tiafoe went up two sets to one on Alcaraz, he seemed ready to back his smack talk in the most emphatic possible fashion.

As a child Tiafoe had devised his strokes against the hitting wall of the tennis center where his father worked and lived as a custodian. Young Frances observed, then mimicked in the quiet hours what he'd seen the rich kids do during their lessons. Eventually coaches realized how good he was and welcomed him into the grind of conventional training. His lonely experimentation left him with unorthodox strokes. The forehand and backhand were a study in contrasts: the former a grand circuitous loop, the latter a succinct little bunt, one spinny, one flat, both of them deadly on a good day. This was a good day, maybe the best day he'd ever had on a grass court. Alcaraz staggered around on the defensive for most of the first three sets.

In set four it was clear why these two made such wonderful sparring partners, in a slightly different way than Sinner and Alcaraz were such wonderful sparring partners. With Tiafoe there was a shared taste for improvisation, for confounding the normal rhythms of a rally. They both had a knack for ad hoc shots conceived in the heat of a rally, the sort that cannot possibly be drilled in practice. They often tumbled into shifty cat-and-mouse exchanges, luring each other forward and then backward, one player attempting an unclassifiable touch shot—was that a half-volley with the wrong grip?—and receiving an unclassifiable reply in return. They seemed to live by a credo: quick hands or die. Grass courts, with their low and unpredictable bounces, are a lush home for such exchanges, for those with that lightness in their feet and softness in their hands, the ones to whom the word "talent" is most often appended. Alcaraz was in a dire spot in the fourth set, at 4-4, serving at 0-30. Two strong returns from Tiafoe could have delivered him the win. Instead Alcaraz rampaged ahead with his serve, fully committed to his offense, and blew out Tiafoe in the ensuing fourth-set tiebreak.

When they arrived in the fifth set, it was hard not to hear the echo of the five-setter the two had played two years earlier, in the semifinal of Alcaraz's maiden U.S. Open title run, which remained the high-water mark of Tiafoe's career to date. Then as now, Alcaraz was in his happy place: the crushing, benthic pressures of a fifth set. He'd recently won two of those to close out his Roland-Garros campaign, his tennis clarified and concentrated by the stress, and against

Tiafoe at Wimbledon, he did it again. He won five games in a row, finishing it, fittingly, with a drop shot so good that Tiafoe didn't run for it but started walking to the net for the handshake. With that win, Alcaraz had assembled a 12-1 career record in five-set matches. A small sample, but no one else's win rate came close; Sinner's was 6-8 heading into Wimbledon. Composure under duress had already become central to Alcaraz's identity, a veteran calm—which was funny, because so many other aspects of his life were still aligned with his age. He was still getting haircuts dubious enough that his fans had begun to construct conspiracy theories, linking the most egregious trims to his most disappointing losses. He'd said earlier in the tournament that he still got goose bumps—pronounced like "ghost bombs"—when he walked onto Centre Court. He'd said after his previous match that he had been trying to make his habits a little more professional, optimizing all 24 hours of his day for his tennis, stripping away the 21-year-old aspects of his lifestyle. "I try to use less the phone. Has been difficult for me," he said, smiling. "Going to go to bed early. Try to respect the hours of sleep."

On the other side of the draw was Djokovic, chugging along, moving better by the day. He was deploying a powerful technique honed over his many years on tour. No player with his level of accomplishment— a strong greatest-of-all-time candidacy—has ever seemed to relish nega- tivity from a crowd, provoking them back, drawing energy from their disdain. And even imagining the disdain, if need be. The mere arrange- ment of facts boggled the mind: a 37-year-old, 24-time major cham- pion, just a few weeks removed from knee surgery, but hungry to fight on, to have the privilege of antagonizing the Wimbledon crowd for an- other day.

In the 2019 championship match, Djokovic saved two match

points to defeat permanent crowd favorite Federer, who was basically the aesthetic-slash-erotic ideal for the average Wimbledon attendee. Afterward, Djokovic described his capacity to turn opposing crowd noise into positivity. "I like to transmutate it in a way," he said. "When the crowd is chanting 'Roger,' I hear 'Novak.' It sounds silly, but it is like that."

In 2024, Djokovic and his rehabilitated knee met No. 15 seed Holger Rune in the fourth round. Djokovic had met the pugnacious Rune many times before, including in the first round of the 2021 U.S. Open. There, he'd gotten his initial exposure to the low, drawn-out way in which the Dane's supporters bellow their man's name: "Ruuuuuuuuuuuune." After winning the match, Djokovic said he thought they were booing. In fairness, it was an easy mistake to make. But he was corrected by a reporter who had better deciphered the chant.

Nonetheless, Djokovic either forgot or pretended to forget that detail. After routing Rune in straight sets in their 2024 Wimbledon meeting, he chastised the crowd. "And to all those people that have chosen to disrespect a player—in this case, me—have a goooooooooooood night," Djokovic said during his on-court interview, elongating the word just as they had the name Rune. "Goooooooooood night, goooood night. Very goooooooooood night," he continued, never one for subtlety in these moments of pique. The interviewer pushed back, suggesting that the boos were in fact just "Runes," but Djokovic insisted he could see through the ruuuuuse. "They were, they were, they were [disrespecting me]," he said. "I don't accept it. No, no, no. I know they were cheering for Rune, but that is an excuse to also boo. Listen, I've been on the tour for more than 20 years, so trust me, I know all the tricks." The crowd issued a bleary, muddled noise in response. "I've played in much more hostile environments, trust me. You guys can't touch me."

It was a prime example of Djokovic's expertise at identifying, exaggerating, or, where necessary, inventing an outside antagonist to use as motivation. His battles with the crowd sometimes strike viewers as a little unseemly, coming from a man who had already proven his supremacy in the sport. His peers Federer and Nadal never took quite this angle with the crowds, even in those rare instances where they were booed. But this behavior is a large part of what makes Djokovic such a fervent competitor, and in that sense, it is also a large part of his appeal. He summons some of his best ball when playing from a place of spite; he is most magnetic and authentic when playing the heel, too.

Jannik Sinner looked ready to lose consciousness during his quarter-final against Daniil Medvedev. His face looked flattened and slack, like a pillowcase emptied of its pillow. He said he'd gotten ill, slept poorly, and woken up in disrepair. That was the physiological story, though there was a psychological one too, to be revealed months later. What was clear in the moment was that he was playing through severe discomfort. Conditions were already difficult. The roof was up on Centre Court and the rain battered it like a timpani. For the players it was stuffy, humid, and loud. "You don't hear anymore the sound of your shots. It's like something is falling on your head constantly, so it's not easy," Medvedev reported after. The two players split the first sets and early in the third, Sinner was sickly enough that he had his pulse taken. Despite Sinner wanting to play on, a physiotherapist whisked him away for further assessment off court, holding the player by the crook of his arm. Sinner was gone for over

10 minutes. His team fretted in the player's box. While away, he was dizzy but did not vomit.

He returned to fan applause. It was hard to imagine this version of Sinner, who was spending his changeovers under the bleak shroud of a towel draped overhead, threatening Medvedev. But he rebounded and played some tennis worthy of the No. 1 seed, pushing the contest to five sets and four hours. It was Medvedev, however, who imposed his style on the match, entrapping them both in the long, patience-testing rallies he preferred. After Medvedev had won, he pointed out the subtle difficulty of playing an unwell opponent. Like a wounded animal, he can act erratically. Such a player might limp along haplessly in one game and hit as hard as he can in the next; he also might suddenly feel better. "At one moment I could feel that he doesn't move that well. It's always tricky, because you want to play more [and longer] points, to make him suffer a little bit more—in a good way!" he clarified, as the crowd laughed. "And at the same time, you know at some point, he is going to say, okay, I cannot run anymore, so I'm going to go full power." That was indeed the pivot that Sinner made at the end of set three, and he managed to get two set points before losing it anyway. That moment could have turned the match.

Later in press, reflecting on those critical points, Medvedev brought it back to their first meeting that season and walked us through some counterfactuals. "In Australian Open, I think fourth set I had a break point. If I'm not mistaken, he made ace. He makes double fault, maybe I win Australian Open. Never know," he said. "That's why people love tennis. That's why people get crazy watching tennis. That's why we tennis players sometimes get crazy playing tennis," said the man who personified that truth as much as anyone on tour.

Those old doubts about Sinner's endurance, which he'd banished over a year of playing so well that his endurance was rarely tested, began to resurface. The previous month, his rival had overwhelmed him in the fifth set at Roland-Garros, deepening the chasm between their performance in marathon matches. After this Medvedev loss at Wimbledon, Sinner noted that he used to retire from matches a lot two years ago but didn't want to do that anymore if the illness was minor. He said he was feeling the ball well all tournament; this result was a disappointment.

With this victory, Medvedev managed to reverse the flow of their rivalry after five straight losses. He had emerged, triumphant, from a familiar circle of hell. His reward was a promotion to a different circle of hell: a semifinal against Carlos Alcaraz. That was the same challenge Medvedev had faced in the Wimbledon semifinal the previous season. That time he had been flattened in straight sets. This time around he at least took the first set.

After the loss, Medvedev was asked to compare Alcaraz to the Big Three, because tennis loves to conceptualize its future in terms of its past. Medvedev acknowledged that he'd played those three only late in their careers, but he gave the question a crack, anyway. His answer, in which he ruled that Alcaraz was probably the most challenging opponent he'd ever faced, was fascinating:

> So Roger plays on the [baseline]. Hits beautiful technique shots, goes to the net. Novak plays also on the [baseline], but completely different. Amazing defense, like pinball player where the ball comes back faster to you. Rafa, completely different. He can stay 10 meters behind, but he is going to run to every ball, banana shot, lefty.
>
> Carlos, I don't think he has anything from them. It's a different game style. I think where Carlos is different from many

players, we all have a little bit our preferences: someone prefers defense, someone prefers counterattack, someone prefers to be super-aggressive. He can do all of it.

With Medvedev out of his way, there was only one more obstacle between Carlitos and his second consecutive Wimbledon title. Just like last year's final, it was Djokovic. The great champion had played no warm-up tournament. He had arrived straight from surgery and rehab, and played well enough to move through his forgiving draw, eased along by the injury withdrawal of his quarterfinal opponent. He slid into this final without much resistance. It was a testament to how far removed Djokovic was from the rest of the tour on grass.

Even the walk-in was a little jittery. The two finalists lingered in the innards of the All England Club, preparing to march out to Centre Court. They stood side by side with their tennis bags slung over their shoulders. Who would lead the way? Which man would arrive on court first, and which man would follow? There's more prestige in being second. The unspoken calculus whirring in their heads was this: Should it be the defending champion, Alcaraz, or the seven-time champion, Djokovic? For all the ritual baked into Wimbledon, the tournament staffer escorting them onto the court left it up to them. "Whichever you like," he said, as if the decision were well above his pay grade. Both players hesitated, and started jabbering over one another. "No, no, no, you go first, I don't know," said Alcaraz, gesturing for his elder to lead the way. The man who had played this championship match 10 times said, beaming, "I don't know what the rules are." It was a joy to see them like this for a change, keyed-up and stumbling over their social graces. Djokovic led the way.

Once they started playing, there was no question of who was

first and who was second. It would not be a repeat of their five-set classic from the previous season; it was all Carlitos. It was clear-eyed, ecstatically good tennis. To the extent that there was any critique of Alcaraz at that juncture of his career, it was the lapses in concentration. In the micro, those lapses might lead him to attempt a demented drop shot when he should have hit an overhead smash, fail, and fling his head between his forearms in humiliation, as he'd done in his semifinal against Medvedev. In the macro, those lapses might lead him to throw away a sloppy set here or there, as he did throughout the tournament. But Alcaraz did not dawdle at all on that final Sunday.

After his easy run to the finals, Djokovic was crashing up against limits that nobody else had been able to expose. Alcaraz got Djokovic on the run, then decided to slot a pluperfect backhand down-the-line into a thin corridor of space, just to wrong-foot him. He banged big first serves and followed them with unanswerable drop shots, condensing into two shots the force-finesse mix that was his stamp on the modern game. He was himself undroppable—way too quick. He ran up a two-set lead before Djokovic had even acclimated himself to the match. Usually, coach Juan Carlos Ferrero needed to soothe his fiendishly talented charge into playing less spectacularly and more efficiently. So focused was Alcaraz that early in the third set, he was talking sternly to his player's box, pointing at them and then himself, asking *them* to focus more on *him*.

The third set contained the only competitive portion of the match. A revitalized Djokovic kept the set level until he stepped up to serve at 4-4. Then Alcaraz delivered his most blissed-out sequence of the day. First was a point of steady pace and depth; deep return, deep backhand down-the-line, deep forehand winner. As he hit that winner, Alcaraz's head was stable, as if pinned to a point in space, even as the force of the stroke hurled him into the air, the rest of his body coiling around him, his aim so true that Djokovic didn't even step toward the ball—0-15. Next it was a return that nicked the baseline, followed by a juicy mid-court forehand—0-30. Then Djokovic tried to serve-and-volley, executed to perfection, arriving at the net in time to prod a volley down the right sideline. It caught Alcaraz in an awkward position in the middle of the court, the area called "no-man's-land," because it's too far from the front to volley comfortably and too far from the back to hit a standard forehand. Most players would have scrambled backward to escape this spatial purgatory and catch Djokovic's volley after it had bounced. Not Alcaraz, who avoided the laborious brute-force option in favor of the most direct and elegant solution. He took two springy strides sideways and swiped the ball out of the air. In that hybrid space, he hit a hybrid shot, halfway between a volley and a forehand, pure funk and audacity—0-40. Two points later, Alcaraz scorched a passing shot, and it was his time to serve for the trophy. The seven-time winner of that trophy barely sat down in his chair on the changeover. He took a quick sip of water and walked to the other side well before the end of the allotted rest and stood there, chuckling darkly to himself, as if having already accepted his doom.

Alcaraz had the benefit of new balls, which move faster through the air. Despite running up a 40-0 lead in the game, earning himself three chances to finish the job, he finally lost focus, for the first time all day. On his first championship point he double-faulted. In the player's box, his 15-year-old brother Sergio started rubbing the back of their stressed-out mother. On the second championship point, Alcaraz sent his second serve straight at Djokovic's body, only for him to neatly sidestep it and smash it back—too good. At this point the crowd was in full tumult. On the third championship point, Alcaraz got exactly what he was looking for: a wide serve at 132 mph, so fast and well-placed that Djokovic could only flop at it, the ball drifting high into the center of the court. It was a ball that Alcaraz would destroy 9,999 out of 10,000 instances. But this particular ball Alcaraz hit out. He might have been distracted by the fan who screamed while the ball was floating over the net, a horrid shrill scream not unlike the ones made by London foxes cavorting in the middle of the night. Alcaraz went on to lose the game, and intrigue crept back into the match for roughly 15 minutes, only for the kid to snuff it out again with a confident tiebreak.

Alcaraz didn't collapse on the ground after the last point, the way he had the previous year; he just threw up his arms, smiled, bared his teeth, and yelled. His parents, who were teary last month in Paris, had conspicuously drier eyes this time around. After the young champion arrived in his box, he was once again absorbed into the blob of jubilant men, but it wasn't as raucous as it was when this type of win was still a novelty. Even his victory speeches in English were starting to settle into canned rhythms rather than showcasing the peppery idiosyncrasies of his diction. Carlitos and those close to him were getting used to these victories and their attendant feelings. And with good reason, because these wins would become an annual fixture of their lives.

"I've never seen him serve that way, to be honest. 136 [mph]," Djokovic marveled after the match. "Maybe I was missing something this tournament, but I've never seen him serve that fast." For his part, Alcaraz said he was still working to make his name, to someday sit alongside "those guys who are eating at the big table," referring to the sport's winningest champions. He was, in fact, already seated, his Hall of Fame candidacy already secure, but this was his standard show of humility. He was the youngest man ever to own four major titles. He was only the sixth man to win Roland-Garros and Wimbledon back-to-back. Not many can manage that transition, the stamina to play seven rounds at each tournament with only a few weeks off in between and the footwork versatile enough to succeed on those two very different surfaces.

As I watched Alcaraz lift the trophy, a hefty golden cup topped with a tiny pineapple—the tournament says it doesn't know why, just that the fruit was a sign of luxury back in 1887—I was reminded again of his admission at the start of the fortnight. He'd been watching videos of himself. Why go elsewhere for knowledge? Plato once theorized that people have immortal souls, full of knowledge accrued from past lives, so learning is actually just rediscovering that forgotten knowledge buried inside. Perhaps this has only ever been true of Carlos Alcaraz. How quickly we'd arrived at the juncture where there was so little for him to learn from other people's examples, where he was writing the future of the sport by himself, expanding its possibilities with every half-volley and high-pressure triumph. He was eating at the big table already, and ravenously.

CHAPTER 10

Hoard of Gold

Over the course of the season, some tennis fans had joked that Jannik Sinner was a sickly Victorian child. This had something to do with his pallid complexion, princely bearing, slender build, and constant procession of maladies. I was getting suspicious when Sinner still hadn't announced his arrival in Paris by late July, with the Olympics just days away. Soon enough he confirmed the worst: This time, it was tonsillitis that got him. All work, extreme athletic exertion, nonstop travel, and little rest had made Jannik a sick boy. He wrote on social media that he had been strongly advised by a doctor not to play and said he was sad to miss out on one of his main goals for the season.

It's difficult to pinpoint the Olympics in the prestige hierarchy of tennis. For many sports, the Olympics represent the apex of accomplishment. But tennis has its own major tournaments to fill that void, and their format—seven rounds, each best-of-five sets—is more strenuous than the Olympics: six rounds, each best-of-three sets. But while an Olympic medal might lack the allure of a major, it does have a nationalist tinge that appeals to a lot of athletes.

And while majors occur four times a year, the infrequency of the Olympics makes the medal a scarcer commodity. The 2024 Games would be even more challenging than usual. Having just finished the grass season, players were making a rare transition back onto clay. Medvedev said he hadn't done things in this order since he was 18. Whatever footwork and visual adjustments had been made for Wimbledon would have to be rapidly unlearned. They were all going back to Roland-Garros.

Well, not all of them. A good chunk of top players, including Americans like Frances Tiafoe and Ben Shelton, and Russians like Andrey Rublev and Karen Khachanov (both of whom would have had to play without a flag, due to sanctions), decided that cramming Olympic clay into their overscheduled summers wasn't worth it. Unlike normal tour events, there's no prize money at the Games, just potential glory. They opted instead to head straight to the hard courts of North America. Carlos Alcaraz was not one of those players. All season the 21-year-old had been looking forward to his first Games. He even decided to eschew the luxurious cocoon of a hotel or rental that he would typically inhabit during a tournament. Instead, like a common Olympian without an eight-figure bankroll, he wanted to enjoy the experience of living in the Olympic Village. He shared an apartment with his fellow tennis players, and even shared a room, where they slept on sustainably made cardboard beds.

There were consequences to his pursuit of normalcy. The attention on Carlitos, both wholesome and otherwise, was incessant, as seen in the deluge of photographs from civilians and fellow Olympians. On the wholesome end of the spectrum, video was circulated of him sitting alone at a Village cafeteria table, eating what appeared to be paella. (He ate his breakfasts at the cafeteria until the Spanish team captain David Ferrer directed his over-popular prodigy to start eating in his room instead, according to *El Mundo*.) On the coarser end of things was a crude meme that depicted a car's gear shifter, broken and askew, asserting that this would be Alcaraz's fate after his fortnight in the Village. The joke was referencing that notorious aspect of Village life: the world's fittest bodies often find themselves carnally entangled.

To the delight of many tennis fans, Alcaraz himself "liked" the scandalous meme on his own official Instagram account. The journalist Sebastián Varela overheard Alcaraz telling his Spanish teammates that he'd pressed the like button by accident—but too late, Carlitos, the world already saw you as the dog you are!

Judging by the sheer volume of images—the Egyptian table-tennis player, the Malaysian badminton player, the fifteen members of the Dutch field hockey team—it must have been difficult for him to walk a few paces in the Village without getting detained for a hug and photo. To a less patient or pleasant man, that would have been an oppressive fate, but in each of these pictures, Alcaraz's smile is disarmingly consistent and convincing. This was what he signed up for, and it was a fruitful pairing of animal and habitat. The Olympics were, at least in theory if not always in corrupt reality, the ultimate celebration of amateur sport. Alcaraz was the rare elite athlete who seemed to optimize his own pleasure at every moment on court. Sinner, too, spoke often about how treating tennis as a hobby was critical to his glacial cool in decisive moments, but the pleasure was less discernible on his face. With Alcaraz it was unmissable in that joyous, vacuous grin, making every passerby's day. Here, as always, he looked adept at having fun.

Among the many swooning Olympians who stopped Alcaraz for a photo was a 37-year-old curmudgeon named Andy Murray, who captioned his image "My favorite athlete." Murray himself was about to retire for a second time. His career had ended, first, in 2019, at the Australian Open, after a chronic injury left him unsure of his fate and sobbing at a press conference. At that point I wrote out a full eulogy for his career. I saw Murray as a relatively normal person interceding in a time of three deities. Djokovic, Nadal, and Federer lorded over the fray—and then there was Murray, entering the fight quite mortal and a little pissy. In truth he was no normal man. He had speed, stamina, a scholarly attunement to tactical nuance, and some of the fluffiest lobs the game had ever seen. Even when his tennis was at its purest, though, he always looked like a wretched goat on the court, snarling and haranguing himself and his team. He didn't enjoy the effortless offense of Federer or the imperious topspin of Nadal. Djokovic played a somewhat similar style to him but had elevated it to perfection. Murray, though not their equal, was still well superior to every other player in their era. And to go right at the three greatest and come away with lots of wins over them, plus three majors (restoring Wimbledon glory to the home kingdom), two Olympic gold medals, dozens of lesser titles, and months at the No. 1 ranking—that was a beautiful career in itself.

Murray went on to have a hip-resurfacing surgery, which coated the end of his femur with a smooth metal alloy, and after an arduous recovery, this cyborg Murray returned to the tour. He fought his way as high as No. 36 in the world. In 2021 he beat a young Alcaraz on the cusp of breakout and a young Sinner who had just broken into the top 10. He often flirted with near wins over top players, offering intermittent glimpses of his former self. This comeback was tantalizing, turbulent, emotionally messy—an apt coda for a career full of the same. He announced before the Olympics that it would be his last-ever event. Though he wasn't healthy enough to play singles, he got on court for the doubles. His last matches ever were with his countryman Dan Evans. Together they fended off match point five times in the first round and lost in the second. Though Murray waved his goodbyes to the crowd at Roland-Garros, the man known even among his peers as a tennis obsessive wasn't long absent from the tour. He didn't know it then, but a few months later he'd be coaching his rival: Djokovic.

For his part, Djokovic was approaching these Games with the zeal of a completist collector. An Olympic gold medal was the only meaningful absence from his vast hoard of tennis winnings. He'd claimed every title of note, many of them multiple times, but this specific gleam had eluded him. Nadal had won singles gold back in 2008, during one of the great seasons in history, and added a doubles gold in 2016. Federer had gotten his gold in doubles in 2008. Murray was the only tennis player ever to win two singles golds, which he managed in 2012 and 2016. But Djokovic hadn't yet been able to improve upon the bronze medal he won in 2008. He had been twice deprived even of bronze by the big, doleful Juan Martín del Potro. He had burnt out in the bronze-medal match in 2021, sending his racquet clattering into the pandemic-empty Tokyo stands. But all through the 2024 season, Djokovic had said he hoped to "peak" at the Olympics, to build his year around the pursuit of this precious metal. For a less committed person, a meniscus tear might have revised that plan, but it didn't deter him from making the Wimbledon final, so there was no reason to believe it would stop him in Paris.

In the second round, Djokovic faced Nadal. While Federer-Nadal was the more famous rivalry, to a certain type of tennis purist, the Djokovic-Nadal rivalry was superior, the one that thrust the men's game into its power-baseline future, laying down an impossible template for every future talent to follow. My internal terminology for the best Djokovic-Nadal matchups is Wide Tennis. It takes two—and really, only *these* two—to produce Wide Tennis. When playing lesser opponents, its full parameters cannot be glimpsed. Nadal can spend most of a match perched near the center of the baseline, imposing his entire will on each ball, cracking one cross-court forehand, then putting the next into the cavernous opening left behind. Djokovic can spend most of a match sitting directly on top of the baseline, taking the ball early, batting it to opposite corners until the end of time. When together, however, they are both hell-bent on hijacking the other from their seat of comfort. The result is a version of tennis that is as visually striking as it is physically baffling. The legal area of play for singles is fringed by two strips known as the doubles alley, which extend the court wider for two-on-two play. But Nadal and Djokovic sprint behind, through, and even beyond these alleys in their singles matches. They travel out to remote locales, then recover back to the center of the court just in time to begin their next far-flung foray. Thus their tennis took on different dimensions. It looked distorted, as if reality's projectionist had made an error with the aspect ratio.

In these matches, their distinctive shots—Djokovic's backhand down-the-line struck with legs opening into a side split, Nadal's "banana" forehand that curls left to right in midair—speak to how gifted they are at pummeling a ball that other elite players wouldn't reach at all. Each man hybridizes offense and defense in a way that commands constant vigilance from the other. Each ball is struck with a reasonable expectation that the next ball will be coming back over the net, perhaps even harder and more angled. Both men intimately understand how difficult it is to hit the ball somewhere that would bother the other. Watching this version of tennis is like reading a text stripped of punctuation marks. Where you'd expect a point to reach its natural conclusion, it simply refuses, instead flowing out into a sequence of shots and sprints and shots and sprints that leaves no room for breath or error.

Had the Djokovic-Nadal contest taken place in any prior Olympic cycle, it would've been an intoxicating display of Wide Tennis, but it was nowhere to be found in 2024. By that time, the lifelong rivals no longer stood on the same plateau. Djokovic was still capable of hauling in the runner-up trophy at Wimbledon; Nadal was losing to lesser players on a mostly feel-good farewell tour. The only question was for how many minutes the Spaniard could keep the action compelling. The answer, until he was down 0-4 in the second set, was very few. And then Nadal broke serve twice, the second time with the shot of the match, a quick improvised swipe at a ball skying overhead, as if pawing an apple out of a high branch. The match seemed to be twisting toward the past, but that vision was fleeting. At 4-4 in the second set, Djokovic stopped his foe's momentum with a harsh break of serve. He walked to his chair for the changeover, identified the haters in the crowd—real or otherwise—pointed to his ear, and savored a round of quite real booing. Then he served out the match.

By defeating Nadal 6-1, 6-4, he closed the book on their rivalry. They had played 60 times, more than any pair of opponents in history; he had won 31, to Nadal's 29. Later, speaking to Serbian media, Djokovic reflected on the texture of their two-decade relationship. "No, there is no brotherhood. We are more rivals and colleagues," he said. "There is a lot of classified information. At this level you cannot be too close to your rival." He hoped they could improve their relationship in the future.

Nadal, meanwhile, acknowledged the realities of his present body. "I haven't had the shot quality to create problems for him," he said. "I don't have the legs I had 15 years ago either. So without the shot quality and the legs I had 15 years ago, you're not going to create problems for the best in history, right?" He had begun to affix that superlative to Djokovic, his toughest rival. While Nadal still would not clarify whether this was his last singles match at Roland-Garros, his language made it clear this would be his last Olympics. This meant that his chance for one more medal rested in his doubles partnership with Alcaraz. If torch-passing could be expressed in a single event, it was this: Nadal and Alcaraz on the doubles court together, the last two decades of Spanish men's tennis alongside its next two decades.

Among top singles players, Nadal was an unusually strong and intuitive doubles player. He was known for his volleys, which he hit with an atypical choked-up grip, sliding his hand higher up the handle of his racquet for more control. Whereas Alcaraz was a doubles buffoon. For all his fluency and untrammeled expression on a singles court, Alcaraz on a doubles court could look antsy and uncertain of his position, like a wild animal put into a pen. Doubles follows different patterns than singles and has a strategy all its own. Speaking broadly, one teammate stays close to the net, while the other teammate plays at the baseline, each one protecting roughly half of the shared turf, working in tandem to get the net player an easy volley. The components of an eventual doubles great were lying dormant in Alcaraz. He was already the best volleyer in singles. But he had yet to suss out the finer points of doubles strategy. To watch Carlitos pick up a new skill was one of tennis's most reliable pleasures. Every coach he'd ever had was astonished by his capacity to integrate new information into his play. To see him do that with Rafa Nadal as tutor, muttering wisdom and tactics in his ear between points, was some of the headiest fan service in recent history. The beaming Alcaraz appeared, at times, like an uncommonly gifted fan who'd won a raffle to play next to his idol. Before the tournament, he said that he planned to "keep my mouth shut and just listen to him."

Their early matches were sloppy, sporadically brilliant, and well-received by the roiling crowds in Paris. "We have been suffering but of course we are enjoying playing together," said Nadal, expressing an extremely on-brand sentiment. "We are having fun in general. I think we have a positive relationship outside of the court that helps inside." They beat an Argentine duo in the first round, then took out the Dutch team in the second. In the quarterfinals, they came up against the American team of Austin Krajicek and Rajeev Ram. That match laid bare the difference between a team of two singles virtuosos stapled together and a practiced doubles team used to operating as a unit. Ram and Krajicek were masters of positioning, poaching tidy volleys at the net. And they were unruffled by a crowd so passionate about the star duo that it teetered into outright disrespect, as the umpire tried to browbeat them into silence with ceaseless shushes and pleas. The Nadalcaraz team had flown this far on the fumes of raw talent, but they could not get past the eventual silver medal team. Nadal bade farewell to Court Philippe-Chatrier for the second time that summer. This time his exit involved no interview, and it was far more satisfying than the one in June, with one detail that appeared almost art-directed. Alcaraz, trailing Nadal on his last steps out of the stadium, laid a hand of support on his idol's shoulder, the future reassuring the past.

Alcaraz's own singles journey was less complicated. He'd been dealing with a groin injury he'd picked up at Wimbledon, but he said he knew how to manage the pain. Clad in a red top and yellow shorts that evoked the Spanish flag—and perhaps also Winnie-the-Pooh, as some fans observed—he did not drop a set in his first five matches.

In the gold medal match, his opponent was Djokovic. While Sinner was still coming into his own, this was already the richest rivalry at the top of the tour, all the more so for its built-in scarcity. Observers might have wanted it to last forever. But one small fact—the inexorable march of time—put bookends on the era when they'd be truly competitive on the court. One man was on his way up the mountain (as hard as it was to imagine significant improvement on his present mastery), and the other had begun his gradual descent (as hard as it was to imagine his supremacy ever fading).

Old archetypes were often applied to new superstars, and in those formulations, Alcaraz was most often seen as the love child of Federer and Nadal, blending the former's extempore all-court play with the latter's brawn and vigor. Sinner, meanwhile, was the one seen as a power-injected, neo-Djokovic. But if you spend a match watching Alcaraz and Djokovic dance on opposite baselines and freeze the frame to appreciate the gummy absurdity of their contortionist poses, it's clear that the Spaniard had taken after the Serb, too. Both men have prepared their bodies to smoothly enter and exit all manner of splits, crouches, and coils; the range of motion in every joint affords them a freedom of expression not available to their peers. As tennis got even faster, shots needed to be retrieved from even more demanding court positions, which often necessitated even weirder body configurations.

Djokovic and Alcaraz played a trilogy of classic matches in 2023, one on each surface. The first volume was their semifinal at Roland-Garros. Expectations for that match were colossal, since it was their first meeting after Carlitos had ascended to major champion. As they split the first two sets, all those expectations were met; I was settling in for an epic. And then at 1-1 in the third, Alcaraz was overcome by cramps. This was beyond the standard cramp, which a player might gut through, limping in between points. Alcaraz was unable to play. Per an obscure corner of the rule book, he conceded a whole game in order to call on medical treatment before the usually permitted window of the changeover. The remainder of the match was a glum formality, a hobbled Alcaraz winning just one game, possibly out of Djokovic's mercy.

"I disappointed myself," Alcaraz said afterward, "ending the match like this, coming into this match feeling great physically, and then cramping." He said he felt the cramps first in his arm and eventually across his entire body, immobilizing him. And he attributed them not to a lack of conditioning or nutrition, but to the sheer psychological pressure he felt. As his trainer Juanjo Moreno put it later: "I can prepare Carlos any salt supplement or a similar drink to prevent cramps, but it's difficult to get inside his mind." Alcaraz said he started the match already nervous, and the physicality of their play didn't help his cause. "Tough rallies, drop shots, sprints, it was a combination of a lot of things," he said. "The main thing was the tension." Asked if that tension was specific to his opponent, he was frank. "If someone said that he's getting into a court with no nerves playing against Novak, he lies."

By the time they met again, five weeks later at Wimbledon, Alcaraz appeared to have resolved the issue. He also appeared to have solved grass-court tennis despite minimal experience. Two days before their Wimbledon final, Alcaraz made a remark I found bizarre at the time. "It's going to be the best moment of my life, probably," he said, referring to a high-pressure contest against a man who had spent the duration of Alcaraz's conscious life siphoning his opponents' joy with his tennis. A blip in self-translation, I figured. While a Wimbledon final against Djokovic might wind up the best moment of Alcaraz's life, it could also take any number of painful forms. Straight-set annihilation, or even full-body cramps, to take a non-hypothetical example. The reality—a five-set triumph that announced his talent to millions of people—made his remark look like prophecy. That may well have been the best moment of his life. After the cramps at Roland-Garros, Alcaraz had asked his team to explain why it happened and kept up his work with a sports psychologist. Before the Wimbledon final, he lay on a physiotherapy table for over 30 minutes, listening to music and trying to calm his muscles and emotions.

Carlitos learns so fast that it generates unintentional humor, best seen in his post-Wimbledon remarks. "I am totally different player than French Open. I grew up a lot since that moment," he said, sincerely, about a match played five weeks before. He undergoes emotional and professional transformation in a span of time when most people his age might only fill a laundry hamper.

When they met the next month on a hard court in the final of the Cincinnati Open, there was little mystery between these two, tactically speaking, but the match did involve a new environmental adversary: the humidity of Ohio in August. Djokovic was already in disrepair after dropping the first set. He screamed at his box for a creatine drink, had his pulse checked in a medical time-out, took refuge in an icy towel. Alcaraz found a match point in the second-set tiebreak, but Djokovic nullified it with a big serve and forehand, and went on to win the tiebreak. In the third set, it was Alcaraz's turn to fend off four match points—one of them with a nutty forehand slap—and push the match to a deciding tiebreak. There the nasty specter of cramps returned. Alcaraz's right hand seized up during a long rally, forcing him to try a gawky, futile forehand with two hands on the racquet. His resources depleted, he took bigger risks on the remaining points but couldn't steady the scoreboard in time. After shaking hands, Djokovic grabbed his own collar with both hands and tore his sweat-saturated polo shirt open, right down the middle. Alcaraz wept, and continued all the way through his runner-up speech. For Djokovic, this match restored an old memory. "The feeling that I have on the court reminds me of facing Nadal when we were at our prime," Djokovic said after. "Each point is a hassle, each point is a battle—you feel like you're not going to get five free points in the entire match." Although it was played on a quick hard-court surface that keeps points shorter, their three-hour, 49-minute match was the longest best-of-three tour final since that format was invented in 1990. If every point was a hassle and battle, here were 261 of them, played at the highest level man had yet discovered.

The gold medal clash, at the Olympics, would join this lineage of matches. Having dispatched the actual Nadal, Djokovic had to dispatch his successor. He had to see if he could undo the judgment he himself rendered after Wimbledon: that he was no longer on the same level as Carlos and Jannik. One aspect not working in Djokovic's favor was the wear-and-tear of this summer schedule. As recently as his Olympic quarterfinal, Djokovic was concerned about his ability to play on. It was the knee, again. In that match against Stefanos Tsitsipas, he said he'd felt "déjà vu" of the meniscus tear. The pain lingered for three or four games, then subsided. He looked untroubled in his next match, and by the time he lined up across Alcaraz, it was clear that no degree of pain was going to interfere with his agenda.

The Alcaraz drop shot is an instant test of the opponent's movement, and from the first minutes of the match, Djokovic met it constantly, refusing to let his young rival dictate the terms. He got himself to the net on the drop shot and volleyed cleanly upon arrival, no easy feat when the ball in question had just been singed by the

Alcaraz forehand. The first set lasted an outrageous 94 minutes. For context, many two-set matches in the tournament had concluded well within that time frame. If Alcaraz left that set with any regrets, it would be the 4-4 game, where he had five break points but capitalized on none. The players collided instead in a tiebreak, a place of comfort for Djokovic, who had fashioned himself into the best tiebreak player in tour history, winning over 65 percent of the time.

In tiebreaks, every point is precious. Players take turns serving. First to seven points, win by two. The high-pressure format conforms to Djokovic's exact strengths. Whenever a tiebreak begins, he seems to retreat into a mental fortress. From there he emits no unforced errors. Because his natural style of play is to gradually accumulate the advantage in a rally by hitting a series of relatively safe shots, he never has to assume too much risk with any individual shot. He can rely on the sturdiness of his legs and mind. It's airtight, hermetic tennis. Later in his career, once he'd shaped his serve into one of the tour's best, more due to placement and spin than raw power, he had even more security to work within. Reeling off these unreturnable first serves, he could float through tiebreaks until he saw a good juncture to attack.

In this particular first-set tiebreak, that juncture was at 3-3. Alcaraz fired a topspin kick serve. Bouncing high, it was intended to land directly in front of Djokovic—a body serve. It's slightly counterintuitive, but a ball served right at the returner is difficult to deal with; a player needs to be far enough from the ball's path to extend his arms and swing a racquet cleanly. When the ball is hurtling right at his chest, a returner gets "jammed," often resorting to an oafish, abortive half swing. That said, a body serve that misses its target, even by inches, can backfire, because it is close to a returner but not close enough to jam them. This particular serve from Alcaraz was a dud, hanging in the ideal strike zone for Djokovic's forehand, waiting for him to deliver a verdict. Gladly he delivered: a crosscourt winner tucked well inside the service box, so artfully angled that Carlitos wasn't even standing within 20 feet of the ball when it blew by. That was all the margin he needed to take the tiebreak. After claiming the first set, Djokovic walked off court for a bathroom break, leaving his foe to stew in his sweat with head in hands.

Frustration began to worm its way into Alcaraz's play. In the second set Djokovic built his points with fastidious, subtle patterns, daring Alcaraz to break through these cages with his own inventions. Typically he relished that challenge, but most of this match looked joyless for the 21-year-old, aside from the occasional finger pointed to the ear. He cursed at himself. He mimed throwing his racquet—but never actually did it. Even the presence of his coach Ferrero, who was on vacation for the Olympics but got to Paris in time for the gold medal match, didn't settle him down.

The second-set rallies began to resemble corporal punishment. There was one late in the set that left Djokovic keeled over as if he'd taken a kidney punch, retreating to his water bottle in the middle of the game, before he was technically allowed to do so. (Umpires have some discretion here; they don't want players to drop dead.) If Alcaraz could keep the match this physical and drag it into a third set, his legs would likely fare better than his elder's. But Djokovic kept pushing, using his crisp serve to win him no-fuss points, and with both players unbroken, they hurtled into another tiebreak. There was a ragged yearning in Djokovic's body language, but a crystalline refinement in his actual strokes. In that tiebreak he hit the best individual shots of his season, both of them forehands struck on the run, both sliding onto his right foot—applying a lot of stress on that dodgy right leg—and both breathtakingly rude crosscourt winners that Alcaraz could only track with despairing eyes. It seemed as though Djokovic would trade in that knee joint for a gold medal, if it came to that. After an impeccable second-set tiebreak, the medal was his. He began sobbing immediately, put his rapture on pause to hug Alcaraz, then collapsed onto all fours. His entire body, right down to his thumbs, trembled furiously, as if a localized earthquake were rumbling only his patch of the clay. He made the sign of the cross and threw a kiss to the sky.

Alcaraz gamely attempted his on-court interview through tears but was interrupted by his own intense, shuddering quiet. He'd spoken throughout the tournament about how badly he wanted to bring home gold, and kissed the flag on his shirt after each win. In this solipsistic game, it was rare for Alcaraz to get to play for something larger than his personal advancement. He had to be comforted by his interviewer, Alex Corretja, a Spanish star from the nineties. For Alcaraz, this silver medal was a sole letdown in a summer of delights. He said he'd felt a different kind of pressure than he'd felt in the four major finals he'd played (and won). In those Roland-Garros and Wimbledon runs, the throughline was how he scrounged up his most ingenious tennis in the most stressful scenarios. He admitted that he didn't live up to that ideal in this match. "Tiebreaks, for example, he increased his level at the top and I couldn't do it, so probably a bit sad thinking about those moments," he said.

That was also a testament to the level that Djokovic reached that day, which hardly any of his contemporaries would have matched. Minutes after the win, the highest achiever in men's tennis said the feeling of winning gold "supersedes everything that I've ever felt on the tennis court." He also offered a peek into his inner life. "That's probably one of the biggest internal battles that I keep on fighting with myself . . . that I don't feel like I've done enough, that I haven't been enough in my life, on the court and off the court. So it's a big lesson for me. I'm super grateful for the blessing to win a historic gold medal for my country, to complete the Golden Slam, to complete all the records."

As a pure athlete, Djokovic might have taken a step down from his apex, but he was still supple enough to fend off a man-child who'd just won back-to-back majors. Time had sanded away some of the Serb's physical advantages, but it granted him fresh technical and psychological ones. After five tries at the Olympics, at 37, he became the oldest man ever to win a gold medal in singles. He was the only gold medalist ever who did not drop a set in the tournament. Most meaningful for Djokovic, he was also the first Serbian tennis player to win a gold. He had not stayed in the Olympic Village that fortnight, but later that day he arrived there to dance with his medal around his neck and his flag draped across his shoulders, surrounded by his countrymen. That evening, when he went into town for a celebratory dinner, he was still wearing the medal. For months after, he took the medal everywhere he traveled.

Two days after the closing ceremony, all the Serbian Olympic medalists were feted in the Belgrade city center, with patriotic anthems and blinding flares. But there's a different video from that visit that offers the clearest window into his bliss. Djokovic is in the back seat of a car, driving through the streets of the capital, leaning out the window with his gold around his neck, singing and praising his nation, reaching into the crowd to receive high fives and at least one kiss. He had spoken of feelings of inadequacy that had survived even his decades of dominating tennis. But it'd be difficult to conjure a simpler image of contentment, of radical adequacy, a man who had completed the full checklist of his career and no longer wondered if he'd done enough.

CHAPTER 11

Damage Control

There's a good joke baked into the very structure of the professional tennis schedule. The tour travels from Melbourne, to Palm Springs, to Miami, to Monte-Carlo, to Madrid, to Rome, to Paris, to London, to Montreal—then alights briefly in the suburbs of Cincinnati, Ohio—before taking off again for New York and Shanghai and Paris (again). The players are aware of the anomaly. Daria Kasatkina, a funny and sharp-tongued player who criticized her native Russia and defected to Australia, composed a video on this theme. At the start, she acknowledges what a privilege it is that her job lets her see the world. Then she barges into her Marriott hotel room, throws open the curtains, and pretends to be flabbergasted by the vista: eighteen-wheeler trucks lurching along the I-71 interstate.

Sometimes the tennis tournament is just one of many happenings in town. The Cincinnati Open is a pilgrimage for tennis fans across the American Midwest, who arrive not to pursue other off-site diversions but to absorb as many matches as possible. Usually when I'm covering the tour I seek out pockets of time to escape the tournament grounds, breathe in civilian air, and have a meal that hasn't been peeled out of concession-stand cellophane. In Mason, Ohio, that temptation is considerably milder. In August 2024 I was content to sink deep into the microculture of the tournament itself: the sunburnt parents toting around lanky tennis-playing preteens, the large immigrant families still locked in Federer fanaticism even after his retirement, the squadrons of country-club moms, all of us adrift in a sea of Dri-FIT polo shirts, wraparound sunglasses, sweatpants, and sundresses.

And yet, of all the teeming metropoles, full of vice, where professional tennis is staged, it was a suburb a half hour outside Ohio's third-biggest city, with a population of roughly 35,000, where both of our protagonists finally complicated their immaculate public images—in very different ways, and to very different degrees.

These days, to talk to a player in a truly relaxed state, you often have to catch them at the outset of a tournament, before the churn and toil begin. That hasn't always been the case. The membrane between journalist and player was more permeable back in the day. The veteran tennis journalist Jon Wertheim told me that at the turn of the millennium, he could speak to Venus Williams privately for half an hour in the middle of a tournament; my eyeballs plopped out onto my keyboard. Curry Kirkpatrick, who wrote fizzy profiles of players for *Sports Illustrated* throughout the eighties and nineties, told me stories about ambling up to Andre Agassi at a swimming pool and bickering with John McEnroe on a walk after he'd written something not quite to the hothead American's liking. The notion of a player today submitting themselves to the critical eye of a journalist, for meaningful conversation, was essentially unthinkable. Tournaments have whittled away the zones where players and writers could commingle. Storytelling is consolidated in the hands of the players.

Sports media is dead; most of what's left is window dressing for on-line sports gambling firms.

Print journalists have become unnecessary middlemen for athletes who can instantaneously transmit their idle thoughts to fans on social media. To expand his popularity, a player relies not on a ferrety writer, but on a well-cut highlight reel or a high-end photo shoot. I understand the calculus: When your own time becomes so valuable, why give away access to your life story for free? There has to be something in it for them, too. A brief, canned sit-down interview might be an acceptable cost to promote a needy sponsor, or to secure a sumptuous cover shoot, which yields photos that can be tossed on Instagram to slake thirsty fans. The image has fully stomped out the written word in sporting culture, if not culture full stop. Players with enough clout can even partake in another current pastime: the hagiographical docuseries, where the player gets full editorial veto power. As noted, Netflix cameras trailed Alcaraz for chunks of the 2024 season. What we lose, in this new media ecosystem, are the thornier narratives that the players themselves don't want to share.

Aside from this broader societal shift, there's also been a tennis-specific shift: The athletes have gotten a lot more sophisticated about whom they hire for their "team." Top-ranked players have become business executives, constantly hiring and replacing personnel. Typically, the team consists of the following. There is the agent, to secure the endorsement deals, sponsorships, and appearance fees. The coach, to hone tactics and technique—sometimes two, with different emphases, as Sinner has in Darren Cahill for the bigger picture and Simone Vagnozzi for the fine details. The strength-and-conditioning coach, to keep nudging the body toward its optimal state. The physiotherapist, to help a banged-up body recuperate after matches. There might also be a sports psychologist and a nutritionist. Much of this staff travels the world with the player, and unlike in team sports, where a franchise handles the overhead, players have to pay their employees out of their own earnings. In a 2021 interview with Sports.ru, Andrey Rublev estimated his annual expenses were about $600,000; even that was on a down year for travel, and more than a few players have an even larger full-time staff than his.

The rapid expansion of the player team is a consequence of rapidly increasing prize and sponsor money in the sport. The titles won them glory, and the agents leveraged that glory to win the player even bigger checks. Winning Roland-Garros in June, for example, earned Alcaraz €2.4 million from the tournament. But a few weeks earlier, he had signed a long-term contract with Nike that paid him roughly $15 to $20 million a year, according to the Spanish outlet Relevo. Sinner had signed a similarly structured Nike contract in 2022, about $150 million over 10 years, before he had won much of note. The apparel companies were already flinging around the sorts of sums they had paid to the Big Three. In a famous round of corporate bidding, Roger Federer had been lured away from Nike to Uniqlo with a 10-year, $300 million contract. Even apparel companies outside of sport wanted a piece of the new kids. Sinner became an ambassador for Gucci, and in 2023 the luxury brand had to persuade Wimbledon to permit a brownish duffel bag that broke the tournament's militant all-white code. The Italian's leggy frame and glassy expressions hold up surprisingly well in the context of a fashion shoot. Alcaraz's brawnier build, meanwhile, had him modeling underwear for Calvin Klein.

Armed with these bankrolls, the Big Three could afford to reinvest in personnel to help prolong their careers and earning potential. This became a new template for the present stars to follow. But as the tennis journalist Ben Rothenberg told me, young players ensconced in these huge teams can also become "siloed and isolated," spending most of their lives around people on their payroll, marinating in a tour culture that is increasingly sterile. The personalities are becoming a little less freewheeling and inquisitive, a little more coddled and calculating. We cherish someone like Daniil Medvedev because he is an outlier to these trends. He seems to be one of the last people speaking his truth at all hours, sometimes to his financial detriment, always to our delight.

There's a lull before every tournament called "media day." Players have arrived on the premises, and they're practicing, but not yet playing official matches. They are thus ripe to be turned into Content. They spend a decent chunk of that day recording clips that will be circulated on social media to promote the tour. Part of the day is set aside for journalists. Select players of interest are trotted out for a casual roundtable discussion, which at the Cincinnati Open was taking place in the dining area of a little golf club across the street from the tournament venue. These discussions, which were each set to last around eight or nine minutes, were also susceptible to starting eight or nine minutes early, as Sinner's did; the player's schedule overrules all others'. He popped into the golf club looking tanner than I remembered, as if his skin were bronzing to match his hair, and wearing a white-and-black hoodie that seemed like overkill for the 84-degree afternoon. He talked us through his summer of ailments—hip pain in the clay season, an unnamed illness at Wimbledon that left him woozy, the tonsillitis that knocked him out of the Olympics—and ended with a bit of Zen. "You know, sometimes you have to accept this." The hip in particular had looked sketchy in his most recent match in Montreal, a loss to Rublev, where Sinner had been clutching at it for the better part of an hour. When I asked if it was still bothering him, he said it wasn't, and he was "not afraid."

But he wrapped up on a muted note, as if he just wanted to get some match reps in Ohio to get in shape for the imminent U.S. Open, the year's last major.

In Cincinnati, Sinner and Alcaraz were the first and second seeds respectively and could meet in the final. Djokovic was still recovering from his Olympic bliss and would not play the role of the chaperone at the teen dance making room for the Holy Spirit between the youthful duo. Alcaraz showed up on media day in the boxy white tee that had become his pre-tournament staple, speaking fondly about the "epic" final he'd lost to Djokovic at last year's tournament. Asked whether the suburban environs relaxed him, he laughed; this was still a 1000-level tournament, and he was fighting to end the year as the No. 1 player in the world, a race that Sinner still led despite Alcaraz's rare double at Roland-Garros and Wimbledon.

Alcaraz was asked once again about playing alongside Nadal at the Olympics, and I was vaguely depressed to hear him recycle almost verbatim an answer I'd heard before. I felt for him, and for those trying to coax a tasty quote out of him. Every journalist seemed to want the Nadalcaraz doubles to have been a transformative experience for the junior Spaniard, and while I'm sure it was on some level, it might not have been the Yoda-like transmission of wisdom we hoped to depict it as. Again I was reminded that sports writing isn't so much tracing the truth as telling a story with a satisfying shape. I could almost mouth the words as Alcaraz repeated what he'd learned from Nadal on court: "Sometimes when we were down, he was there in a positive way, talking to me like, 'Well, right now they are gonna feel the pressure. We have to just stay there, putting some balls in, trying to get them in trouble.' Some situations, some things that you probably don't see—or is difficult to see—he sees very clear." Alcaraz was always cooperative with reporters, and he didn't switch on autopilot the way Sinner sometimes did. It was hard to blame a 21-year-old for reusing an old line. Maybe today's players had reason to prefer recording breezy video clips about who the funniest or most handsome player on tour was, when the alternative was talking to us obsolete scribes with our little recorders.

Both Sinner and Alcaraz had a first-round bye, earning them an extra day of rest. Local fans flocked instead to their countryman, Frances Tiafoe, who seems to have a biological response to the tour's return to American hard courts. His concentration improves, his tactics firm up, and he sponges up all the attention. I caught him for a chat a few minutes after his second-round win over Lorenzo Musetti, when he was still beaded with sweat. All professional athletes are confident—some amount of self-delusion is in the job description—but there are still levels of differentiation. "Brimming with confidence" wasn't a sufficient metaphor for Tiafoe in a superb mood. Standing next to him, I felt irradiated with confidence, as if it were beaming out of the portal in his gap-toothed grin. The restorative effects lingered afterward, giving me a little extra pep in my step as I ascended four flights of stairs.

In Musetti, Tiafoe had dispatched one of the best players of the summer, fresh off a Wimbledon semifinal and Olympic bronze medal. The American celebrated the win by hovering one palm low over the court: the "too small" celebration, one of many flourishes Tiafoe has imported from basketball, and almost certainly its first usage in the history of pro tennis. While some of the prudish and crypto-racist corners of the tennis internet moaned about the gesture, I cracked up at his showmanship. And I could understand why he was so elated; he'd just begun to turn around an abysmal season.

I asked Tiafoe whether he felt any pressure to make the most of this window of time, when the Big Three had receded and the Sincaraz era was just beginning. Tiafoe said what was coming wasn't nearly as "brutal" as what had just passed. "Even though Sinner and these guys are playing really well, obviously you still wanna do really well, because you feel like when their game is complete, it's gonna be very, very tough," he said. "Granted, it's a little different. They're younger than me, I don't have that fear factor. When I'm playing Novak, Rafa, these guys—man, I've been watching those guys since I was a kid. So you can't get over the Mount Rushmore."

Even in this off year, Tiafoe had taken Alcaraz to five sets in the third round of Wimbledon before finally giving in. It was the second time he'd taken the Spaniard to a fifth set at a major. Why was he so good at making Alcaraz sweat? "Well, I mean, I think"—Tiafoe took a sharp exhale through his teeth, as if measuring out his self-belief into nonlethal doses—"we're probably two of the more talented guys. I mean, obviously, he's probably the most talented guy here. And myself . . . look, man, at my best, I can do special things." He rattled off the features they had in common: quick feet, great hands for volleys, good defense, a knack for twisting defense into offense, shot variety, and great intangibles. "We kinda can do all similar things, it's down to who wants it more in the end, or who takes those moments better." I was reminded once again about the bell curve of sports commentary. High-decibel talk-show shmucks say it's all about who wants it more; middlebrow commentators like myself try to offer sober technical analyses; transcendent athletic geniuses say it's all about who wants it more. "At the Open when we played, I was hanging on for dear life," he said, of their 2022 five-setter in New York. But the recent Wimbledon match had been different: "I think I was the better cat that time." Tiafoe cited that match as a "spark" that awoke his tennis, and it was true that he had looked far better since. Some gifted but lesser players seemed to have this reaction to Alcaraz. He invited them into stimulating, inventive exchanges that reminded them of their own capabilities. Sinner, on the other hand, might just remind them of how far they were from the mountaintop.

Alcaraz played his opening Cincinnati match against a lanky, roguish acrobat—Gaël Monfils. For nearly two decades, Monfils has been one of the fastest and best-liked players on tour, a friend to every player and every crowd. Whenever he sees an opening, he opts for flash. No man in tennis history has ever jumped quite so high. He can spurt into the air like a geyser to smash a lob; he can match Djokovic's rubbery side splits. He'll go between the legs or behind the back; he'll swing without even looking at the ball. He likes to follow these trick shots with a conspiratorial wink or grin, as if inviting you (and several thousand others) in on a secret. But his playing style, for all its joys, can also confound his supporters. He often lapses into a defensive mode, forgetting his formidable offensive gifts, and he can wither away in a long match, because his endurance is not on par with his agility. Sometimes he seems cursed to wander between the style of tennis that can win him the match at hand and the style that most enraptures the crowd. In this way, Monfils was a cautionary tale for someone like Alcaraz; he'd had a long and successful career, but it was hard to shake the feeling that he could have done more if he'd been willing to play boring. That's the gloomiest possible reading of the matchup. As for the sunnier one: Here was the most natural showman of the '10s taking on the best of the '20s. The match started ugly, and when rain suspended play in the second-set tiebreak, it was almost a mercy. Let them return tomorrow and have more fun with it, I thought.

When play resumed the next day, Alcaraz lost the tiebreak and they moved to a deciding set. I peeled away from the match to transcribe an interview. But I stepped back out to watch at an opportune moment, because right then, at 2-1 in the third set, I witnessed something I never would have fully believed had I not borne direct witness. I would have ruled it a deepfake, a trick of the machines. Monfils had hit a volley, one that Alcaraz typically would have tracked down. But he was sluggish to react, lost the point, lost the game, raised the racquet above his head, and—unlike the dozens of times he'd raised that arm in mock rage, only to immediately relax it—smashed it against the court. He swung four times, and each time I could hear the crisp clatter all the way up in the nosebleeds. The first strike broke the frame on one side. The second and third deformed the oval shape of the racquet completely. The fourth folded the oval in half like a quesadilla. As befit its perpetrator, it was one of the most athletic racquet destructions I'd seen, a fully committed and coordinated act. Alcaraz sank into a deep lunge, driving with his hips and core, shoulder loose, every link in the kinetic chain conspiring to send that black-and-yellow Babolat to hell. Walking to his bench, his shoulders were high and tight, his face flushed as bloodred as his T-shirt. He chucked the ruined frame and grabbed a fresh one as the crowd whooped.

Because of his popularity, fans wrote half-ironic paeans to the tantrum. Even his first racquet smash as a pro was an aesthetic feat—he really was a prodigy in all things. Where did it rank in the annals of past smashes? To me it doesn't beat the clean Grigor Dimitrov number from 2015, when he slung his racquet at the ground and on impact it split the handle from the string bed. I'm also partial to the Stan Wawrinka one in 2016, when he held the racquet at its top and bottom and placidly snapped it over his shinbone, a marvel of leverage and economy. Others are partial to the Mario Vilella Martínez master class of 2019, where he took six shuddering smashes that each jolted his body forward on the clay, casting up a dust cloud, then flung the ruined frame at the back fence, his coda a clean ping. There's quite a bit of moralizing in tennis around the racquet smash. Famously, Rafael Nadal never smashed one in his entire career, on principle, but most players have caved in a moment of pique. Some, like Nick Kyrgios or Benoît Paire, seem to smash as often as they can to burnish their tedious bad-boy personae.

But Carlitos is the consummate good boy. For an hour afterward I remained in shock, as if I'd witnessed some kind of natural disaster at a remove. My colleague Patrick Redford, watching at home, said it was like watching a puppy smoke a cigarette. With his four smashes, Alcaraz shattered an enduring image of professional happiness. As a kid, he'd had quite a temper, and while he'd managed it well enough to win four majors, perhaps he hadn't exorcised it completely. Later that day, after losing to Monfils in three sets, he arrived at his press conference in a checkered polo and baggy denim shorts, looking like a repentant schoolboy at the principal's office (if you ignored the fact that the shirt was Louis Vuitton and the Rolex on his wrist cost more than the principal's car). Almost immediately, he told the press that it was the worst match he'd played in his career. Though he'd been training well, he was surprised to find the court surface on the main stadium was much faster than the practice courts, like playing "a totally different sport."

Somehow, well into the press conference, nobody had asked him about his out-of-character tantrum, so I risked the wrath of the new Dark Carlitos and phrased it delicately: That whole racquet situation, have you ever felt that way on court before? He had, he said, but he'd been able to check himself. "Today, I couldn't control myself, because, as I said, I was feeling that I was not playing any kind of tennis. So it was really frustrating for me that at some point I want to left the court. I don't want to be on the court anymore." Almost every press conference with Alcaraz produces an appealing neologism—"it was a really heartful moment for me," he said in this one—but none of them had ended on this dour a note. "I will forget it," he said of his day, "because I think it is impossible to get any good things about this match." With that, he was out of Cincinnati, just as soon as he'd arrived. Only one other time this season had he lost his opening match at a tournament, and that was in Rio, when he'd liquefied his ankle two games in and retired. By flaming out of Cincinnati he would lose a big chunk of the ranking points he won the previous year when he came runner-up to Djokovic.

On the flip side of every upset is a very happy man, and for Gaël Monfils it was the best win of his silver era, a virtuosic day of serving. He didn't get a moment to relish it, because the rain delay had wrecked the schedule and forced him to play his next round later that same afternoon. Despite a good effort, at 37, the double-header was too much for Monfils, and he lost in three sets against Holger Rune. I caught him afterward to get his read on Alcaraz, a fellow track star on the court. "Years ago we could compete together, but now he's extremely, extremely fast," he said. "His reading of the game on defense is insane. So he puts a lot of pressure [on you] to choose wisely, to come in, to attack." Was Alcaraz the fastest opponent he'd faced? Right now, "Yes." Ever? He rattled off the usual names—Djokovic, Federer, Murray—but only the elder Spaniard was mentioned twice. "He's up there, of course, Carlos, but you know . . . Rafa, at his age or so, was crazy fast." It was affirming to hear the testimony of a man who understood speed, who had battled many generations and could correct some of the hyperbole of the present. There were physical outliers before Carlos Alcaraz, and there would be others after him.

With Alcaraz out, the draw opened up for Sinner, who got a day off in the third round because his opponent withdrew. That day off happened to be his 23rd birthday, and the tournament sent him a carrot cake, which he later revealed he didn't eat a bite of but handed over to his team instead. Even though his identity was fatefully entwined with the carrot, Sinner said he preferred cakes with cream, fruit, and chocolate. One of the perils of being a public figure is that your public persona can condemn you to receiving the wrong kind of cake.

Although he said at the outset of the tournament that his goal was just to prepare his body for the U.S. Open, Sinner found himself pushing through complex matches in some of the roughest conditions I've ever sat through. Like Indian Wells before it, Mason, Ohio, was experiencing plague-like weather. Within the span of a best-of-three tennis match, players and fans alike could experience pulverizing 87-degree heat; winds so fierce that every ball toss was sent askew; and rains that suspended play for hours. An evil trifecta, even before factoring in the slick court surface that had bedeviled Alcaraz. In his quarterfinal, Sinner conquered the self-flagellating Rublev, who had beaten him earlier that month in Montreal. Afterward, Rublev told me that of all the aspects of Sinner's tennis, it was his mentality that had improved most during this past year of self-actualization. Rublev needs to learn the equanimity he admires in his fellow redhead, given his notoriety for beating his own limbs bloody with his racquet.

In the semifinal, Sinner took on Zverev, the only elite player he had yet to face in the ascendant post-puke phase of his career.

Zverev controlled their head-to-head record, 4-1. The matchup between them demanded unearthly focus and execution, because both players were trying to win points from the baseline, and both could tolerate long rallies. It was like watching two Sisyphuses roll a boulder back and forth. When Sinner prevailed in the third-set tie-break, he keeled over and unleashed a long roar—I counted to three Mississippi—a far more colorful celebration than he has mustered after winning whole tournaments. When I asked about the yell, he played it cool and vague for a moment, before admitting that he'd been thinking about his specific troubles with Zverev. "The head-to-head, he was up quite a lot, and you know that in your mind."

The yell was a rare moment of catharsis in what had been a conspicuously wordless and gruff week for Sinner. While he typically looks to his coaches for motivation during matches, he'd barely cast them a glance all week. It wasn't for lack of trying. Darren Cahill and Simone Vagnozzi had been offering the full cheese board of multilingual tennis cheers: "attaboy, "allez," "molto bene." They'd been embracing one another with uncommon vigor after each Sinner victory. But Sinner toiled on in quiet. Between points he bore the expression of a man who'd been food-poisoned. He walked in the creaky cadence of a man who'd been thawed from a great block of ice. He said that hip had a niggle, but not the same one that had worried him during the clay season. And yet, for all his malaise, physical or spiritual, he was still eking out wins over his peers in the top 10.

As a study in contrast, Tiafoe had been capering through the draw, happiness incarnate. Late in his semifinal against Holger Rune, he benefited from two shots that bobbled off the net cord in his favor, including one that would have lost him the match. Later he said he saw those lucky bounces as omens. He dropped a jubilant f-bomb in his on-court interview and signed the camera: "Why not me?" All week he'd been pulling off scrappy late-night wins, after which his team bounded around the tournament grounds, hugging, greeting fans, high off the momentum. I could see the accretion of their joy over the course of a good week on tour, the virtuous cycle that kept a good feeling alive. With those wins, however, Tiafoe earned one of the most terrifying tests in tennis: Jannik Sinner in a hard-court final.

Pinkish cocktail, orange slice swimming in it—Tiafoe arrived at the post-tournament press conference with consolation in hand. There was no shame in losing to Sinner, given his 48-5 record in 2024. Tiafoe was joining a large club. When asked what made Sinner so hard to beat, Tiafoe quipped: "Ask everybody else on the tour— motherfucker can't lose," before elaborating. "He moves so well, and the average pace of balls is big, and he has great depth. So you feel like you gotta overplay to match his medium." That aligned with my own read of the championship match. While there were brief, dis- crete moments where Sinner strained for his most outlandish shots, mostly I was awed by how good he looked with his ordinary tennis. Every Sinner rally ball landed within a few feet of the baseline, at hellacious speed, and as he himself indicated, Tiafoe had to explore the outer limits of his talent just to keep up with that man's normal. To Tiafoe's credit, he did well in the first set. But in the second set, no matter how gingerly Sinner walked between points, once the ball was in play he was floating all over the court, smooth and wraithlike, whipping his racquet to a blur.

There was depth in the simple words that Tiafoe offered to Sin- ner at the net during their handshake. "Fuck, man, you're a good player," he said. "I'm not used to playing as many matches as y'all do." Later he copped to some mental fatigue, which made sense. Winning five matches in a week and having to play a sixth for the title was the rarefied lifestyle of Alcaraz and Sinner. On any given day, Tiafoe might stumble into some magic, serving big and mixing in enough finesse to unsettle a top opponent. But he couldn't do it on command like the very best were doing, week in and week out, flying somewhere new, doing it again. The feeling seemed to strike him some days and abandon him other days. The art of winning a title like the Cincinnati Open was consistency, conserving energy on the good days, salvaging the bad days. Hazy serendipity had to be converted into a solid routine. The genius had to be repeatable.

That repeatability may be the central feature of Sinner's tennis, and perhaps even of his spirit. In Cincinnati, as he'd acclimated himself to the surface, weather, tennis ball, and other particularities, he refined that capacity. Day by day he homed in on the pulse of the hard court itself, and once he'd locked into that beat, no one in the world could hang with his tennis. He made every moment uncannily like the last one, the next shot just as pure as the one last struck. After Tiafoe left the pressroom, Sinner arrived, this time with a big swirly vase of a trophy perched next to him. His answers were clipped and opaque; he was less chipper than he'd been at the outset of the tournament. Judging solely by the ambiance of these two press conferences, it was hard to discern that *he* was the winner.

The next morning, it was easy enough to understand why. The International Tennis Integrity Agency, which monitors doping in the sport, announced to the public that Sinner had twice tested positive for a banned substance, an anabolic steroid called clostebol. Both samples had been taken in March, at Indian Wells. Tests had detected a steroid metabolite, just under a billionth of a gram per milliliter, which the

ITIA report described as a "tiny concentration" that would not have had a performance-enhancing effect. It was still prohibited. Sinner's team had supplied authorities with an explanation of how that clostebol had gotten into their player. In their account, the sequence of events went like this. Sinner's fitness trainer had purchased a spray for healing wounds, back in Italy, where these over-the-counter sprays often contain clostebol. That spray was brought on their trip to Indian Wells. There, Sinner's physiotherapist cut his finger on a scalpel used for treating the player's calluses. He used the spray on his cut. The physiotherapist, thus treated, gave massages to Sinner, who had a form of dermatitis that caused small sores on the skin of his feet and back, creating a path for the clostebol to pass into Sinner's body.

Tennis has an illustrious history of elaborate excuses for drug contamination. Some hall-of-fame examples include: kissed a woman at a nightclub who had been doing cocaine; ate tortellini prepared by mother who accidentally dropped cancer medication into the food; performed intimate acts with boyfriend who had been using a sexual-performance-enhancing steroid. Sinner's gruesome tale—physiotherapist unintentionally mashed his steroid-covered wound into my skin sores—ranked among them, in terms of prima facie absurdity. But certain aspects of it could be verified externally. Medical experts consulted by the anti-doping tribunal found the story scientifically plausible. The fitness trainer produced a receipt for the clostebol spray purchased in Italy. Contemporaneous photos showed that the physiotherapist did indeed have a bandage-wrapped finger that week. The anti-doping tribunal had conducted interviews with all the staffers in question. And they ruled that Sinner had not intentionally ingested the substance, had taken all necessary precautions, and was thus at "no fault or negligence" for having it in his system. That said, because tennis has a standard of "strict liability," where a player bears inarguable responsibility for having a banned substance in the system, no matter how it got there—otherwise support staff could be a convenient, reusable scapegoat—Sinner was stripped of the ranking points and $325,000 in prize money he had won at Indian Wells, where the two urine samples were collected. But otherwise, for now, he was free to go on with his career, with only reputational damage as a long-term consequence.

All this had been playing out for months, in private, even while he'd been competing on tour. Later, in an interview with *Esquire UK*, he reflected on the moment he found out about his violation. He was hanging out at his flat in Monte-Carlo when his manager called him and said, "Jannik, you are positive." As Sinner remembered it: "And I'm thinking, yes, Alex, I'm always positive. 'No,' he says, 'you are positive for doping.'" He said his mind went blank. What followed was months of fast and sophisticated legal work to overturn temporary suspensions and eventually win him his relatively painless outcome.

Here was an after-the-fact explanation for Sinner's demeanor over the course of the season. He'd spent much of it in a bureaucratic purgatory. He drew a link between the stress and his assorted maladies. He had played matches without having slept the previous night, including his Wimbledon quarterfinal against Medvedev, where he arrived ashen-faced and had to be medically evaluated midway. In an interview with *Sky Sports*, he described feeling socially trapped. He would win a match, and people would ask him why he was feeling so down, and he'd been unable to explain himself with the case ongoing. One type of court had offered him refuge from the other: "The moment I go onto the court and put on my cap, for me only the tennis ball exists."

In particular, this clostebol revelation explained his sullen mood while winning the title in Cincinnati that week. The final hearing took place during the tournament itself. As Darren Cahill later explained, Sinner had spent one of his rest days sitting on a six-and-a-half-hour video call with authorities. Even as he lifted the trophy, he would have known that the news was about to break. In this unremarkable suburb, both protagonists had their first taste of scandal, at very different scales: baby's first racquet smash, and baby's first doping violation.

I learned the news on the way to the airport to fly out of Cincinnati. I wondered if I'd see Sinner there, since we were both headed to New York for the U.S. Open, and soon enough, I was standing on a people mover and staring at the reddish back of his head as he ate at a casual Italian restaurant, sitting at a table with his two coaches. As a human being, I knew that it was the worst moment of his professional life. As a journalist, I knew that I had a lot of questions. As a writer of this book, I felt I needed to play the long game, not to be the first of a thousand pests to needle him. Some of Sinner's colleagues had already started to take potshots at him. Among them, a consensus had emerged: outrage that Sinner had managed to continue an almost uninterrupted touring schedule while his doping case was adjudicated behind closed doors. Many players in the past had to derail their careers to get out from under a doping suspension, with the entire process unraveling in public. "Different rules for different players," wrote the fading Canadian star Denis Shapovalov, suggesting that Sinner had gotten preferential treatment as the top player on tour. The fact that he was in the middle of one of the best seasons in tour history made the optics even worse, and it had surely made some colleagues more eager to discredit his wins as the treachery of a doper. Under a post that Tiafoe shared about his runner-up finish in Cincinnati, the tour's perpetual troll Nick Kyrgios asked a spicy question: "Do you get the title now?"

I had been blindsided. On my phone in the car to the airport, I pinched and unpinched my fingers to navigate the fine print of the official report. Earlier that week, a friend in the know had tipped me off to some unease between Sinner and his team, but we hadn't suspected anything this consequential. No journalist had managed to break the story that had been simmering undetected for four months, but also, there weren't all that many journalists in the sport anymore. Once the news was public, however, those still in existence had plenty of questions and theories. Some used the Sinner news to explore the possibility of widespread microdoping in tennis; I never thought that the risk-reward calculus made all that much sense for a top player. Nor did I think those players were naive and unsophisticated. I suspected they were tiptoeing right up to the line of the banned substance list, eating every legal supplement to squeeze out every unpunishable advantage. (My suspicion would be confirmed later that season when Iga Świątek, a top player on the women's tour, who also got busted for a banned substance and claimed accidental contamination, was revealed to have been taking 14 supplements.) Mostly, though, I was trying to understand how the staff of the world's No. 1 player could have made an error this elementary, if indeed their account was truthful.

At the airport, I briefly spoke to the Sinner table at the Italian restaurant, not to grill them, but to assess the vibes. I congratulated them on their title and discussed the U.S. Open, as if oblivious to the news. Perhaps this was even more awkward than addressing it head-on. Sinner was wearing his usual nondescript sweatsuit and the heavy-rimmed black glasses he dons off court, which lightly anonymize him, giving him the look of a morose architect. The atmosphere at the table was calm, perhaps a bit watchful, but far from paranoid or funereal. The meal, even in the grim circumstances, was a little celebratory. Sinner had said in an interview the previous night that he toasts his titles not with booze but with a Coke. On the receipt on the table, I did see a Coke Zero, along with a pepperoni pizza, a prosciutto pizza, and a prosciutto and fig panini. Let the historical record show that this was Jannik Sinner's last supper before hurtling in earnest into a hellfire of scrutiny and skepticism from his entire industry.

Sinner put up his hood and walked to the gate, where he posed for a photo with two fans. Though I'd assumed someone of his means and airline points would've ranked a little closer to military personnel or people with children, the world's No. 1 player boarded his American Airlines flight in group six, among peons like me. He settled into the aisle seat, first row. Later I spotted him at baggage claim, keeping a distance from his two coaches, strolling aimlessly and stretching his hip flexors. Once everybody's cargo had been piled onto a cart, he pushed it himself, trudging all that baggage out to the curb, into the daylight.

CHAPTER 12

Digestion and Indigestion

In general, there's not much to relish in the wan fluorescence or threadbare carpeting of a conference room, but in this one instance, days before the 2024 U.S. Open, I detected a crackle in the atmosphere, a faint whiff of ozone. My fellow journalists and I were waiting for Jannik Sinner. At the head of the room was a wide white podium, a vase of orchids to one side, and an unopened bottle of water awaiting a potentially dry-mouthed speaker. Sinner might have arrived in such a state, had he been a different sort of person, possessing a more fragile mind. It had been three days since our shared flight from Cincinnati to New York. This was his first-ever appearance before the press since the world learned about his two positive tests for a banned substance. He'd explained how the infinitesimal amount of clostebol had gotten into his body, but there was so much more to ask him.

Sinner had still not appeared 20 minutes after the appointed start time. I wondered: Was he intending to run out the clock? Would he miss his press window completely, leaving the tournament's public relations apparatus to mumble about how they had to keep moving on with the schedule because other players were due to appear? And then without ceremony he walked into the room, his often chaotic red curls looking coiffed for the occasion, and his eyes narrowed slightly.

At first there was a beat of silence, as if no journalist wanted to be the first to ask about the only topic that anyone wanted to ask about. Then one tactfully vague softball question on the doping issue was lobbed his way, and Sinner fielded it with a brief answer, and there was an interjection from the conference's moderator. "Okay, we won't be entertaining any more questions on that subject," he said, with the gruff demeanor and tone of an umpire in a baseball movie for children. "If you have a question about another subject . . ."

Another subject! The assembled journalists dissolved into murmurs and objections. We all recognize that question-and-answer sessions are stilted and not much of a way to get to know a person—but at the very least, our questions aren't screened in advance. For all the ways that traditional media has been squeezed out of the picture, we still have the freedom to ask what we want. I found myself blubbering the words, "No, you can't." But it was former player and current TV commentator Mary Carillo who truly led the counterattack, and the rest of us marshalled behind her. We simply pressed on. We asked questions about his interactions with the anti-doping authorities, and with the same cool precision that characterizes his tennis, the 23-year-old Sinner kept answering them.

Often in his press conferences, Sinner takes on a funny, slightly harried tone that suggests he finds the question daft, that he wishes you were as good at your job as he is at his, that having to answer this question is the terrible price of being a great tennis player and the math is starting to look iffy—but in that moment, he was unfailingly patient and clear. He spoke about the trainer and physiotherapist on his team, both fired after the story went public, who made the criti-cal errors with the steroid spray: bringing it on a work trip at all, ap-plying it to a cut on the physiotherapist's finger, allowing that steroid to enter Sinner's bloodstream through sports massages. He thanked the staffers for their help over the last two years and said he was now in search of "clean air." He said he was relieved to have all this out in the open, after months of grappling with the authorities. He said he hadn't taken any shortcuts to circumvent the standard process; it was simply that his team had been able to quickly suss out the source of the contamination and mount their appeal. He pronounced "anti-doping" as if it were an Italian digestif, made with walnuts, good on ice cream. He talked about his reputation and said he was learning "who is my friend and who is not my friend, no?" He even tested out an uncharacteristic bit of stagecraft: When describing the amount of steroid metabolite found in his urine sample, he chuckled and said, "0.000000001," counting off eight zeros on his fingers and thumbs. It was so smooth that I wondered if it had been workshopped ahead of time, drilled as studiously as his backhand down-the-line. If he had been prepped, his PR team only forgot to remind him to use a unit of measurement (grams per milliliter) after the number, for extra credit.

After 10 minutes of answering questions, the moderator brought the conference to an end. Dozens of journalists with raised hands like sunflowers in a field lowered them dejectedly. Despite the ini-tial attempt to cut off all doping-related questions, it was obvious that Sinner had ended up doing the best thing for his credibility—he'd answered the inquiries head-on. "I like to dance in the pressure storm," he had said in January, after winning the Australian Open final in a comeback from two sets down. Here he was, dancing again.

• • •

Four days later, Sinner was playing rather poorly, getting pieced up by the world No. 140 Mackenzie McDonald. This was not a match anyone flagged for upset potential. The undersized American was better than his ranking suggested, and he'd even played a solid three-setter against Sinner the previous season, but there was nothing about his arsenal that should have threatened the year's undisputed hard-court master.

Sinner, in a mossy-green outfit that almost camouflaged him into the court, looked ruinous. He spilled 14 unforced errors in the first set and saw his serve broken thrice. When he went down an early break in the second set, I began to speculate about the real psychological damage of recent events, but then he suddenly restored order, and all the doubts jotted in my notebook gave way to blankness. There was nothing to say as Sinner thrashed McDonald for the remainder of the match, winning 18 of the last 22 games. It was, surprisingly, his first-ever victory in Arthur Ashe Stadium, the main court at the U.S. Open, where the superstars play. He won there again in rounds two and three, floating right through his opponents.

Carlos Alcaraz, for his part, seemed to have recovered from his tantrum in Ohio, having already issued an endearingly formal apology on social media: "As a human being, there is a build-up of nerves inside and it is sometimes very complicated to control yourself when you have a very high pulse," he wrote. He seemed in a sunnier mood in New York and had been spotted walking around Manhattan like a common tourist, alone and unflanked by his team, waiting respectfully at the crosswalk instead of jaywalking. When he did his press conference before the Open, like every other player he was asked about the Sinner situation. But as his rival, the comments were going to be more closely inspected. He picked his words carefully, as if filling a cup one grain of rice at a time. "In English it's going to be difficult for me to explain myself, but I try," he said. "I believe in a clean sport. So I don't know too much about that. I am pretty sure that there are a lot of things that we don't know, inside the team or inside everything. But if they let Jannik to keep playing, is for something. They said he's innocent. So that's all I know and that's all I can talk about." The two fan bases babbled about the tepid support of Sinner indicated by Alcaraz's response, wondering if the friendly rivals had fallen out. Soon enough they were seen on the practice courts, side by side, Alcaraz razzing his rival, saying that his older brother Álvaro, who does not play on tour, had a better serve than Jannik.

The U.S. Open crowd is loud, quite drunk, and immune to shame. American, basically. These are double-edged qualities, as sometimes they enhance the tennis and juice the entertainment value, both in person and on TV. The mood is one of perpetually confused rowdiness. As a New York City institution, the tournament has always been something of a scene—Anna Wintour's sunglasses are a near-nightly presence—but it reached new levels in 2024. The Open transcended tennis and became a larger cultural spectacle: part sporting event, part nightclub, part corporate retreat. Influencers recorded footage of themselves traipsing around the venue; businesses treated their clients to the finest seats; ticket prices spiked preposterously. The tournament's melon-themed vodka cocktails, called Honey Deuces, generated $12.8 million in revenue over the tournament. At an evening match, where the fans slurped down several of those under the bright stadium lights, the party ambiance intensified. It was an apt setting for Alcaraz, who was more or less a nightclub in the form of a tennis player. He also had thematically apt fashion, a swaggy all-black getup reminiscent of bygone Nadal outfits. After winning his first-round match in a kit that bared his striated shoulders and biceps, Alcaraz admitted that he liked to go sleeveless "to make fear to the opponents." This strategy was sound. After losing to Alcaraz in the first round, his opponent, Li Tu, joked in a TV interview that he'd watched Alcaraz remove his jacket before the match and thought, "This guy's a specimen."

On the evening of his second-round match, which headlined the U.S. Open's Pride night, Alcaraz walked out in his black tank top to the pulsing electro-pop of Troye Sivan and a kaleidoscopic light show. He tried to keep the party going with his tennis. But in the first set he found himself struggling against the world No. 74, Botic van de Zandschulp, who was as dispassionate as Alcaraz was passionate. Alcaraz appeared almost too pumped up, verging on twitchy, and his lack of rhythm was immediately obvious. He hit no winners while losing the first set in half an hour. Best-of-five typically gives him enough time to tidy up and find a decent level for the crucial moments. And a decent level from Carlitos was fatal to all but a handful of foes—it was too quick, too clever, too powerful. That had been the defining feature of Alcaraz's summer: his newfound ability to claim the sport's biggest prizes, despite drifting quite far from his A game for long passages of play. In a roundabout way, it had been the most convincing thing about his season with regard to his long-term career prospects. He'd played at a more consistent level for much of 2023, but in 2024 he proved that he had such a high skill ceiling, and such a reliable intuition for when to dial up his focus, that he could get away with these temporary lapses.

But there was no sense of best-of-five inevitability in that second-round match at the Open, no timely recovery for the pivotal points. There was not even enough of a basic technical foundation for that hypothetical comeback to build on. Alcaraz couldn't consistently land three solid forehands in a row. He struggled to return both first and second serves, and failed to defend out of the corners. His shot selection, which can be quixotic even at the best of times, can look delirious when he's down two sets and trying to volley a defensive lob that is about to land in the back third of the court: a brutally risky shot with apparently scarce reward. Taken as a whole, the image was difficult to reconcile with past experiences of the 21-year-old's charmed career. I never thought I'd see Alcaraz, down two sets on Arthur Ashe Stadium against a player ranked outside the top 50, with the crowd utterly checked out and conversing among themselves. Usually the crowd is his renewable energy source. Smiling, which Alcaraz has described as the "key of everything," was something he attempted only late in the third set, in the game where he broke back to level at 3-3. Later he tried to point to his ear and rile up the crowd, but he couldn't find good enough tennis to substantiate his late-night showmanship.

After pulling off the bewildering straight-set upset of the No. 3 seed, the soft-spoken Van de Zandschulp, who had been pondering retirement from tennis earlier that summer, was asked what emotions he was feeling. "Actually right now not so many," he told the assembled press, chuckling. And I believed him. While the 28-year-old Dutchman plays some smooth and cunning tennis, his foggy, tranquilized affect would be more common among SoundCloud rappers than among people in his profession. His victory over tennis's happiest boy was basically a test of ascetic willpower: Is it possible to feel nothing after defeating the player who just strung together Roland-Garros and Wimbledon titles and an Olympic silver medal? Does one not shout after handing the boy-king his first genuinely bad loss at the majors? No: He gives a light fist pump, a few firm blinks, and shakes of the head as if emerging from a trance. Buddha would envy the blissful nonattachment Van de Zandschulp modeled throughout the evening.

Afterward I asked Van de Zandschulp what was different about this match, compared to his losses to Alcaraz in the past. "Normally when he is striking the ball, you feel like the ball is coming with such impact. So you get stressed a little bit like I want to hit harder, or it's tough to control the ball," he said. "Today I felt I had much better composure during the hitting." He also said his game plan was to get to the net before the net-happy Alcaraz could do so. He'd been successful there: I couldn't remember the last time I saw an opponent outfox Alcaraz so thoroughly in the frontcourt, besting him in the improvisational points he loves so dearly.

Alcaraz sounded frustrated with himself and mystified as to what he should learn from this loss, just as he'd sounded after the loss in Cincinnati. He praised his opponent and said he'd expected to get free points off errors; once he realized that he wasn't going to get those, he couldn't find a way to step up his game. He was reluctant to attribute his loss to the lingering disappointment of falling to Djokovic in the Olympic match, though he did concede that he came to New York with a lower-than-usual energy level due to his busy summer. He said it was one of those days when he simply didn't know what to do out there, or how to adjust. "It was a fight against myself, in my mind during the match. In tennis you are playing against someone that wants the same as you, to win the match, and you have to be as much calm as you can just to think better in the match and try to do good things," Alcaraz said. "It was a roller coaster, let's say, in my mind." While it was still hard to discern what exactly was in the mind of Botic van de Zandschulp during that tournament-altering upset, rest assured that it was not a roller coaster. Probably more like a sun-dappled brook running over pebbles on a cool summer day. He lost his very next match. He seemed unbothered.

Djokovic soon joined Alcaraz in the realm of untimely upsets, losing in the third round to the No. 28 seed Alexei Popyrin. To hear Djokovic tell it, having gotten even that far was a triumph. "Honestly, the way I felt and the way I played from the beginning of this tournament, third round is a success. I mean, I have played some of the worst tennis I have ever played, honestly, serving by far the worst ever," he said. He admitted that his Olympic exertions had taken a lot out of him mentally and physically.

At the outset of the tournament, I'd asked him a question. Did beating Alcaraz have any effect on the way he's thinking about retirement? Did it inspire him to fuel up the private jet for another year on the tour? Or did it make him feel closer to ready to hang up his racquets and live life as a centimillionaire full-time dad? The answer was muted. He said that his rivalries with Sinner and Alcaraz in particular, before tossing in a few other top players, spurred him to "push myself to perfect the game and to give myself an ability to be able to run for hours with them." But his biggest incentives to keep playing had nothing to do with specific opponents. One was to continue representing his country, which he had done, with euphoric results, at the Olympics. The other was to win more major titles.

With his U.S. Open loss, 2024 became only the second year since 2011 that he had failed to win a major. The other was 2017, when he had played through an elbow injury that eventually needed surgery. Now it was because he had two rivals in their twenties who were just too good. His exit from the Open yielded another bold statistic, one that reflected the sea change in the game: 2024 was the first year since 2002 that *none* of the Big Three took home a major. Their two-decade hegemony was over. The Sincaraz era had begun.

With Alcaraz and Djokovic out of the draw, Sinner became the prohibitive favorite to win the tournament. The doping-specific questions had thinned out—we journalists were asking him about other inane things again—and Sinner seemed to have returned to some measure of calm. That's not to say there weren't things I still hoped to learn about the scandal. I tried to find out how it had felt for him to continue working with his trainer and physiotherapist for several months even after their severe steroid-related errors, but he ducked the question and said he was going to hire new ones soon. (A few weeks later he'd hire two longtime Djokovic staffers as their replacements.) I didn't get much further than that. It was an odd feeling, trying to facilitate a conversation with someone by asking them a maximum of one question, in a public setting, every two days. In general, he spoke a lot about narrowing his world to the people he cared about and trusted most.

Though Sinner was keeping his head down and presumably shutting down his social media intake, there were figures in the sport who were wading around the apps, hungry for provocation. One was Nick Kyrgios, the quasi-active Australian tennis player who was serving as an ESPN commentator and on-court interviewer for the Open, and who was about as opposite from Sinner in disposition as is possible. Kyrgios had been leading the charge for Sinner skepticism—in a characteristically loud and factually loose manner. "You should be gone for two years. Your performance was enhanced. Massage cream . . . Yeah nice," wrote Kyrgios, in a social media campaign that would lurch on for months to come.

In press after round two, Sinner was asked how he'd feel if he had to be interviewed by Kyrgios. "I don't want to respond on what he said. Everyone is free to say everything, so it's okay," Sinner said, initially cracking into a smile about as wide as he'd shown in months, despite the gravity of the subject matter. "But, no, I'm always quite relaxed. I'm someone who forgets quite fast something." The gist: *I don't think about him at all.*

Tommy Paul, Sinner's fourth-round opponent, also appeared to take a dig at the Italian the week before the tournament. He posted a photo of himself getting a massage from a physiotherapist wearing black latex gloves—a pointed joke about the tainted massage. Paul, who has hovered at the threshold of the top 10, tends to lure spectacular tennis out of elite opponents. He's such a versatile athlete that he can almost mirror their qualities for a passage of play, best seen when he's facing Alcaraz. Even in a cohort of the most coordinated people in the world, Paul stands out with his fast-twitch jitteriness, deft hands, and elaborate yo-yo-style racquet tricks to kill time between points.

Paul stayed nose-to-nose with Sinner for two sets, bringing out the red-bloodedness of the lower-bowl crowd at Arthur Ashe Stadium. A broadly dispersed group of men who had probably spent about $70 for their mild buzz and red faces were chanting, "USA! USA!" Occasionally I could make out calls of "cheater," too. But in time, the differences between Paul and Sinner started to tell. Sinner's best tennis feels both languid and violent; it can be difficult to connect the cause with the effect. In between shots his lank frame looks almost floppy, and as he skids and scrambles and makes his little adjustment steps around the court, you wonder if those feet will give out from underneath him. But right when the ball is approaching, all that ambient floppiness is aligned into one sublimely synchronized chain, from foot to hip to wrist, as he readies his full-body slingshot groundstrokes. A compact backswing, a snap, and the ball is gone. The visual is loose and jangly, but the sound is like someone hucking a billiard ball against a garage door. Real power in tennis comes from relaxation and timing, rather than pure muscular output. Sinner's what you'd get if you made a whole tennis player out of that axiom.

"E-las-ti-ci-ty," intoned the longtime tennis writer Chris Clarey, snapping off every syllable, as he watched Sinner dismantle Paul. Jannik was pinging shot after shot off the precise center of his racquet's string bed, dozens of pristine hits in a row. It was difficult to believe that his origins lay in the province of man. His play aligned suspiciously with the popular cinematic depiction of aliens: slender, possessed of a strength irreconcilable with our understanding of human anatomy, demure in affect, capable of lethality without visible exertion. I found it hypnotic.

Paul decided that he couldn't hang in the rallies with such an error-proof organism and hauled himself to the net, only for Sinner to deliver an eclectic feast of passing shots. The Italian ended up winning the first two sets in tiebreaks, then took the third set in a breeze. He had won 14 of his last 15 tiebreaks, approaching a Djokovician degree of comfort in that space. Afterward I asked Paul about the feeling of playing against Sinner. "Unreal out of the corners," he said, calling Sinner "the best ball-striker on tour"—a claim that felt spicy but, as I rolled it around in my head, also true. Judging from that performance, it would be difficult to argue that anyone else on the planet was better at the simple, terrible task of placing a tennis ball heavy and deep into the opposing court, over and over. In his interviews, Sinner fixates on improvement, and his coaches say that one of the hardest parts of their job is tearing him away from the practice courts. But it was hard to conceive of how any entity could possibly get much better at this task.

The quarterfinal between Sinner and Medvedev—the only two major champions left in the draw—felt like it might be the de facto final. Medvedev had lost to him in the finals of the Australian Open and Miami Open, but struck back in the Wimbledon quarterfinal, dispatching a sleepless, stressed Sinner. But at this U.S. Open, Sinner's secret was out, both men were healthy, and they had cruised through their previous round, suggesting a classic to come.

While I wish I could illuminate the page with such an epic story, you're better-off left in the dark. These men never played well at the same time. Medvedev showed some of the best tennis of his season in the second set, but otherwise laid a mystifying egg on Arthur Ashe Stadium, a court where he believes his forehand gets some added sting. The enduring image of this match was a backhand-to-backhand exchange, at about 40 percent pace, until one man hit it into the net. Sinner won in four sets, and Medvedev was out, stumped by a familiar puzzle.

Sinner's semifinal managed to be even more unpleasant, though in a different sense. He had to play his close friend Jack Draper, a lefty with a murderous serve who was making his first deep run at the majors and had not yet dropped a set in the tournament. This being Draper's first match with these stakes, there were some nerves at play, which would eventually manifest themselves in various displays of extreme moisture.

It was only 78 degrees out, but quite humid—not nice to sit in, but unremarkable conditions by the harsh standards of pro tennis. Draper was becoming, before my eyes, the sweatiest entity I'd

ever seen in person. He is a sweaty man by reputation, but this was
alarming. He soaked through his oversized shirt until it seemed to
have the weight and sheen of a leather jacket. At one point he had
to briefly pause play to change into new shoes, because he had fully
saturated those, too. At another, he bent down to mop up the court.

My assumption was that he had managed to create a hazardous
pool of sweat just by standing in one place for too long. But the reality
was gnarlier: Draper had vomited twice, so subtly that I had not reg-
istered it despite sitting only a couple of rows from the court. Footage
later revealed that while preparing to return serve, he'd barked up the
puke without ceremony—blap, blap—immediately gone to his towel,
cleaned up the mess, and thrown the towel back from whence it came.
His ability to do all this, swift and undetected, struck me as one of the
most impressive athletic feats I'd witnessed all week.

Draper vomited twice more over the course of the match. He
wiped his face with the same towel he'd used to mop up the vomit.
Stalking around the court with a starved look in his eyes, he seemed
like he needed to be hosed down and administered an IV, stat.

Sinner started to suffer too, during the most surreal and over-
stimulating point of the entire tournament. He ran up to fetch a
drop volley, ran all the way back to retrieve a lob, slipped and hurt
himself at the back of the court, and scrambled to his feet just in
time to intercept what should have been a point-ending overhead
smash, which he ripped back at bloodcurdling speed right past a
dumbstruck Draper. After this Herculean effort, Sinner keeled over
in pain to massage his wrist while the crowd howled its appreciation.
Too many things were happening at once. A minute later, both men
sat down for the changeover and were visited by medical staff, one
for the wrist and the other for reaching new frontiers in on-court
vomit. Through it all, the tournament's catchphrase, "The world's

healthiest sport," was overlaid on the periphery of the court in the TV broadcast.

Sinner's painful fall on his wrist didn't seem to compromise him, the way it had at Indian Wells; he also wasn't playing an opponent quite like Alcaraz. Here at the Open the top seed prevailed in straight, if bleary, sets. Afterward, a freshly, mercifully showered Draper described the misery he'd endured. "I'm definitely someone who is, I think, quite an anxious human being," he said. I felt for him, and didn't envy the experience of being unable to keep food and fluids down while playing a brutally taxing major semifinal. Mid-match vomiting might have rescued Sinner in his infamous match in Beijing, but the technique had not helped Draper in quite the same way.

Over on the other side of the draw, I heard optimism from the surviving American players. Throughout the second week of the tournament, Taylor Fritz and Frances Tiafoe talked about how the field had opened up for them. They were deep in a major, and for the first time in 22 years, the Big Three were nowhere to be seen. That, plus Alcaraz's early loss, made this U.S. Open feel like it was for the taking. But those optimists might not have fully grasped the austerity of life under tennis's new youthful regime. Here were the Next Two, and one of them was very much alive in the tournament.

As juniors, Fritz and Tiafoe once sat on an airplane and talked about how they'd be the two leading Americans in their generation. Tiafoe recounted that story ahead of their semifinal clash, which would guarantee the first American men's finalist at the Open since 2006. Their match was nerve-racking, and in the fourth set, while close to closing out the match, Tiafoe succumbed to anxiety cramps. He later likened it to what Alcaraz had suffered the previous year in Paris. Fritz not only survived, but speculated that the final would actually be less stressful than having to play his friend Tiafoe. He even said he was looking forward to playing Sinner. "I don't know . . . he's like a very strong ball-striker, but I feel like I always hit the ball really nice off of his ball," he observed. He and Sinner had split their previous meetings 1-1, so perhaps he could find reason for belief.

Fritz, a laid-back and wavy-haired Californian, can beat a lot of players with first-strike tennis. He has a powerful serve, and he makes sound tactical choices, which he can walk you through clearly after the match. But he's a limited mover, and against the best, who can reliably put him on the defensive, his game always looks a bit precarious. To have a chance at the title, he would have to serve flaw-lessly and hit ambitious targets from the baseline.

Instead he had his serve broken in the first game of the match. Sinner tempted Fritz to overhit, made him totter forward for the oc-casional drop shot, and then exposed the chasm between their lateral movement skills. I'm not sure I've ever seen anyone besides Fritz make such pure contact with a tennis ball while on the verge of top-pling over face-first. A few brilliant rallies notwithstanding, the first two sets sped toward the expected outcome. The stirrings of Taylor Swift, seated a few sections over from me, received about as much attention from the crowd as the swings from the Taylor on court. Fritz had a chance to serve for the third set, but Sinner foreclosed on the comeback attempt. He moved through the endgame with a finality reminiscent of Djokovic, as if he'd done this a dozen times and would do it a dozen more.

After winning in straight sets, Sinner threw his hands in the air and left them there, in keeping with his low-impact style of celebra-tion. Nothing frenzied, no loss of control—just a young man taking in the cold, clean air at the top of a mountain. He went off to hug his coaches and girlfriend Anna Kalinskaya, and, since the true hallmark of every big-time tennis player is having a totally non sequitur celebrity in your player's box, he also hugged the musician Seal, whom he met through a mutual friend.

In Sinner's post-match remarks, he proactively brought up the doping incident and the pall it had cast over this phase of his career. He also dedicated the title to his ailing aunt, letting down his guard for a teary moment. "I don't know how much longer I will have her in my life," he said. "If there was a wish I could make, I would wish good health on everyone, but unfortunately it's not possible." Later in press, he talked about how his experiences with his aunt helped him differentiate between tennis and "real life." He is a quiet presence, but his answers can sometimes be meditative and disarming, making the listener feel like they have all the wrong priorities. Nowhere in his post-championship words could one find a passage of overt, uncomplicated joy. It wasn't that sort of tournament.

Alcaraz's 2022 win in New York had felt like a young star zealously bursting into public consciousness; two years later, Sinner's felt something like the opposite. A young man, already private and modest by disposition, had found himself under suspicion from colleagues and online hordes alike. He'd burrowed inward to avoid the noise, and emerged seven matches later, triumphant. He wasn't fully in the clear, however. Though tennis's anti-doping authority had let him play on with light penalties, the World Anti-Doping Agency, the top watchdog in international sport, could still push for Sinner's suspension. Reputational rehabilitation would also be its own slow and imperfect process. In the interim there would be syringe emojis in the comment sections of Instagram, grumbling in the locker room, and lingering questions in the press. There were jokes, too, about whether we were witnessing a Sinner heel turn in real time. That still felt unlikely—Draper had quipped that Sinner's one weakness was being too nice—but if it did happen, its origins would be traced back to this murky juncture of his career.

On my way out of a major tournament for the last time in 2024, I almost walked right into Sinner. He was holding his trophy at his side, letting it dangle slack like a gym bag full of dank sneakers. Trailed by handlers, he walked out of Arthur Ashe Stadium and toward the huge rectangular fountain in front of it. The crowds had long since emptied out of the venue. He stood up on the ledge for a photo shoot, smiling intermittently into the strobing camera flashes as plumes of water burbled behind him, and Curtis Mayfield's "Move On Up" blared over the desolate grounds.

A hamburger was the key detail of his post-championship celebration, according to his appearance on *The Today Show* the morning after. (There was no official word on whether it had been accompanied by a Coke or Coke Zero.) Having digested that along with everything else over the previous fortnight, Jannik Sinner would assuredly step back onto the treadmill of improvement and continue to perfect what already seemed so uncannily close to perfection.

CHAPTER 13

Changeover

My favorite linguistic tic among tennis players is their affection for the term "level." If you were to analyze a corpus of press conference transcripts, it would be one of the most overrepresented words. "Level" means quality of performance, but that doesn't capture all the nuances. A player might be dissatisfied with his own level in a particular match. He might be astonished by the opponent's level. A match, as a whole, can have a level, determined by the level of its constituent players. A player might say that his level oscillated up and down over the course of a single match. A player might pine for his bygone level, now impossible to recapture due to injuries or age. Everyone knows that a player's peak level is not necessarily their standard everyday level.

Level is separable from the player; it can be commented on at a remove, as if a player were holding their own tennis out at arm's length, putting it up to the light to study it more closely. Level is an instantaneous snapshot of where a player stands—their accuracy, ferocity, ingenuity at a given point of time. It is the result of their training, but also their jet lag, their love life, their legal proceedings, their last meal. When I hear players talk about level, I imagine them in a blue expanse, standing atop flat clouds, occasionally leaping up to a higher one or plummeting to a lower one, landing next to another player to meet them where they are.

I love to examine a player's peer evaluations at a time when his level is untouchable. It is one thing to trigger awe in an ordinary spectator; it is another to see that awe written all over the faces of his colleagues, who are themselves capable of extraordinary feats. It's as if we are as far removed from them as they are from him. A few weeks after the U.S. Open, this was how the tour was talking about Carlos Alcaraz again. Nobody was reaching his cloud.

In late September, Alcaraz went to Berlin to play in the Laver Cup, an exhibition tournament that doesn't count toward tour rankings but still pays good money. It is a team event, where some of the top players from Europe take on some of the top players from the rest of the world. (The groups are rather straightforwardly called Team Europe and Team World.) The 2024 edition, as usual, featured a strong field of players, including Fritz, Tiafoe, and Shelton for World, and Zverev and Medvedev for Europe (though not Sinner, who has never participated). Even in that context, Alcaraz lorded over his colleagues. He wound up winning the decisive singles match that tilted the cup in favor of Team Europe. Andy Roddick, the 2003 U.S. Open champion, was struck by how many players at the event said, without flinching, that the Spaniard had the best top level in tennis. "The general feeling seems to be that once he finds it, and has it, you have a massive problem," he said on his podcast.

You could see this reverence play out in real time. The Laver Cup being a team event, the players liked to treat one another to pep talks and tactical advice during changeovers. But as the journalist Tumaini Carayol observed, they tended to leave Alcaraz alone in these lulls when he was playing a match—as if they were unqualified to advise him. After Team Europe won, Zverev wasn't shy about expressing his admiration for a man six years his junior. "Don't listen to what I'm going to say, because you're like 12 years old, and I shouldn't say so many nice things about you," he said to Carlitos. "But yes, it's a privilege to share the court with someone who's already a legend in our sport." Zverev reflected on the "special" feeling of having played doubles alongside Roger Federer at the Laver Cup in 2019 and said that playing alongside Alcaraz was "also special." He wasn't the only one to link those two luminaries. Team World, tasked with solving such a player, had also apparently been referring to Alcaraz as "Fed '05," a reference to Federer's 81-4 performance in 2005, one of the dominant seasons in tour history, when he was coming up with beautiful, sinister, heretofore-unseen shots on a nightly basis. "I'm too far from that level," Alcaraz said sheepishly when confronted with the nickname in an interview. But everyone around him seemed to disagree.

Even the great man himself had words for Carlitos. Federer, whose management team co-owns the Laver Cup, had retired two years earlier. He was hanging out at the 2024 iteration, describing the pangs of being off the tour, wondering if he was still allowed to walk onto the court surface or if that was an honor reserved for those still on active duty. Surprisingly, though he had practiced with Alcaraz when the latter was a junior prodigy, this Laver Cup was the first time Federer had ever seen him play a full match live. Watching on TV, however, had been enough to convince him of Alcaraz's potential, especially the way he won his first Wimbledon final over Djokovic—a scenario where Federer himself had lost three of four times. "That's when he showed he's 'the Guy,' and he's going to be around for a very long time," he said in an interview with Australian

TV ahead of the Laver Cup. He also offered a grain of wisdom. "He's got to be careful, you know, [that] he doesn't run basically for every ball, because it's not necessary," he said, as if describing an overactive pet. "But he'll learn that with age and with time. And [he's] also very strong [mentally] when it matters the most."

It was hard not to laugh at the contrast between his peers' faintly religious tributes to Carlos Alcaraz and the actual observable behavior of Carlos Alcaraz. Anytime he wasn't playing tennis, he was partaking in horseplay. As much as he intimidated other players with his talent, he still remained chummy with them—hugging them, backslapping them, whispering stupid things into their ears. From the bench, he cheered on their successes, writhing in his seat like a rascal, humping the air in delight. He was the star pupil conjoined to the class clown. In this lonely sport, players occasionally talk about craving camaraderie, which they get, in small doses, during team competitions. For Alcaraz, it was like a healing balm after his twin disasters on American hard courts. He'd been complaining a lot about the density of the tour schedule, hinting at burnout. "Probably they are going to kill us in some way," he said, smiling. "Right now they are showing up a lot of injuries because of the ball, because of the calendar, because a lot of things." (We'll hear more about the ball shortly.) But getting to goof around with friends, play relatively low-stakes singles and doubles, and make some easy dough—it was like a restorative spa visit.

I was reminded of an anecdote about a much younger Alcaraz, who was getting too good for the competition and experiencing some social growing pains. His lifelong friend and training partner, Pedro Cobacho Sanchez, could no longer keep up. As a friend of Carlos's father recalled to Tumaini Carayol, it was very hard for the budding genius to say goodbye to Pedro. "Why isn't this kid going to train with me anymore?" Carlos wondered.

"Well, he doesn't have your level," he was told.

"But he's my friend. I'm not going to practice if I'm training without my friend."

"But he can't track down your shots."

Not all players need that communal aspect. Jannik Sinner, for example, had a different orientation at a similarly tender age. His second skiing coach, Klaus Happacher, said that once Jannik really began to take the sport seriously, he requested that he leave his group lesson and train solo with the coach so he could better focus.

Some people see more clearly where friendship and the pursuit of excellence diverge.

In 2024, the Sincaraz rivalry had settled into a pleasing symmetry. Alcaraz won half of the majors, the two played on the "natural surfaces" of clay and grass; Sinner won the two played on hard court. The Rivalry Industrial Complex, whose outputs include even the book you now hold, was in full thrum. The clear supremacy of these two players over the rest of the tour had me wondering how the game might evolve during their reign, and I invited some sharp observers of the sport to inhale the oracular fumes and describe the Sincaraz future. According to the analyst Gill Gross, we were headed for an era of bulletproof, balanced offense and defense. Its hallmarks would be extreme court coverage; a lack of exploitable weaknesses (think about the vulnerability of Federer's one-handed backhand); and "violent weight of shot." That is, the blend of speed and topspin that can make a ball feel like an immovable melon on an opponent's racquet. That had been the hallmark of

Nadal's game, but the new duo were already hitting heavier than their predecessors.

As the coach and analyst Hugh Clarke saw it, this style of play was an outgrowth of the technologies they'd grown up using. Even our most singular artists are, in the end, still the product of their historical context. Alcaraz and Sinner belonged to the first generation of tennis players raised on lighter carbon-fiber racquets (which allowed for faster swings) and polyester strings (which generated even more spin). Their technique and tactics had developed in symbiosis with their racquet tech. Their setups were slightly different in the particulars, as the gear expert Jonas Eriksson explained to me. Alcaraz's racquet was lighter, good for heavy spin, and maneuverable enough that he could manipulate the racquet face at the last second to deceive a foe. Sinner's was slightly heavier overall, with that weight distributed more toward the top of the racquet, rendering it head-heavy the way a hammer is, which suited his whippy groundstrokes driven from the hip. But both configurations rewarded moving the racquet as quickly as possible. The long, sleepy strokes of the distant past had been replaced by violent, blurry slashes.

These new techniques gave way to new tactics. Every time Sinner and Alcaraz saw an opportunity to attack, they seized it. Gone were the cagey, slow-burning rallies of Djokovic versus Nadal, each man hunting for a momentary lapse in stamina or focus. For the new kids, the game plan was to attack first, attack second. There was little taste for playing in a safe, error-reduction mode, the kind that Djokovic mastered in tiebreaks. Instead, Sinner said in an interview with *Sky Sports* that his tiebreak philosophy was to consider all the various attacks he'd tried over the course of the set and commit to those he felt had worked best. Sinner and Alcaraz were pioneering an era of "point-and-shoot" tennis, as Clarke put it, evoking the visual grammar of a first-person-shooter video game. If the ball was there to be hit, it would be hit—and hard. Sinner laid out his prophecy for the sport in that same interview: "In my opinion everything will become faster. To play at a faster pace, physically you have to be stronger."

But one part of the game was moving slower, according to a pet theory held by many players on tour. The "dead ball" theory, articulated by Daniil Medvedev and since taken up by others, held that the ball had degraded in quality during the pandemic. It had become much harder to hit it clean past the opponent for a winner. "They're a little bit like a shuttlecock," Sascha Zverev told me. "They fly very, very fast through the air the first two, three meters, then they just slow down." A tennis ball is a pressurized rubber core covered by felt, and Zverev believed the core was being manufactured with lower-quality material and was prone to losing its pressure. He also thought that this had increased the rate of elbow and wrist injuries on tour, as players strained to impose power on a ball that seemed to refuse it. Alcaraz had referenced the same injury theory. Medvedev felt that the ball's decline had sabotaged the game plan of low-powered counterpunchers like himself, who now struggled to end points on their own terms. And he thought that Sinner and Alcaraz were exempt because they had the surplus power to attack a "dead ball" and still hurt the opponent.

All the while, that power-baseline Wide Tennis mastered by Djokovic and Nadal had started to expand along the vertical axis. After so many years of old-timers bemoaning the loss of net play, the tour had rediscovered the all-court game. With players like Medvedev and Nadal pushing their return positions far behind the baseline, suddenly serve-and-volley became a viable strategy again, as a counter. As for the drop shot, Alcaraz had become a living argument for its value. The more powerful players became from the baseline, the more effective it was to subvert the expectation of power with a soft drop shot. Those looking to take servers by surprise might try the "crush-and-rush"—big aggression while returning a second serve, followed by a foray to the net. In 2024, to reach the very top of the rankings, it was essential to have a sound slice, sound volleys, and a sound drop shot, which wasn't necessarily true a decade earlier, when the game was more stubbornly fastened to the baseline. Every generation thinks it has seen the apotheosis of the sport. And yet the bodies, technologies, and tactics keep evolving in a rich interplay. Sinner and Alcaraz are now leading the way, but someday soon there will be a player who has grown up watching *them* and has something new to say.

But why get ahead of ourselves when the present offers so much to chew on? The tournament following the Laver Cup was in Beijing, and both of our protagonists were in the draw. This was the same court where, one year before, Sinner had fatefully ejected the contents of his stomach into a trash can during a quarterfinal match.

Sinner and Alcaraz entered as the No. 1 and No. 2 seeds, respectively. (Djokovic wasn't playing.) In the head-to-head matchup record, Alcaraz held the edge 5-4. If they both made it to the final, it would be their third time playing this year, and only their second-ever title fight. Early in the tournament they were spotted in the gym together, Carlitos cycling away on a stationary bike, holding one hand pinched and pointed up in a stereotypically Italian gesture. He waggled the hand and beamed at Jannik, who stood nearby and replied with a limper version of the same gesture. (The sense I get is that the gesture does not figure in Sinner's home region of South Tyrol.) It was a nice moment of levity, in a week that was actually quite unpleasant for Sinner. The World Anti-Doping Agency announced during the tournament that it was challenging the prior "no fault or negligence" ruling in Sinner's case and pursuing a ban of one to two years.

Sinner said that he was disappointed and surprised, having already gone through three hearings in the previous phase of this process, all of which went well for him. "Maybe they just want to make sure that everything's in the right position," he said diplomatically. Though Alcaraz had spoken more cautiously about the doping saga at the U.S. Open, here in Beijing he offered fulsome words of support, wishing that the process would be over with soon so that "Djannik"—he always hit that first syllable quite hard—wouldn't get too down. This was the fraught context for the 10th installment of their rivalry: Indeed, they both marched through the draw and arrived at the final. Would this be the last chance to see the best matchup on tour for 12 to 24 months? If the rivalry was forcefully put on pause for that long, would it ever be the same? The stakes seemed anomalously high for a 500-level tournament.

The two players were at last dressing to their personae in ways that distinguished them: Alcaraz in a tank top with hues of orange and raspberry sherbet, Sinner in a set of muddy greens with his canopy of curls tucked under a black cap. Sinner stole away a first set where Alcaraz had holistically played better tennis. The second set was defined by a desultory, fascinating 15-minute game locked in deuce, the advantage bobbling back and forth. Alcaraz alternated between lunkheaded decisions and messianic epiphanies. He leveled the match at one set apiece.

Between these rivals, I could see each one mapping out the other's tendencies, and then figuring out how to exploit the map the other had made. Specifically, in that second set, I came to appreciate a new wrinkle in the Alcaraz attack. He would rear back to hit a forehand, switch his grip as if to massage a drop shot—any savvy opponent would see that grip change and start shifting his weight to run forward—only to drive a slice deep through the court instead. He used this trick in two mesmerizing rallies, and each time it startled Sinner, perhaps the most balanced player I've ever seen. Both times he lost his footing and the point. With this mischief, Alcaraz had grafted another limb onto the decision tree in Sinner's mind. The next time he moved his racquet that way, Sinner would remember what had happened before and wonder whether he should sprint ahead or stay put. To burden your opponent with additional uncertainty is to win the mind war.

The absolute best tennis induces laughter in audiences. This rivalry induced laughter even in the participants. Throughout the match, each player had to take a moment to appreciate the absurdity of the other one, with a smile, a hand of applause struck against the strings, or a full-on chuckle. In the third set, the tennis went spiral-eyed. It was some of the best I'd seen in years, reminiscent of their seminal 2022 U.S. Open match. If you heard only the sounds of his mid-rally grunts, you might have thought Alcaraz was power-lifting or giving birth. Even Sinner, usually so sleek and soundless on the court, shouted in self-exhortation. It was not quite Wide Tennis but tennis smeared, like butter on toast, all over the court surface. It was something all its own. Early in the third set, Alcaraz broke Sinner, who swiped his racquet against his leg in disgust, worried he'd lost his chance. But he needled away at the still-vulnerable Alcaraz serve and forced a tiebreak. The first one to seven points would take the championship.

Sinner served first to open the tiebreak. His service games are elegant in the simplicity of his agenda: Line up a juicy forehand as early as possible. He aims the serve already thinking a move ahead, then perches right on top of the baseline and maybe even a step inside it—all his weight moving onto his front foot—to complete the deadliest one-two punch on tour. Once he lands that forehand, the damage to the opponent is irreversible. That's exactly how he won the first point. 1-0, Sinner.

For the next point, on Alcaraz's serve, Sinner torched a forehand and followed it up with a lush drop shot. Even if he lacks the mother-tongue fluency of Alcaraz with the shot, he is getting much savvier with it. A wardrobe malfunction made it even harder for Carlitos to keep up. While chasing down that drop shot, Alcaraz's sneaker ruptured, one side flapping open. Tennis, like basketball, now involves exertion of forces so strong that shoes do occasionally explode. If the players of antiquity, ambling around lawns in cable-knit sweaters, learned such a future was coming, it would have chilled them to the bone. Alcaraz stalked away from the court mid-rally, knowing he wouldn't get to the next ball, and Sinner tapped the ball past his sullen and half-shod opponent. 2-0, Sinner.

Alcaraz retreated to his bench to find fresh kicks. He pulled out the crumpled paper stuffed into them, slid his soft blue orthotics out from his old pair, and placed them into the new one. All this fiddling took him two full minutes—which Sinner spent bouncing on the soles of his feet to stay warm. Alcaraz finally walked up to serve, but he'd gone cold. His second serve was so feeble and ill-aimed that Sinner drilled it right back at the server's feet, so hard that Alcaraz could only flail the ball into the net. 3-0, Sinner.

Sinner had gained a big edge by winning both points on his opponent's serve, and for a player with his pristine record in tie-breaks, it seemed a near guarantee of victory. But the actual points still had to be played. Sinner served, opening up a calm rally, when Alcaraz decided he'd had enough. He ripped an inside-in forehand, bellowing as he swung, and then he shrewdly anticipated Sinner's next shot, gliding up the court to cut it off with a sumptuous half-volley. 3-1, Sinner.

The next point was an ode to persistence, or perhaps insistence. Alcaraz thumped the return and followed it to the net, parrying Sinner's usual one-two punch. But instead Sinner poked back a lob that sailed high over Alcaraz's head, sending him scampering in retreat, until he was standing outside the doubles alley, repelled to the back of the court. After a brief exchange of neutral shots, Alcaraz tore open a new angle with his forehand, moved forward again, and caught a devious low volley so sweetly that the ball went to sleep in the middle of the court, irretrievable to all but a handful of humans. Sinner was one of them, and surged forward to not just retrieve the ball but bat it hard down the sideline. But Alcaraz was too quick again. His body lurched to intercept the ball, as if moved by some primordial instinct. Lunging low, his hip, head, and racquet all in a horizontal line, he flicked a volley into open court. On the way back to the baseline, the crowd noise a deafening mesh, he roiled his fans with a finger pointed at his ear. 3-2, Sinner.

An unreturned first serve from Alcaraz leveled the tiebreak at 3-3. Emboldened on the next point, he introduced a peculiar new variation on the serve-and-volley. He followed his serve forward, even though it wasn't all that good, and was standing just a few steps in front of the baseline when Sinner's return hissed right at him. Alcaraz had tried to sneak forward when there was no advantage to press—but instead of panicking, he simply created the advantage out of whole cloth, with an audacious volley from no-man's-land. Then he kept creeping forward to the net. His talent overrode his error in judgment; the gambit paid off. His next volley was as conventional and decisive as the last one was speculative and bizarre, and Sinner couldn't touch it. 4-3, Alcaraz.

It was Sinner's turn to serve again. Alcaraz returned the ball and then the two mirrored each other, hitting right down the middle of the court. Who would break the pattern first? Alcaraz, as you and I both knew he would. He sprang for a clean forehand winner, only the ball hit the net cord. Since fortune in the tiebreak had all begun flowing in his direction, the ball stayed on its course and kissed the sideline. Sinner flicked up his arms in momentary resignation. So much for his cushy tiebreak lead. 5-3, Alcaraz.

On the next point, Sinner made an error from the baseline. After the point was over, he whacked the loose ball into the cosmos. 6-3, Alcaraz.

Alcaraz, with match point in hand, required just one serve and one forehand to finish the job. He screamed at his box, head-banged, and bared his teeth in their usual post-victory big-cat snarl. After a friendly hug, Sinner walked away looking almost as green in the face as he did while puking on this court. But by the trophy ceremony, he was in good enough spirits to take the blue plush toy he was given by the tournament and toss it into the cup of Alcaraz's trophy as they had their photos taken. "I respect you a lot as a player but even more as a person," Alcaraz told him in his speech, reusing a compliment, almost verbatim, that he often offered Sinner.

The Beijing final fully revived their rivalry. Unlike their last choppy meeting in the Roland-Garros semifinal, which showcased just how uncomfortable they could make one another, this match had all the rapturous shot-making and scoreboard volatility that fans had come to expect from these two. The tactics were ultra-aggressive, with perhaps two minutes of neutral rallying across the entire three-hour, 21-minute affair. Each player selected their shots more ambitiously than they normally would, because they knew their opponent was not normal, and was instead capable of gummy and acrobatic feats of court coverage. It was the sort of match that made a highlight reel feel thin; it should instead be experienced in full, as an accumulation of absurdities. It's not so much about gasping, "How did they do that?" a few times over the course of a match, but rather, "How are they doing all this over and over, for hours, without lapsing?"

They both played true to their reputations. Sinner maintained a cruising altitude from start to finish, a level of tennis thousands of miles above most opponents, but not this one. Alcaraz's level dipped and bobbed, but ultimately surpassed his rival's in critical moments. As brilliant as the match was as a whole, it was that last decisive stretch of Carlitos in the tiebreak that rang on in my head. Here was another instance of him responding to scoreboard duress with his bravest tennis, living and dying by his reflexes and gut intuitions. Nobody was better when cornered. And it hadn't always been this way. The previous summer, playing Djokovic at Roland-Garros, his body had gone rigid with anxiety. Just 15 months later, the pressure seemed to liberate him, to sweep away the indecision and send him to the net, where he has always belonged. Down 0-3, he strung together seven straight points against the tour's premier tiebreak player. On paper it was vanishingly unlikely, and yet as it played out in real time it felt almost inevitable.

After the victory, Alcaraz was asked if he was aware that Sinner had won 18 of his last 19 tiebreaks heading into that third set. Yes, he answered, of the gist if not the specific numbers. He knew his chances were minimal after sliding into that early deficit. He still considered Sinner "the best player in the world, at least for me . . .

physically, mentally, he's a beast." He was proud of their matches, and he'd begun to suspect that they were so good that they could haul ordinary citizens off their sofas. "I think for the people who don't watch tennis, probably thanks to these kind of matches, [they will] start to watch tennis or even practice it." Sinner said it was one of the best matches he'd ever played.

The kid who seemed so fussy and overtired in August was back on top in October. His coach Ferrero cried after the win. "I guess he got emotional at the end because we all know what we went through the last month or the last two months. It was a really difficult moment on the court, off the court," Alcaraz said. His American misadventures had made him not want to touch a racquet or travel, and his team had slowly talked him back into form. Along with Indian Wells, it was the second time this season that Alcaraz had snapped out of a prolonged emotional funk by winning a title. Perhaps this pattern would persist. He was a player for whom every single shot was physically possible, and when he lost, he tended to frame failure in emotional rather than physical terms. He might be a hunter always in search of a good feeling, capable of peerless play when he found it, but liable to sulk when he lost it.

Two hours after the match, the rivals shared a private jet to their next tournament in Shanghai. There's a picture of them squeezed into the plane's cabin with their teams, the Sinner camp nearer to the camera, all a-grin, and on the other end Alcaraz's camp, nobody's face visible except Carlitos's, mugging and throwing up a peace sign. "It is weird. It's a weird thing," Alcaraz later admitted about the flight. "But I think tennis is different than other sports because of it. Because we are fighting each other, three-hour match, really close— he could win—at the end I got the win. And then two hours later we are in the same plane, having some laughs, making jokes, talking about life, acting like nothing happened before. . . . Probably in other sports, it could be impossible to do it. But I think in tennis, we have a really good relationship off the court as well."

Novak Djokovic had been relaxing far away from the twin terrors. He hadn't played any tournaments since losing in the third round of the U.S. Open. By this point in 2024, he had basically become a part-time tennis player, who happened to still be one of the best in the world. It was a charmed life. But he decided that the Shanghai Masters was worth his time, and after arriving, he bumped into Alcaraz in a hallway of the tournament venue. "Titanito," or little titan, was how he greeted his junior colleague. He joked that he'd been enjoying his time off, and that Alcaraz was way too much to deal with. Maybe this was modesty. Djokovic had, of course, won their most recent meeting, the gold medal match at the Olympics that left both fighters bawling and proved that the Big Three had yet to be rendered fully obsolete.

Other veterans of Djokovic's generation, however, cheerily announced their obsolescence. Gaël Monfils, who had upset Alcaraz in the Cincinnati racquet-smash match, was asked by a reporter if he could repeat the feat in Shanghai. "No, no. I think he will beat me. He will crush me a hundred percent, you know. I think I was just lucky, as I said. Last time I was very fortunate. . . . I will do everything to not be crushed too easy, in a way. But everything is bonus." Alcaraz went on to beat him 6-4, 7-5—not crushed too easy, a respectable fight from Monfils.

There was potential for another Sincaraz matchup, but it was foreclosed by a funny Czech man in short shorts. Tomáš Macháč, a player nearing his 24th birthday with a dangerous top level and an irregular track record of producing it, played a spectacular match to dispatch Alcaraz. Afterward Carlitos congratulated him on Instagram. Macháč reposted it and added a caption: "Sorry for my level today." Macháč also tested out his jokes on Sinner during their otherwise businesslike semifinal. "Too fast! The rallies is too fast! The racquet is broken," yelled Macháč in mock protest, while swapping out his broken frame for a new one. Sinner, too locked in to register the attempt at humor, jogged up to the net to see what was amiss, inspected the frame, said "Ah!" and jogged back to resume throwing bombs at Macháč's feet, securing a straight-set win. Sinner then went on to beat Medvedev in similarly casual fashion.

In the middle of the tournament, the great Rafael Nadal, who hadn't played a match since the Olympics, made an announcement, inevitable but long deferred: He was officially retiring. For his last stand, he would represent Spain in international play at the Davis Cup the following month. Because tennis players live in a kind of benign viral-video-farming surveillance state, the tour circulated a clip of an unsuspecting Alcaraz standing in an exercise room, watching the Nadal retirement announcement video on his phone. He stood in an intimate huddle with his brother, physiotherapist, fitness trainer, coach, and agent, all of them staring at the same screen, looking a little fragile. "It's tough to accept it. I was in shock, a little bit," Alcaraz said of his initial reaction. "It is a shame for tennis." He'd get a chance to play alongside Nadal, though, for Spain, one more time.

One legend announced his exit, but the other one announced that he was very much still in the mix. Djokovic, always popular in China, hadn't played in the country in five years. He'd won Shanghai four times in the past, thriving on its quick court surface, and this year was no exception. He arrived in the final having dropped just one set. He would take on Sinner, whom he hadn't encountered in eight months, since losing to him in the Australian Open semifinal. The first set in Shanghai ended in a duel between two tiebreak artists; Sinner won it. Some unexpected fans had come to see the match and hunkered down right behind Sinner's player's box. Alcaraz and Ferrero apparently had stuck around in China even after falling out of the tournament, and there too was Federer, who had joined them for a practice earlier that week.

Even though the retired 43-year-old had walked onto the practice court with his tennis bag and wondered aloud, "What am I doing here?" his strokes still looked tour-ready. Perhaps his knees didn't. After two of tennis's great offensive savants finished trading punches, Federer approached Alcaraz, wondering if the kid had gotten enough. "You happy, or anything else?" He jokingly proposed they play a practice set. Alcaraz had gotten his chances to play (and beat) Djokovic and Nadal on tour, but this particular intergenerational bout would always remain a hypothetical. Carlitos later relayed that Federer had given him career advice that he intended to keep to himself, and that it had been a privilege to talk to him.

The two of them and Ferrero looked like they were enjoying themselves, watching Sinner slay Djokovic in the second set. "There are three legends watching me—and I played one legend," said Sinner in his victory speech, gesturing to the runner-up. One year before, Sinner had an 0-9 combined record against Medvedev and Djokovic, two of the best players of the era. Now he had an 11-11 record against them.

The very end of the season—late October through November—is a bit of a choose-your-own-adventure. Most players are somewhat beaten down by a year of traveling on tour. They might pack up their bags early to enjoy what little exists of the tennis offseason. Players with a big enough name, however, will grab some cash by play-ing exhibition events, which are not official tour matches and offer no ranking points, and are thus played at low effort, purely for fan amusement. Some players will make it a priority to represent their countries in international competitions, like the Davis Cup, where Nadal did finally retire, losing his last-ever match to the chilled-out Botic van de Zandschulp.

All these late-season events are played indoors, which gives the tennis its own flavor. The indoor hard courts are typically faster than their outdoor analogues, and the conditions are consistent. Same temperature, same humidity, no wind to sabotage the ball toss, no sun to make you squint, no clumps of turf or dirt to send the ball bouncing at a weird angle—just a stable environment, no matter the time of day, and honest bounces off quick surfaces. There are play-ers who savor these laboratory conditions. Big servers, for example, who know every ball toss will be undisturbed by glare or breeze and can simply focus on hitting their spots. Or big hitters, who like to see a consistent ball over and over, and a surface fast enough to end points decisively. Sinner loves to stay indoors and keep time with his fine-tuned, metronomic groundstrokes. Not so much Alcaraz, who prefers a slower court, higher bounces, and unpredictability. He seems to enjoy the various problems posed by the natural world, and has yet to find the same success indoors that he has outdoors.

The rivals met in an exhibition tournament in Saudi Arabia, whose sovereign wealth fund had spent a year sinking big money into tennis. That same fund had recently captured golf. The Profes-sional Golf Association mounted a brief resistance, saw much of its top talent get poached by a rival Saudi league, and eventually caved, desperate to collaborate. Tennis had apparently decided it was bet-ter off unfurling the welcome mat at once. In 2024, the logo of the Public Investment Fund was plastered all across the signage at some of the tour's biggest tournaments; during changeovers, crowds were often treated to a short video extolling the royal kingdom. Fans who preferred to keep human rights abuses far from mind while watching tennis weren't overjoyed by this development, which was just one prong of a broader soft power strategy often critiqued as "sportswashing." But the individual tennis players themselves had always cashed Saudi checks without too many misgivings. That year, before he retired, Nadal had even accepted a post as an ambassador to the Saudi tennis federation.

This particular exhibition event, set in Riyadh, was called the Six Kings Slam. In the final, inevitably, it was Sinner and Alcaraz. As an exhibition, it wouldn't hold weight in the official record of their rivalry, but there was still plenty to play for. After Sinner prevailed, he was in an uncharacteristically chatty mood—possibly because he had just won $6 million, the largest purse ever handed out at a tennis event of any kind. He jabbered to on-court interviewers about how difficult it had been to film the ludicrously overproduced, CGI-heavy promotional video for the event, where Medvedev was depicted riding an armored bear. Sinner explained how hot he'd been in his costume—a vaguely Renaissance getup, with big ruffles and a cape—and how frizzy his hair had gotten in the humidity. Before the trophy photo shoot, he reached over to pick the confetti out of Alcaraz's hair. "I wake up in the morning trying to understand the ways how to beat him," Sinner said while cradling the trophy in his arms. The interviewer, bless his attention to detail, followed up to clarify: "Did you just tell us that every day you wake up and think about him?" he said, referring to Alcaraz. "Well . . . no," said Sinner, first caught in an awkward pause, before smiling. "It would be strange, no, in a way." Over at the podium, Alcaraz was cracking up.

Ten days later, Sinner was asked in an interview what it was like to get back from a work trip with another six million in the bank, knowing he could just go on vacation for years if he wanted to. "No, I don't play for money. It's very simple," he responded, straight-faced. "Of course, it's a nice prize and everything, but for me, I went there because there were possibly the six best players in the world. And then you can measure yourself with them." Later, at a press conference in Paris, Alcaraz was asked if his motivations were similar. "Well, I mean . . ." said Carlitos, before trailing off, playing with his microphone stand, and giggling to himself. "If I say I went there just for fun, or to play, and forget the money . . . I'm gonna lie," he said. "I love playing tennis. Most of the time I don't think about the money. I just play for love or for fun. But you have to be realistic. You have to think that you want to earn money, you know, and that's it."

There were certainly two different public relations strategies at play here. At a time when his honesty was already under such scrutiny, I was surprised that Sinner was trying to convince us he'd flown to Riyadh out of pure love of the game.

The season ends in November with the most important indoor tennis event: the ATP Finals, which pits the eight best players in the world against each other to designate one champion among champions. Djokovic, a seven-time winner of the event, had qualified for it but stuck to his part-timer's lifestyle and opted out, citing an ongoing injury; he was spotted lounging in the Maldives that same week. For Alcaraz, it was an opportunity to figure out the one surface that had frustrated him. In October, he'd made an adjustment to the backhand, changing the way he held the racquet at the start of his swing. Instead of keeping the tip of the racquet pointed straight up, as if holding a sword, he pointed the tip of the racquet down, as if putting the sword in a scabbard. It was a conspicuous mid-season change, but simplifying the motion could help on faster courts, when he had less time between shots.

I asked him about the thinking behind an adjustment like that; was it something he tests out with his team before implementing? "I'm a player who makes changes without working on [it]. I didn't speak to Juan Carlos. I didn't speak to anyone else. I just started to feel comfortable doing it—or without thinking, I just did it a little bit different, and I started to feel well," he said. "Sometimes is good. Sometimes is bad. But I do changes without practicing at all." He was a player driven by deep intuition, making revisions based on his own sense of feel, and he did it without any micromanagement from his team. The kid—who, five years ago, stood "mouth closed and ears open" to do whatever Ferrero said, and who, just two years ago, was begging Ferrero in the middle of a huge match to tell him where to serve the next ball—had grown up.

For Sinner, no adjustments were necessary. The indoor courts of the ATP Finals were an ideal canvas for him. My friend Bryan Lehrer coined a revelatory word to describe Sinner's game. He was working by analogy to the term "servebot," tweaking it to describe Sinner's style. Jannik was a "groundstrokebot." With the same ease as a seven-foot bomber of aces, Sinner could blast his opponents away by hitting forehands and backhands more perfectly than they could, over and over again. The venue for the ATP Finals, severe and shadowy, boxy and gray in a way that evoked the Death Star, had courts that were almost purpose-built for Sinner to work this magic.

And since the tournament took place in Turin, Italy, it was also home court. Sinner was one of the most famous people in the country. I walked into a pizzeria for lunch and the proprietor started talking about her love of Sinner, unprompted. A local sportswriter said that while nothing would ever usurp football as a sporting interest in Italy, Sinner's tennis was starting to threaten it. When I walked through the crowds at the tournament, I literally heard the name on everyone's breath: *Seen Air.* Jannik's face was on the lampposts that lined the thoroughfares leading up to the venue. During the changeovers in his matches, a digital Jannik appeared onscreen to advertise coffee. Jannik's ubiquity in ads—from personal finance to skin care to cheese—had recently been skewered on Italian TV, in a satirical sketch that Sinner shyly and begrudgingly admitted some awareness of.

His official fox-shaped Nike logo was emblazoned on orange caps on so many heads. The crowd required only the mildest provocation to break into full-fledged soccer-style chants of "Olé, olé, olé, olé, Seen Air, Seen Air." There were, of course, carrot-themed costumes, and while the charm of the Carota Boys had long since expired, there was lots of bootleg Sinner gear that I found more compelling: neon-orange construction vests, or the elderly gentlemen in orange trucker hats that read "Sinner Seniors," or a whole family wearing headbands with fox ears. I wanted to applaud the man in a fine dark green suit with a vagrant carrot top dangling at least a foot out of his jacket pocket. In this sea of carrots and foxes, everything was set for Sinner to dominate the tournament.

Alcaraz lost so early he missed his last chance of the year to battle Sinner. He'd arrived at the tournament already quite ill, taking antibiotics, cutting short his practice session after a few minutes because his chest was so constricted. Before his matches, wearing a pink nasal decongestant strip on his nose and juggling to prime his hand-eye coordination, he looked like an under-the-weather clown. There wasn't much of a chance he'd perform well physically, and he now cautiously emerging. Even when he was spraying champagne all over his team to celebrate the ATP Finals title, I was still mulling over whether he was happy, the grin on his wet face dissolving some, but not all, of the doubts in my head.

The last image I have of Alcaraz in 2024 was in New York City. For a guy constantly griping about fatigue and overscheduling, he had packed his calendar with cash-grab exhibition matches at a time when he might otherwise have been lazing on the beach. This one was in Madison Square Garden in early December. Rumor had it that the event paid him in the low seven figures just to show up. There was a little party the night before the match. Alcaraz, who still lives at home with his parents, arrived with his dad, Carlos Sr., and older brother Álvaro, who often accompany him on tour. The Alcaraz men have squarish faces, hairlines so robust that they may well be proceeding rather than receding, and the same electric smile as their superstar kin. When Carlitos enters such a party, everyone stares at him out of the corner of their eye. His gaze is like the beam of a lighthouse, and everyone clamors to enter its path. People get a little animalistic, grabbing at his shoulders from all angles, but he handles it as smoothly as he might a tricky half-volley. On this night, he accepted the hugs and photo ops while his agent looked on discreetly from a few feet away, knowing that his own livelihood required keeping this man happy and gatekeeping the world's access to him.

Earlier in the day Carlitos had sat down with a few journalists. "Do you joke with Jannik about the season?" he was asked, because while Jannik had ended as the No. 1–ranked player, Carlos had beaten him in all of their tour meetings. Alcaraz laughed. "I didn't joke with him about it. But I joke with my friends. I can't lie," he said, likening it to stretches of Federer's career where almost all his very rare losses were to Nadal. "It's hilarious and makes me feel good, you know, beating the best player in the world, he has done one of the best seasons ever." The final tally of that season was 73-6 for Sinner—and yet 0-3 against his archrival.

One was mercurial; the other methodical. One was a master of compartmentalization; the other seemed to feel everything all at once. Together they had made the sport anew. They'd completed the changeover in 2024, stepping into superstardom right as the greatest generation slipped out of it—except for Djokovic, who'd proven that he still had the legs to linger and complicate life for these two heirs. But there was no mistaking the transition. Sinner and Alcaraz were the new names to emulate, even in the eyes of their shell-shocked older peers. They were only 23 and 21, and somehow there was already an even younger cohort of pros idolizing them. Like Learner Tien, who claimed to have grown up watching Alcaraz (which instantly aged me a full century), and fellow teen Joao Fonseca, who said he saw himself in Sinner (and had the same unteachable power to show for it).

Sinner and Alcaraz have each refined their tennis beyond their years, yet have so much more to learn. Each has something the other lacks and would like to infuse into his own game. Alcaraz praises Sinner for his capacity to play every point at "9/10 or 10/10" intensity; the unspoken addendum is that he himself can fluctuate between 2/10 and 12/10. Sinner needs to find more comfort in the unscripted moments of feel and daring that are Alcaraz's native habitat; there is more to tennis than the routine. Sinner needs to stay physically robust and avoid illness to withstand the longest fights. Alcaraz has to smooth out his cycles of emotional burnout so he doesn't feel like a "slave" to the sport.

The old problems will continue to haunt them in the seasons

ahead. But the future will surely be defined by these two, interlocked in a joyful and absorbing struggle. They'll get bigger and stronger; they'll get smarter; they'll get hurt; they'll hurt each other. They could become genuine friends. They could drift apart. They might not win 20-plus majors, the way their predecessors did. That sort of longevity and egomania is not lying dormant in everyone. But they are setting the highest heights as their destination, and they will push far. If all they do is replicate the genius of the 2024 season, year after year, that will be enough of a blessing to the game they now reign over.

ACKNOWLEDGMENTS

I'm grateful to everyone at Defector for our happy oasis. Thanks especially to the fellas Samer Kalaf, for being the universe's one true source of editorial judgment, and Patrick Redford, for taking the tennis pill with characteristic joy. Over at the Second Serve, thanks to David Shaftel and David Bartholow, for their unerring taste in all things, tennis or otherwise. Thanks to Owen Lewis for his brilliant research and feedback; he is on an Alcarazian trajectory as a writer and will crank out plenty of books better than this one.

Thanks to my editor, Max Meltzer, for encouraging me to write a book at all, sculpting my erratic text dumps into something I could be proud of and gently lasering away my worst writerly tics. Thanks to my agent, Jim Rutman, for being such a calm steward of this book and its frequently perplexed author. My publicist, Sydney Morris, for championing this book. My copyeditor, Valerie Shea, and production editor, Steve Breslin, for reading the manuscript keenly and teaching me the correct usage of "prior." The designers at Rodrigo Corral Studio, for the cover of my dreams.

Robert O'Connell, for the craft talks and draft notes. Bryan Lehrer, for his tennis mind and excessive belief in me. John Kane, for the generosity in Tom Perrotta's name and many enjoyable hitting sessions. The Vermont Studio Center and my fellow residents, for the clean air and space to start writing. Ben Rothenberg, for sharing your wealth of knowledge with me. The many other cool people I hung out with on tour, including Craig Shapiro, Gerry Marzorati, Vicente Muñoz, Matt Roberts, Tumaini Carayol, Reem Abulleil, Sebastián Varela, David Avakian, Catherine Whitaker, David Law, Aki Uchida, Angela Evans, and Giorgia Mecca. And thanks to Alex Gruskin, Gill Gross, Hrothger Vierhand, Jonas Eriksson, and Hugh Clarke for sharing your sharp insights on this strange game.

I am grateful for every good crowd at a close tennis match, the kind that gets so quiet before the serve that I feel like I've stepped into the woods the morning after snowfall.

Thank you to my whole enormous family. In the interest of saving trees I will name only a few here. Akka, Tim, Eshan, Inaaya, Thara, and all the Shims—I love you guys. Amma, Appa, Amache, and Thatha—thank you for building such a beautiful life for me; sometimes it's hard to believe it's mine.

Jane, thank you for generating every idea in the book and speaking to me exclusively in the voices of these two characters while I wrote it. I almost feel sad publishing this book and exposing our internal lore to the public. To put it in that language: "I'm not gonna lie," I love you and Aruvi "in the best possible way," forever.